A
Generation
in Motion

A
Generation
in Motion

Popular Music
and Culture in the Sixties

DAVID PICHASKE

SCHIRMER BOOKS
A Division of Macmillan Publishing Co., Inc.
NEW YORK

Schirmer Books
A Division of Macmillan Publishing Co., Inc.
866 Third Avenue, New York, N.Y. 10022

Collier Macmillan Canada, Ltd.

Library of Congress Catalog Card Number: 79-63033

Printed in the United States of America

printing number
1 2 3 4 5 6 7 8 9 10

Library of Congress Cataloging in Publication Data

Pichaske, David
    A generation in motion.

    Includes index.
    1. Music, Popular (Songs, etc.)--United States--
History and criticism. 2. United States--Popular
culture. I. Title.
ML3551.P53   780'.42'0973   79-63033
ISBN 0-02-871860-7
ISBN 0-02-871850-X pbk.

This book is for Stephen and Kristin, so that someday they will understand.

"We observe today not a victory of party but a celebration of freedom."
—John Kennedy,
January 20, 1961

"The best thing to be is not apprehensive and not give a fuck."
—Phil Spector

Contents

Motion as metaphysics; Hermann Hesse's *Narcissus and Goldmund*; Henry Thoreau's *Walden Pond*; the passing of the sixties with sixties songs as repository of values

Roots of sixties thought and behavior in the counterculture of the late 1950s; growing up during the Eisenhower-Nixon years: sputnik and the Russian menace; Norman Mailer, Herbert Marcuse, William Whyte, Paul Goodman, juvenile delinquents, James Dean, Caryl Chessman, Jack Kerouac's *On the Road*, Allen Ginsberg's "Howl," the beat generation; comedy and social criticism; Campaign for Nuclear Disarmament; rock-n-roll as revolution and subversion; Elvis Presley, Chuck Berry, Little Richard

Protest in four major strains: nonviolent—Martin Luther King, Jr., civil rights, Vietnam, Pete Seeger, Phil Ochs, Tom Paxton, *Broadside, Sing Out!*, Buffy Sainte-Marie, Joan Baez, Bob Dylan; violent—Malcolm X, Weathermen, Black Panthers, Phil Ochs, the MC5's *Kick Out the Jams*, the Jefferson Airplane's *Volunteers*; holy goof—Abbie Hoffman, Jerry Rubin, Yippies, Procol Harum, Mothers of Invention; artist as social critic—Phil Ochs's *Rehearsals for Retirement*, the Beatles' *Sgt. Pepper*, the Kinks' *Village Green Preservation Society*, the Who's *Tommy*, Leonard Cohen, Simon and Garfunkel's *Bookends*, Bob Dylan's *John Wesley Harding*

The yes behind the no; Woodstock; sixties romanticism; the Beatles' *Magical Mystery Tour*; experimentation and new experience; exploration of self, resistance to structure, feeling as understanding; poverty, love, small is beautiful

Search for a more humane, more flexible life style; dope, Aldous Huxley, Timothy Leary, the Jefferson Airplane's *White Rabbit*, the Beatles' "Lucy in the Sky with Diamonds"; sexual exploration, the Rolling Stones, the Beatles, the Doors, Stephen Stills, David Crosby; flower power; acid rock as the embodiment of the San Francisco hippie philosophy; black power and soul music; experiments in country life and country music, the *Whole Earth Catalog*; the Jefferson Starship, David Bowie, and future rock; experiments in novels, newspapers, light shows, and posters; independent record companies and progressive FM radio programming

5 The Tug of Gravity: Co-option, Absorption, and Shlock Rock 153

Capacity of Western society to absorb any and all alternatives; three tactics used by the power structure to deal with threats: the rub out, the buy-off, and imitation; susceptibility of rock to absorption; Dick Clark and shlock rock, bubble-gum music, Don Kirshner, Tony Orlando, the Carpenters, Muzak, the Monkees; Elvis Presley as paradigm of co-option; Bob Dylan and the walkout

6 Artiness, Absurdity, and Excess 179

Attempt by rock music to turn itself into fine art; folk songs as poems: Paul Simon, Phil Ochs, Bob Dylan, Leonard Cohen: the Beatles' transformations on *Rubber Soul* and *Revolver*, and art songs like "Eleanor Rigby" and "Strawberry Fields Forever"; *Sgt. Pepper* as art and the consequent changes in the Rolling Stones, Joan Baez, Cream, Procol Harum, and Blood, Sweat, and Tears; Van Dyke Parks's ambitious *Song Cycle*; artiness in late Paul Simon, the Jefferson Airplane, the Moody Blues, Phil Ochs, and Bob Dylan; rock and theater: the Doors, *Tommy, Jesus Christ Superstar*; Living Theater, guerrilla theater, street theater; the sixties sense of absurdity and *Blow Up* as a denial of the possibility of knowing; Dylan's sense of the absurd and the Beatles'; Frank Zappa and the Mothers of Invention; Yippies, Chicago Democratic convention, and trial of the Chicago Eight; the dangers of excess, demonstrations and causes, Janis Joplin, the Rolling Stones' concert at Altamont Speedway

7 The Seventies: Looking Back, Looking Ahead 221

Slowing down of motion; Paul Simon's "American Tune"; the Who's *Quadrophenia*; the Rolling Stones' *Some Girls*; retrenchment and privacy; encapsulation of sixties values in private lives; reclaiming the past; Dylan and Rolling Thunder; eyeballing the future

Acknowledgments

Thanks. To Frank Thomas and H. Wayne Wilson of WCBU, to Wayne Tuminello, to my brother Peter, to Columbia Records, A&M Records, Atlantic Records, Vanguard Records, Elektra Records, John Nemo, Robin Currie, Bess Gallanis, Val Beattie, Allen Ginsberg, Robert Bernstein, Mary Meeham, Jamie and Walter and George, Rebecca Sterne. Special thanks to *Rolling Stone* magazine and its editors and contributors, for this book leans heavily on their chronicle of the late sixties and early seventies. Thanks to the Illinois Humanities Council for funding the series of radio broadcasts out of which came the idea for this book. And to Peter Dusenbery for reading this book in rough draft and commenting, at length and in his usual insightful manner.

Preface

A whole generation
With a new explanation
People in motion
People in motion
    —John Phillips, "San Francisco"

Photographs of the sixties flash through my memory: working with SNCC, sitting in a coffee shop somewhere in rural North Carolina with two white friends and a young black journalist, not being served, and refusing to leave until we were served, and still not being served, angry, righteous, anxious, desperate for the courage to continue the journey we had mapped out three hundred miles ago. Knocking on Philadelphia doors, passing out leaflets, and "just talking to people about the war" and about the candidacy of Eugene McCarthy for president of the United States. Rapping with Phil Ochs after a coffeehouse performance in Bryn Mawr. Teaching Thucydides' *Peloponnesian War* at an antiwar teach-in in 1967. Hearing *Sgt. Pepper*, stoned, for the first time. Marching and talking and singing, in large groups and small, in front of cameras and in the solitude of the night, in Philadelphia and Washington and Appalachian villages, on the streets of London, Berlin, Paris, and Rome.

It is, although it has never known a depression or a world war, a tough generation. It arrived in the late forties to understaffed and overcrowded maternity wards and postwar economic dislocations. In childhood and adolescence it fought its way through schools unequipped to deal with either its numbers or its abilities. When, in the middle sixties, it went looking for a college education, it found too few seats in too few universities, so it busted ass to get in and busted ass to stay in. When, diplomas in hand, it went looking for work, it watched a seller's market evaporate overnight and real income begin the protracted decline from which it has never recovered. Now it hustles jobs as it once hustled college dormitory rooms, fighting to hang in there.

When it comes to be buried, it will no doubt find short space at astronomical rent in America's cemeteries.

Which will be no surprise, for it is a generation toughened by fighting for space in a world built two sizes too small, two decades too old.

A generation light on its feet, accustomed to dreaming, experimenting, building and rebuilding, hearing put-downs and watching retreats, and not getting too punched out of shape about them.

(It is in this respect unlike all other generations of native-born, white, middle-class Americans.)

It is a soft generation, kind and generous, contemptous of this world's goods as only people who take them for granted can be. "The best informed, the most intelligent, and the most idealistic this country has ever known," wrote the author of the Cox Commission report on the disorders at Columbia University. It loves hard and plays hard, just as it works hard. It would like to be hopelessly romantic, just as it would like to be nonviolent, tolerant, and pure. But Vietnam, Charles Manson, and the Rolling Stones concert at Altamont Speedway, opened eyes and lumps on the head, have necessitated accommodations. "What we learned in the sixties," a friend told me, "is to help people . . . and kick bastards in the balls."

The generation that grew to maturity during the sixties is a generation given over to some of the noblest causes and some of the most indefensible nonsense in history. It is a generation of great faith and great folly.

It is a generation of experimental rebels. It began by rebelling against irritations close at hand, and before the decade was out the rebellion had spread to virtually all areas of American life. Most of all, it rebelled against the humdrum of middle-class life that annihilated the self in narrowness of vision and smallness of heart. In the end the rebellion of the sixties denied the very essence of Western civilization: liberalism, organization, morality, reason, and deferred gratification.

But negation stands, as William James observed, at the very core of life. While the generation of the sixties was busy denying, it was also busy creating visions by which life could breathe, visions of social justice and personal liberty, Edens of peace, love, freedom, and joy. No to racism meant yes to respect—if not fraternity—among the races. No to militarism was yes to social welfare; no to moral earnestness, an invitation to Rejoice. And the whole fractious, rebellious mass of the decade was lurching its irrational way toward some new and as yet incomplete becoming.

On the way, the generation of the sixties quarreled with everyone and everything—including itself. Weathermen split from Students for a Democratic Society, and women split from Weathermen. SNCC outradicaled the NAACP, and then the Black Panthers outradicaled SNCC. Bob Dylan split from protest folk music for rock-n-roll, then split from rock for country, leaving at each exit booing fans and baying critics. Black Panthers denied drugs and flower children denied the Panthers. Abbie Hoffman and Pete Townshend, mythic embodiments of the new American and British orders, quarreled bitterly and openly at the Woodstock Festival, that emblem of the new consciousness, that celebration of love and understanding.

In *Ramparts* the more ideological New Left militants viciously attacked their ethereal hippie brethren as "liberals gone wild" and "bourgeoisie": "They conform to the reactionary formula of vague protest, hopelessness and fatality. . . . Their work is essentially anarchistic; despairing and destructive . . . rooted in bourgeois individualism." *Ramparts*, in a critique of hippie culture, turned around the Family Dog motto ("May the baby Jesus shut your mouth and open your mind"—a men's room graffito): "Open your mouth and shut your mind."

For their part, counterculturalists often lumped New Left spokesmen with all other politicians, liberal and conservative, seeing in them only more empty politics and more tedious rhetoric. In introducing "For What It's Worth" at the Golden Gate Park Vietnam Moritorium, Stephen Stills proclaimed the bankruptcy of all politics and the truth of his own music: "Politics is bullshit! Richard Nixon is bullshit! Spiro Agnew is bullshit! Our music isn't bullshit!"

In the great mix that was the sixties, two strong-willed and irreconcilable alter egos predominated. Hermann Hesse had identified both thirty years before in a novel that children of the sixties made their own: *Narcissus and Goldmund*. Narcissus, the father and the thinker, the monk, the disciplined moralist, stern and terrible and eternal. Goldmund, the child and the sensualist, the wandering poet and lover, the dreamer and quester locked in his own illusions, incoherence, and spirituality. Each recognizing in the other a completion of his own partial self, each reverencing yet challenging the other, the pair together resonating through periods of separation and conjunction, two truths that are one, two voices that are one. Children of the sixties recognized in both a portion of themselves and in the novel a portrait of their own psyches.

For all the decade's multiplicity, in retrospect one grasps immediately, intuitively, that something *did* happen and continues even now to happen that sets people of the sixties apart from the fifties or seventies generations. But it is not the no or the yes, not the syllogisms of the New Left or the Dionysian vibrations of the west coast: the heart of the sixties was motion and its concomitant, change. Motion made politicians out of folksingers, radicals out of pacifists, activists out of university professors, and dropouts out of businessmen and lawyers. It torched buildings and whole cities, clogged —if only momentarily—the wheels of the war machine, brought love and peace to the Haight, death to Kent State University. The sixties may have said no to everything including itself, but the greatest no of all was to stasis. On that *everyone* agreed. It was motion and change, constant change, change now, that made the sixties as heady and terrifying as they were.

"I can't take boring things."—Jerry Rubin

In insisting on change as wholeheartedly and immediately and constantly as it did, the generation of the sixties insured nothing so much as its own exhaustion and eventually its own demise. People wearied of chaos and confusion. The built-in brakes described by Alvin Toffler in *Future Shock* are real and operative, and they grip us even today. The pendulum *does* swing, and ultimately the Lyndon Johnsons and Dick Daleys were right in sensing that all they had to do was outlast the kids in the street. The dream of Woodstock turned almost inevitably into the nightmare of Altamont. The explosion of energies dissipated quickly into multiple causes, increasingly trivial, increasingly narrow, increasingly untenable.

> "To tell the truth, whenever I hear anyone talking about instinct and being and the secrets of human energy, I get nervous; next thing you know he'll be saying that violence is just fine, and then I begin wondering whether he really thinks that kicking someone in the teeth or sticking a knife between his ribs are deeds to be admired."—Norman Podhoretz, *Partisan Review*, 1958

Motion generated motion, change followed upon change, escalating constantly, until the impossible was demanded as a matter of course. Ultimately the orgy of experimentation led from the modest demand of Dr. King for the right of blacks to vote and to ride in the front of the bus, through the adamant call by Black Panthers for freedom for all black people in federal, state, and city jails, to the theatrical absurdity of the Yippies ("Give me two hundred thousand dollars, and I'll split town"—Abbie Hoffman). Beyond "free everything" could lie nothing but a reassertion of Middle America, the silent majority, the sane center of blue-suited organizers and managers, the defenders of the establishment.

> "While he had existed in perpetual motion, Spector had been invincible. The moment he slowed down, he was lost."—Nik Cohn, rock critic, on Phil Spector, rock producer

But things are not so simple. If the sixties thought that a circle of chanting hippies could raise the Pentagon three hundred feet in the air or exorcise its demons, if they believed that flower power would have political force in terms of elected candidates and revised federal budgets, if they expected the seizure of a library here or a dean there to shake a university's commitment to the Institute for Defense Analysis, then certainly the sixties are dead. However, if the essence of the sixties was not program per se but experimentation, gathering fresh evidence, doing a new and beautiful thing just to show how and that it can be done, then the sixties were not empty sound and fury. We discovered new myths, a new set of heroes and villains. The sixties gave us fresh ways of thinking and talking and behaving.

And we have the music.

A product of the new technology against which both the music and the sixties rebelled, which both it and the sixties took for granted, pop music is the most accurate reflection of the generation in motion. Folk, country, soul, but most of all rock are not merely a record of the age, they *were* the age in all its multiplicity.

> "For the reality of what's happening today in America, we must go to rock-n-roll, to popular music."—Ralph Gleason, *The American Scholar*

> "Rock and roll was the basic revolution to people of my age and situation."—John Lennon

> "Rock 'n' roll music is the energy center for all sorts of changes evolving rapidly around us: social, political, cultural, however you want to describe them. The fact is, for many of us who've grown up since World War II, rock and roll provided the first revolutionary insight into who we are and where we are at in this country."—Jann Wenner, publisher of *Rolling Stone*

Besides being a lot of fun, rock and folk and soul music taught us the sixties, brought us vicariously to Woodstock, Berkeley, Washington, and San Francisco. Where is the sixties child who actually stood outside the gates of Berkeley in 1964 and again in 1969, at Columbia in 1968, at Montgomery in 1963, at Washington in 1963 and 1967, here, there, everywhere the histories and interviews and media recollections take us? He* does not exist; certainly he is not you or I.

Moreover, our chronologies are fuzzed. We came at different times to the Movement. "I never read newspapers until 1968," recalls one child of the decade, "and I stopped again in 1970/71." How was she to know on March 24, 1965, that a teach-in had been held at the University of Michigan that would set the tone and structure for much anti war protest over the next five years? She could not. She did not. And neither did most of America's youth—not even those passionately committed to the peace movement. In time, of course, she attended a teach-in. Somewhere, sometime. But not in Ann Arbor on March 24, 1965. And whatever was said and done on that date by Dr. Spock, Senator Gruening, Norman Thomas, Norman Mailer, Dick Gregory, Malvina Reynolds, and Phil Ochs, though it may have been archetypal, was simply not a part of her experience. The arc of history is a fabrication.

---

*Unfortunately, we lack an appropriate neuter pronoun, and it is awkward to adopt "he/she" whenever a personal pronoun is necessary. Throughout the text I sometimes use "he," sometimes "she," and in each case it should be understood that these terms refer to all human beings.

At this point the music of the sixties saves us. It offers the most accurate record of persons and places and spirits. More important, it provides a common history. We may not have been in Montgomery, Alabama, but we have all sung or heard sung "We Shall Overcome." "We Shall Overcome" created a sense of unity among diverse peoples and purposes, a community of pacifists and hippies and whites and blacks, a bridge between 1962 and 1969. The songs of the sixties give support to sixties history and sociology.

For most children of the sixties, music is inseparable even today from action. Bopping at the hop was itself a form of teenage rebellion. The curious moral ambivalence of a protest demonstration yoked with a folk or a rock concert makes no sense at all, nor does the screaming of fans at a concert for starving children in Bangla Desh. But middle-class white youth of the sixties borrowed a tradition from the poor and the disenfranchised of other ages and other cultures, and college libraries across the country were seized to the strain of guitars.

> Greetings and welcome Rolling Stones, our comrades in the desperate battle against the maniacs who hold power. The revolutionary youth of the world hears your music and is inspired to even more deadly acts. We fight in guerrilla bands against the invading imperialists in Asia and South America, we riot at rock-'n'-roll concerts everywhere: We burned and pillaged in Los Angeles and the cops know our snipers will return. . . .
>
> We will play your music in rock-'n'-roll marching bands as we tear down the jails and free the prisoners, as we tear down the State schools and free the students, as we tear down the military bases and arm the poor. . . .   —Radical Welcome to the Rolling Stones, Presented upon the Occasion of Their First Visit to the West Coast

The music of the sixties was very much aware of its role, self-critically aware, making itself a news bulletin board, interpreting and arguing in song the way medieval scholastics debated in Latin, denouncing imposters and poseurs, commenting on itself as participant and reporter: Dylan's "My Back Pages" (1964), the Who's *Quadrophenia* (1973), the Stones' "Street Fighting Man" (1968). White Panther leader John Sinclair's proposed symbol of "the particular nature of our movement for the liberation of the youth colony" was two crossed sticks representing "a rifle (on the left) and a guitar (on the right), with a peace pipe full of the righteous sacrament crossing them and bringing those two elements together. We can't have the guitar without the gun or we won't survive, we can't have the gun without the guitar or else we'd just be more of the same old shit we are trying to do away with; and without the sacrament that gives us our vision neither the guitar nor the gun would amount to anything worthwhile."

> "We have to differentiate between songs that really make a point like 'Hattie Carroll' and songs that make vague philosophical points that can be taken

any way by anybody."—Phil Ochs on "Eve of Destruction"

The sixties live on in music. The songs do not merely survive, they continue to speak, to vibrate. The movies are quaint, television-pathetic. Most
of the books are dead, from *Soul on Ice* to *The Electric Kool-Aid Acid Test*
to *The Greening of America* to *Steal This Book.*

But the music lives, in record shops and private collections and golden
oldies. In K-TEL's forty-nine oldies for only $6.95, $8.95 tapes, care of this
station, not available in any record store. On warm spring days blasting
from college dorm windows. That's where the sixties are to be found, the
mythology and the passion, the new visions and the revolutions, all the motion and the commotion of the great decade. It's still sung, still played,
still *believed* in spite of the years, creating its own synapse through time.

Those who came of age during the sixties find in each song a moment
and an attitude we cannot and will not bury, a contact with the self and an
experience with others, a vision we can dance at the flip of a record changer.

And to those who ask wide-eyed about the great, good times, who have
unlearned in so short a period all that once seemed precious, who have sold
out or been sold out or perhaps have just not understood, who wonder wist-
fully what it was like to grow up in the sixties—for you I switch on the record machine, to see whether you will dance, to see whether your feet will
move and your asses fidget and your brain bounce, maybe to show you a
vision and trace its birth and death, to brag a little. To remind you.

Chuck Berry does the splits and the duck walk, his trademark since 1956. He is the greatest of the fifties rock-n-roll poets and the voice behind the Rolling Stones. *Photos by Chuck Pulin. Used by permission.*

Buddy Holly, the white root of rock-n-roll, the voice behind the early Beatles, died in a plane crash on February 3, 1959, "the day the music died."

Disc jockey Alan Freed, first rock-n-roll super promoter; died destitute a few years after the payola scandals. *United Press International Photo. Used by permission.*

Fats Domino, a steady, chunky, slightly boogie-woogie and always restrained bridge between rock-n-roll and rhythm and blues. *Photo by Chuck Pulin. Used by permission.*

"My music is the healin' music, it makes the blind see, the lame walk, and the dumb and the deaf hear and talk." Little Richard Penniman. *Courtesy of Michael Ochs Archives. Used by permission.*

James Dean, rebel without a cause and embodiment of the frenetic motion expressed by Jack Kerouac's characters in *On the Road:* "We gotta go and never stop going till we get there." "Where we going, man?" "I don't know, but we gotta go."

Elvis Presley, the white singer with the black sound: "When the record came out a lot of people liked it, and you could hear folk around town saying 'Is he [black], is he?' and I'm going 'Am I, am I?'" *Photo courtesy of Michael Ochs Archives. Used by permission.*

1955 Chevrolet Bel Air hardtop coupe.

Lean, young, and hungry Elvis as outlaw in the 1957 movie, *Jailhouse Rock*. This film, which he choreographed himself, contains some of the finest dancing of his career.

Elvis' body movements on a 1956 television show so enrage critics that, from then on, he is only shown from the waist up.

Woody Guthrie, dust bowl balladeer, an influence on every American folksinger since the 1930s: "It was in the quick sands and muds of the rivers risin', the winds that blew and whipped from east to west in a split second, the lightnin' that splintered the barn loft, the snakey-tailed cyclone, prairie cloud bursts, months of firey drought that crippled the leaves, and the timber fires, and the rights of men against all of these that I was born, the third child in our family."

Opposite page, top: A 1962 demonstration in New York City against nuclear testing, featuring, among others, Pete Seeger (below "LIFE" sign) on the banjo. *United Press International Photo. Used by permission.* Bottom: Beats count their pennies before buying another round in the Co-Existence Bagel Shop, San Francisco, 1958. *United Press International Photo. Used by permission.*

1 | Underground in the Fifties

To understand the sixties, you have to understand the fifties—both the mainstream against which the following generation revolted and the counterculture out of which the sixties sprang full grown except for a splash of color here, a chemical or stray transistor there.

And to understand the firties, you must begin with World War II for that is where the mental set of the fifties began (and ended). Our ride to the Armageddon of 1969 begins with Hitler's blitz of Poland three decades earlier.

The most important thing to grasp about World War II is that it was not fundamentally good for America. Even if we did win handily—or perhaps precisely *because* we won .

First, it's never healthy having millions and millions of husbands and daddies—an entire generation, in fact—processed by the war machine, hair cut, bodies standardized into pressed and polished uniforms, minds standardized into drill field rows and blocks, eyes straight ahead, chin in, chest out, salute and return salute, all part of a finely tuned machine that goes when it's told to go, holds when told to hold, and fetches on command. Even after all due allowances for the usual discrepancies between image and reality, concentrated doses of the military mind tend to kill off victors along with vanquished. Second, when you win as cleanly as we did, without devastating our own backyard, without fully comprehending that war is—really *is*—hell, then a lot of things happen to your head.

For one, the khaki vision is bound to rub off. No matter how screwed up *A Bridge Too Far* may appear at the moment, when you come to step back and take an overview, to balance out as it were, and you find yourself face to face with the blond goddess Victory, you catch yourself thinking, "Well, it *did* work after all," and in the back of your mind you may *believe* in the chain of command, and the organization, and the subordination of man to country, and everybody doing her part cheerfully and obediently.

For another thing, war appears a little too easy, a little too glorious, and—the Second World War having been a righteous war and therefore palpably different from the standard land grab—a little too justifiable. Especially when it pulled us out of a nasty depression. So war, you begin to think, has its advantages, especially if it can be promoted as a holy war, with God on your side. The unthinkable becomes an acceptable tool of foreign policy (Korea, Vietnam), economic policy (a price war), social policy

1

(a war on poverty), or everyday life. Let's make war on racism, bigotry, the Biggees, hippies, fags, niggers, our own kids. Your thinking as well as your vocabulary gets screwed around. Norman Mailer explained this mindset in *Why Are We in Vietnam?*

To a degree we all succcumbed, but mostly the veterans themselves, our fathers and teachers. Not only did they accustom themselves too easily to military aggressiveness, but they developed other bad habits as well, all more or less directly attributable to World War II. Like a certain contempt for alternatives (European, Russian, Oriental) and unthinking devotion to the ideals for which and the methodologies by which they had fought and won. Or a dangerous overconfidence. Or the habit of seeing things in black and white and from lofty heights.

The war filled America's pants with lead, set the moss growing, raised up a generation that wanted nothing more than to marry the little honey it hadn't seen in thirty months, buy a house, and fill it with kids. To protect her and them and General Motors from godless communism, godless socialism, and godless fascism; to take a bath, settle in, hunker down back home in Kalamazoo, forget the Nips and the Krauts, bite into that old, capitalistic apple pie, and just do things right and easy under Ike and Nixon (America was never too sure about Nixon, but if Ike thought he was okay, then he was okay); and to relive the power and the glory with John Wayne as battalion leader.

Our fathers came home from the war and married their pen-pal sweethearts. They went to college on the GI bill, where they obeyed their teachers the way they had obeyed their drill sergeants ("Most dedicated, disciplined, hardworking students we've ever had," the college people will tell you, "although not necessarily the brightest"). They went to church, arrived at work promptly at 8:00, bought homes and cars and life insurance, warmed to *I Remember Mama*, laughed at the wholesome *Adventures of Ozzie and Harriet*, preferred Ed Sullivan's vaudeville two to one over Steve Allen's social satire, and generally got on with the kind of democracy they had made the world safe for.

Having seen Europe once, they had no wish to return or even to trouble their heads with French existentialism or German reunification. Having traveled, they put down their roots. Having sown wild oats across three continents and a thousand isles, they settled comfortably into marital celibacy. Weary of war's confusion and alarm, they sought stability and security. Discouraged by training from philosophical subtleties and intellectual complexities, they left the thinking to the eggheads, elected Ike, brought up their kids right. When threatened, they shot first. Never did they ask questions. After all, a generation that endured the depression, the war, and the postwar economic readjustment was entitled to peace, quiet, and some of the good life.

I don't wish to be severe. I mean only to explain the remarkable cultural and intellectual vacuity, the social rigidity, the pervasive conservatism of mainstream, postwar American life, and thereby both the counterculture that developed far below ground during the fifties and the eruption of the sixties.

Who, seriously, is going to freak out over long hair—except a generation that mandated the military crew cut for all decent American males, despite the obvious and painful fact that it makes men look like bald eagles? And, conversely, where's the rebellion in dancing the twist or the jitterbug or the cool jerk—unless you've been indoctrinated with the basic box and the Arthur Murray rumba? Why should it be so radical to protest the executing of car thieves or the relegating of one-fifth the population to separate johns, restaurants, bus seats, and baseball leagues? Unless the moral sensibilities have been reduced to cowboy-Indian simplicities by something like World War II?

What the golden fifties were really about was the unnatural prolongation of World War II heroism and mindset, both of them narrow and atavistically barbarian during the war years, both of them narrow and anachronistically barbarian in the fifties. It is no wonder that the young were complaining by 1958, rebelling openly in 1963, triumphing so easily— if temporarily—in 1968.

So let us have some fragments, some reminders of the fifties establishment, some evidence from a variety of sources.

Time magazine cover, October 5, 1953: "Proctor and Gamble's McElroy: He Duz the Dishes with a Tide of Joy." Inside, the heart-warming story of "Anne Spada, 29, who reached the finals of the Mrs. America beauty contest but withdrew to be with nine children and a plant-foreman husband." Mrs. Spada is photographed enjoying the "reward of unselfishness," a Florida vacation for self, husband, and all nine kids.

November 1954 *Life* magazine cover story: "Gina Lollabrigida—A Star's Wardrobe." Inside, a series of two-page spreads introducing the 1955 line of Chrysler automobiles.

November 25, 1954: on the front page of the *New York Times*, Ike and Mamie and Montgomery smile for reporters below the caption "President's New Plane Christened, and Is Off for Augusta." The accompanying article elaborates: "The President planned to remain here until Monday, with a minimum of work and a maximum amount of time for golf. The weather forecaster promised mild weather." Monty, his back injured shortly after the war, would follow the presidential foursome but would not play. He would, however, certainly join Ike and Mamie for bridge during the evening.

December 1954: *Flatiron*, a humor magazine at the University of Colorado, is busted for publishing pinups of coeds. The University Publications Board suspends the magazine after three issues, decrying "emphasis on sex and alcohol."

May 30, 1955, *Time* magazine again: "The people of the U.S. had never been so prosperous (*see* Business). Never before had the bread-winner taken home so much money; in March and April, after-tax pay of the average factory worker with three dependents was around $70 a week. Not since the first delirious, mistaken weeks after V-J day had there been so much expectancy—with caution, this time—for peace. The fishing was good, too. In the gulf, off the coast of Louisiana, speckled trout were swarming in the bays and bayous, and tarpon appeared a full month earlier than usual. Said Bill Tugman, editor of the weekly Reedsport (Ore.) *Port Umpqua Courier*: 'The salmon are running and the trout and striped bass, and they even say the shad feel like taking a fly this year. So let Moscow do its worst.'"

May 5, 1958: Five young soldiers are killed when unpredicted winds drag men of the 101st Airborne Division across the ground behind parachutes that will not collapse. One dies of head injuries, the others are strangled. "Sure it was sad," commented a sergeant, "but it's what we volunteered for." The division's commander, one Major General William Westmoreland, also jumped and was dragged two hundred yards by the gusts. "It was part of our business," he explained.

> (Westmoreland believed what he said in 1958, just as he believed it a decade later in Vietnam. It was characteristic of the fifties that the general should not for a moment have questioned that dying absurdly and pointlessly *should* be his job. In 1958 this was understandable because the United States was still frozen in the Second World War mentality. In the sixties, the lights had changed in America.)

"Neck deep in the Big Muddy, and the big fool says to push on."—Pete Seeger

The fifties were a quiet, peaceful time to live—disciplined, ordered, aware enough of the Bomb to buy a bomb shelter but not politicized enough to object to the notion of bombs for every city, bombers for every bomb. An era content to let blacks into white baseball—grudgingly—but not into white schools. (Even when the great awakening came in 1957, Ike persisted in turning the matter of segregation out of a moral issue and into the technical question of *Orval Faubus v. the Law of the Land.*)

The fifties were a good time to be under twelve, to be riding a bicycle or playing baseball in a vacant lot or investigating the decaying house on the edge of town. They were good years for working your way up the corporate ladder, for collecting dividends, for everything that relied on a stable system, on fixity, on 2¾% annual interest.

But once you passed puberty, began to think or ask questions, you were in trouble. Behind the smiles and the callow nonchalance lay a great vacuum and a terrible repression, with much guilt and a lot of nervous tension, most of which was visited upon the innocent young.

Two scenes especially stick out in my mind, each in its way representative of the true temper of the times.

It is May 1956. Junior assembly. For eight evenings, once each month during the school year, an Arthur Murray instructor has drubbed into our uninterested, eighth-grade heads the standard ball-room dance steps: step STEP close, step STEP close, step STEP close, step STEP close; one, two, cha-cha-cha, one, two, step-step-step. The boys have done it, then the girls have done it, then lined up facing each other they have done it, then randomly paired they have done it, breaking for cookies and punch, in lines again and in pairs again. Backs straight, boy's hand held firmly in the middle of his partner's back, none of that cheek-to-cheek, head-to-head stuff ("mixing dandruff," he used to call it, which was certainly enough to discourage *me*). Straight, professional, Mr. Clean dancing that our parents had been convinced by the school board or the dance instructor or somebody who ought to have known better would develop grace and social skills and allow a cool, sanctioned familiarity with the opposite sex.

Now it is a real live dance with a real live band and suits and pastel formals. The gymnasium has been decorated with pink and white crepe paper and little café tables around which couples may sit and sip Coca-Cola or study the engraved dance programs in whose blanks have been presumably written all the young men with whom one's date will dance the evening away. (Mine are mostly empty, of course, so she dances with me or with a last minute swap. "Do you have any dances open?" "Well, yes, do you?" "Which ones?" "Well, only a couple." "How about number twelve?" "What a coincidence!")

There is clumsy grown-up talk, or attempts at grown-up talk—anything other than the school chitchat that would easily fill a less contrived situation.

"The place sure looks nice."

"It must have taken them a long time to decorate it."

"Pretty."

"You'd never think you were in a gym."

"Doesn't even smell."

"That looks like Ken over there."

"With Carol."

"Yes."

"I think it is."

"We could talk to them."

"We could."

"Would you like another Coke?"

"Well, if it's not too much trouble."

"I'll go get it."

"The place sure looks nice. . . ."

There are spot dances ("The couple under the light, right there at the top of the foul lane, wins a silver dollar each; come on up, kids, and get your prize"). And door prizes. The whole ten yards. None of which is enough. By the band's first break, the entire artifice has disintegrated. Boys congregate with boys in the hallways, by the refreshment table, in the can. Their dates are abandoned to girl friends or themselves. Couples must be conned onto the floor with increasing numbers of prize dances, and even then there are few takers. Girls dance with girls. A few try jitterbugging to slow numbers off in a corner, but the band cannot, will not, or is not permitted to play anything but step STEP close and one, two, step-step-step. Rumor has it that Tommy Egan and Candy Moore are in a car in the parking lot making out (rumor also has it that Tommy has actually *screwed* her—a word that I'd not even heard half a year before although the matter now interests me greatly—but no nevermind, he's a young punk most certainly destined to be a car mechanic, and the people at church have been talking to her). In tight knots in the hallway the guys twitter nervously, but nobody will go outside to look. At 10:00 we are directed to dance one last slow number with our dates (spines straight, hands firmly in the middle of the girl's back) before our mommies and daddies come to pick us up.

October 5, 1957. I am shelving books in the Springfield Public Library, at 85¢ an hour, one of the more tangible rewards of being president of the Junior High School Library Club. I'm in the nonfiction section, near 335 books on communism and 527 books on space travel, which in this International Geophysical Year are pretty popular. I have a copy of Willy Ley's *Rockets, Missiles, and Space Travel* somewhere on the truck, or Wernher von Braun's *Exploration of Mars*, along with Daphne du Maurier's *Scapegoat* and James Cozzens's *By Love Possessed* for the fiction shelves.

There is a stir by the door—it's the kind of stir you don't hear in the Springfield Public Library, and I know something's up. Mr. Huddleston, a Saturday morning regular, retired watchman for Westinghouse, who reads a dozen mysteries in a week, has brought a newspaper, over which he and Mr. Hall, the librarian, and somebody else are conferring. Consternation clouds his normally placid face, and even Mr. Hall—wife, two kids, working his way steadily up the comfortable ladder of the Springfield High School administration—frowns darkly.

The Russians have launched a satellite, called a sputnik. The headline reads: "Soviet Fires Earth Satellite into Space; It Is Circling the Globe at 18,000 M.P.H.; Sphere Tracked in Crossing over U.S."

Our thoughts are all the same although we talk around them. "*They* are *there*, ahead of us. The evil ones. Five times heavier than us. Photographing, snooping, doing God knows what. We've been caught off guard. Our team has lost. What will happen to us now?"

The World Series, even at a game apiece for Milwaukee and the Yanks; our chess game; the election of Jimmy Hoffa to the presidency of the Teamsters—are suddenly trivial. This is, and each of us senses it, the end of fishing and golf in fifties America.

My brains will bleed for these Russian sins over the next four years, as the American generals, their egos bruised and their nerves jangled by this greatest of international upsets, filled to their ears with Dulles-inspired angst, thrash my ass in a mad race to bury the Ruskies beneath dollars, programs, and cerebrums, to make sure the United States does not become a second-class power. Overnight the schools are offering special programs of accelerated learning (mostly in the hard sciences, with emphasis also on foreign languages and math) for heretofore unchallenged, undervalued, and mostly ignored eggheads. I do not ask why, I merely study frenetically. Rock-n-roll, hot rods, girls are now not only sinful but unpatriotic as well. By 1959, *Time*'s cover concern will be "U.S. Public Schools: Can They Produce Quality and Quantity?"

I will live a decade in sputnik's long shadow.

> (In the fifties social problems were *always* internalized and personalized. If you didn't make it, it was your fault, never the fault of a bad system. You had not taken advantage of an opportunity somewhere. If your team lost, that was also your fault—you had not worked hard enough, had not done enough to stop the other team. In the short run, this internalization generated guilt; in the long run it generated anger. In the sixties, the anger turned to rage.)

At best, then, the ordinary lives of ordinary people were during the fifties dull, duller, dullest. Often they were painful. Very restrictive. Straight. We have forgotten this in the golden glow of *The Way We Were* and *American Graffiti* and *Happy Days*. A Columbia Records LP called the *50's Greatest Hits* includes Johnny Mathis doing "Wonderful! Wonderful!" Patti Page singing "Tennessee Waltz," Frankie Laine and "I Believe," Joan Webber with "Let Me Go, Lover," Johnnie Ray singing "The Little White Cloud That Cried," Doris Day doing "Secret Love," and a dozen other *Your Hit Parade* specials. How sticky, how gushy, how totally unreal! Of the lot, only Rosemary Clooney's "Come On-a My House (I'm gonna give you candy)" sounds vaguely interesting today.

Let us leave mainstream 1945-1960 thinking with a look at the 1945 version of *State Fair* (or even the 1962 remake, with Pat Boone and Ann-Margret, a movie offered as something wholesome and then some that the by then embattled forces of decency could hurl against their rock-n-rolling, guitar-toting kids; I prefer the original myself—it's purer). Everything is bow ties, formal gowns, carnations, teenagers who look twenty-seven, crew cuts, lush makeup, Rodgers and Hammerstein songs, posed and stylized motions, virginal women. Mother wins a special award at the fair for her pickles, dad wins a blue ribbon for his hog. Daughter loves and nearly loses Mr. Wonderful when he rushes off without warning (to take a job as a Chicago columnist, it turns out—but he comes back). Son falls for a carnival singer only to discover that she's already (unhappily) married. Off he goes to get mildly drunk and then consoled by the barker: "Nobody's perfect. Show folks is just like you folks. Is everybody in your home town perfect?" The kid decides that no, by golly, everybody's *not* perfect (they're allowed to be unhappily married and maybe even to get divorced). So he has her and she has him, everybody wins a big prize, and, presumably, they all live happily ever after in the green hills of Ioway.

> (I think I saw that movie half a dozen times in high school assembly. That one and *Mr. Smith Goes to Washington,* which, until John Kennedy went down, I also half believed.)

To a very considerable extent the anger of the sixties arose directly from the realization that the system, not the individual, might be at fault when affairs get botched, that only in movies does everybody win big prizes, and that America pays largely in paper money. Naturally we were plenty pissed when those small rewards we'd been given turned out to be counterfeit—but we were also liberated, freed from the illusion that work on Maggie's Farm really pays off. And in liberty comes strength.

> (Basically all you got for your twenty years of schooling was the day shift.)

Grown-up smart people of the fifties could have exposed these fictions, but with few exceptions they did not. Mostly they had been bought off by the establishment and just dished out the party bullshit, thereby becoming accessories to the fact. I hold no grudges now: they're sorry, I'm sorry, we've all learned. Maybe I wouldn't have listened anyway. Besides, there were pressures on them, too. On the one hand were the House Un-American Activities Committee (HUAC) and the blacklist, the one official and the other quasi-official, either of which could sink even a tenured professor quicker than Ike could sink a putt. On the other hand were the aid and comfort of working your way up the administrative ladder and the security of much more than $70 a week for intellectuals who got themselves absorbed via a federal appointment into the military-industrial-educational complex. And who, really, could blame them? After all, intellectuals and artists also had hungered during the depression and the war.

But HUAC and the war do not explain the failure of intellectual nerve in America after 1945. Nor, for all its glowering terror, was it the Bomb that totally unnerved everybody. The sellout of intellectuals and artists was more complicated than economics, technology run haywire, or cold war politics. It had been developing over the better part of the twentieth century.

To distill a lot of baroque and very New Left analysis, the failure of intellectual critique stemmed from four processes. All were well under way by 1945 and would probably have brought America to something closely resembling its fifties zero with or without the war.

The first was the failure, somewhere around World War I, of the socialist alternative, which, beginning in the late nineteenth century, had offered a fairly comprehensive blueprint for thorough reform of American society. At the outset of the First World War, it is comforting to remember, the country was crawling with populist-socialist-Marxist visionaries: 79 socialist mayors in 24 states, 1,200 socialist officeholders in 340 American cities, the poet Carl Sandburg, and the politican Eugene V. Debs, who in 1912 polled 6% of the popular vote in the presidential election. These fellows had a plan to fix this here country: nationalize the railroads and telegraphs, tax the hell out of land speculation profits (would you believe, America, 100%?), form labor and farm cooperatives, build unions, enfranchise women and blacks and poor. The program was zapped by the old left-right of factionalism within and wartime prosecution without. When it went down in the early twenties, it took with it the whole left wing of the American political spectrum, except for Haywood's IWW, which flourished more as an idea than as a political force.

> "During the Dies, McCarthy and Feinberg Law investigations," Paul Goodman wrote, "our professors shivered in their boots and our 'radicals' hid like roaches."

The second reason for the lack of intellectual criticism was the rise under Franklin Roosevelt of classic work-for-reform-from-within-the-system liberalism. Although it looked good at the time, liberalism did not work out well. Not only did it distract intellectuals who might have offered valuable critiques of the status quo but it effectively buried their modest visions under a mountain of federal machinery as well. And the further it went, the bigger it grew and the less effective it became. By the fifties, liberalism was absorbing most of the nation's brainpower and, tangled up in its own systems, producing almost no effective reform.

A third important factor was the neutering of the humanities. Literature turned its attention from truth, morality, and even beauty to morally neutral (but pseudoscientific) technique, literary history, and textual and linguistic analysis. Political scientists and sociologists turned the world into tables of *yes, no, often, sometimes,* and *maybe,* on which laws of statistical predictability and correct footnote form counted far more than whatever the numbers and the footnotes measured. Psychologists abandoned their study of man—or, rather, they sold out to the establishment. Half of them studied man to find new ways of selling General Foods cereals, General Motors cars, and General Eisenhower Republicanism to people who wanted none of the above. The other half busied themselves refining the tools of psychoanalysis so that the dissident few could be worn out against the passivity of the analyst and the neurotic many could be reconciled to their unhappiness. "Therapy," as Marcuse said in 1955, "is a course in resignation."

The dominant school of philosophical thought was, by the end of the Second World War, existentialism, which reduced the world to a highly intellectualized nothing before laughing at it and then irresponsibly but heroically committing suicide.

Finally, the artists—who might have spoken over, under, around, and through this cotton filter—found themselves virtually without audience. Some were cut off, absorbed, or patently misrepresented by slick systems of distribution manned by the hired guns of the mainstream and intent only on profits and preserving the status quo. Others despaired, cut themselves off from the distributors *and* the masses, and produced art for artists. Either way, serious art disappeared from the lives of those Americans who needed it most.

The old values and the old virtues (humanism, truth, morality, ethics) interested no one. Pure and morally neutral technique interested everyone. But *that* was part of the problem.

So where, I ask, was the leadership in all of this?

Nowhere.

Yet underneath the cotton candy was developing a counterculture as international as the American plasticity it opposed, formulating for itself very different axioms, and poopooed by every voice of the establishment as cheap, thin, decadent, trivial, vacuous, immoral, mindless, juvenile, unhealthy, undisciplined, uncivilized, unfit for human consumption, and generally un-American.

> "I feel the hints, the clues, the whisper of a new time coming. There is a universal rebellion in the

air, and the power of the two colossal superstates may be, yes, may just be ebbing, may be failing in energy even more rapidly than we are failing in energy, and if that is so, then the destructive, the liberating, the creative nihilism of the Hip, the frantic search for potent Change may break into the open with all its violence, its confusion, its ugliness and horror."—Norman Mailer's last column for the *Village Voice*, 1956

And those voices were right. For the counterculture of the fifties, often in schizophrenic fashion, attempted to be everything that mainstream America was not. The establishment offered institutionalized Christianity and the traditional Western values of rationalism, technology, organization, control, temperance, deferred gratification (especially sexual), and liberalism; the counterculture answered with Eastern mysticism, studied disorganization, self-indulgence, immediate and conspicuous gratification (especially sexual), and—when it came to politics—either flaming radicalism or strict abstention.

Whereas the mainstream had intellectualized itself to abstraction and absurdity, countercultural heads were frankly, actively, flagrantly (although not purely) noncerebral. What the mainstream tried to conceal, the counterculture flaunted. What the mainstream tried to ignore, refine away, and otherwise purge from human experience, the counterculture explored openly, delightedly, and tauntingly: noise, homosexuality, speed, sex, psychopathy, ugliness, excrement, death.

This was no "persuasive program for social reconstruction, thought up by many minds, corrected by endless criticism, made practical by much political activity," as Paul Goodman once described the socialist alternative, but it was *an* alternative, alive and real and rambunctious.

At first it was a buried alternative, rumored in the alleyways, fathered by legendary figures who drifted from New York to San Francisco, to Denver to Mexico to Paris, to Algiers, more elusive even than the black subculture on which it patterned itself. It might have been intuited, perhaps, from some of the realistic fiction being written—Mailer's *Naked and the Dead*—but not until the middle fifties did it really escape the closet in the guise of rock-n-roll music, the cult of James Dean, the movie *Rebel without a Cause*, Herbert Marcuse's *Eros and Civilization*, William Whyte's *Organization Man*, and the essays of Paul Goodman that would become *Growing Up Absurd*.

(This delayed process of discovery and the subterranean quality of fifties counterculture, especially in contrast to that of the sixties, is an important measure of the Eisenhower chill. Whereas in 1965 the news media devoured anything that was new and moved, the attitude of the fifties was such as to repress motion, minimize alternatives, screen out the unusual. In 1955 you had to go looking for novelty; a decade later you could not escape it.)

The year 1955 saw the publication of Marcuse's *Eros and Civilization*, an insufferably Germanic analysis but an important early warning against an age that had become, with assistance from neo-Freudian analysis, "totalitarian where it has not produced totalitarian states." In Marcuse's view, civilization, almost of necessity, demands that aggression and sex be sublimated into Protestant work. In fact, Marcuse saw the complete annihilation and alienation of individual expression by efficiently functioning systems. There are alternatives, however. Marcuse reflected on "alternative reality principles" that might reduce "the social demands upon instinctual energy to be spent in alienated labor." What the West needs, he argued, is a change of goal and a change of myth, something that could accept the material goodies generated by a repressive "performance principle" and use them as a basis for a "qualitatively different, nonrepressive reality principle" that might loosen up the controls on fantasy and sex.

In this case, the quantum of instinctual energy still to be diverted into necessary labor (in turn completely mechanized and rationalized) would be so small that a large area of repressive constraints and modifications, no longer sustained by external forces, would collapse. Consequently, the antagonistic relation between pleasure principle and reality principle would be altered in favor of the former. Eros, the life instincts, would be released to an unprecedented degree.

Translated this means, approximately, let's let the machines do the work, and let's get loaded, sing, dance, and screw.

Pleasure principle, life instincts, the collapse of external forces—within Marcuse's awkward academese one recognizes the germ of the liberated sixties, their slogans, their metaphysics, their world. Marcuse's *One-Dimensional Man* would become a mainstay of sixties New Left analysis; *Eros and Civilization* described the hippie ethic ten years before that group's emergence: "The Orphic Eros transforms being: he masters cruelty and death through liberation. His language is *song*, and his work is *play*." (The italics are Marcuse's.)

Other fifties critics came at the problem from different directions. William H. Whyte's *Organization Man* is a less mythological-philosophical-psychological, more commonsense analysis of Marcuse's repressive performance principle in action. In a tone that wavers between sympathy and contempt, Whyte followed a young modern bureaucrat through the many phases of his developing relationship with the organization: his training for, and election to, successively higher levels of authority (and absorption), his adjustment to phony "belongingness" and "togetherness" and "well-roundedness." Organization, system, bureaucracy: in Whyte's view they are dangerous, counterproductive, necessary, useful, tyrannical, but most of all inescapable. They are everywhere: in clubs and churches and work-places and schools and sports arenas. In a casual evening spent with friends. In dining out and in making love.

Whyte's conclusions are guarded.

> This book is not a plea for nonconformity. Such pleas have an occasional therapeutic value, but as an abstraction, nonconformity is an empty goal, and rebellion against prevailing opinion merely be-cause it is prevailing should no more be praised than acquiescence to it. . . . I am going to argue that he [the organization man] should fight the organization. But not self-destructively. He may tell the boss to go to hell, but he is going to have another boss.

Whyte is a liberal, then: "Organization has been made by man; it can be changed by man."

If Marcuse's Eros represents one-half of the sixties, Whyte himself is the other: the crusader and the demonstrator, the worker through the system, or the worker to replace The System with another system that works better, but always an individual conscious of organization and the way it might be used to affect the behavior of whole populations.

Whyte's unthinkingly acquiescent organization man is the prototype for a favorite sixties caricature—the Beatles' Nowhere Man, Ray Stevens's Mr. Businessman, Bob Dylan's Mr. Jones, who all live in little boxes made of ticky-tacky.

> Little boxes on the hillside,
> Little boxes made of ticky tacky,
> Little boxes on the hillside,
> Little boxes all the same;
> There's a green one and a pink one
> And a blue one and a yellow one
> And they're all made out of ticky tacky
> And they all look just the same.
>
> And the people in the houses
> All went to the university,
> Where they were put in boxes
> And they came out all the same,
> And there's doctors and lawyers,
> And business executives,
> And they're all made out of ticky tacky
> And they all look just the same.

And they all play on the golf course
And drink their martinis dry,
And they all have pretty children
And the children go to school,
And the children go to summer camp
And then to the university,
Where they are put in boxes
And they come out all the same.

Little boxes on the hillside,
Little boxes made of ticky tacky,
Little boxes on the hillside,
Little boxes all the same;
And the boys go into business
And marry and raise a family
In boxes made of ticky tacky
And they all look just the same.
    —Malvina Reynolds

The third major rationalist critique of life in the fifties is Paul Goodman's *Growing Up Absurd* (1959). Goodman neither apologized for nor attempted to hide his attitude toward his subject, "the disgrace of the Organized System of semimonopolies, government, advertisers, etc., and the disaffection of the growing generation." In magnificent, rolling prose, Goodman unloaded both guns.

> For it can be shown—I intend to show—that with all the harmonious belonging and all the tidying up of background conditions that you please, our abundant society is at present simply deficient in many of the most elementary objective opportunities and worth-while goals that could make growing up possible. It is lacking in enough man's work. It is lacking in honest public speech, and people are not taken seriously. It is lacking in the opportunity to be useful. It thwarts aptitude and creates stupidity. It corrupts ingenuous patriotism. It corrupts the fine arts. It shackles science. It dampens animal ardor. It discourages the religious convictions of Justification and Vocation and it dims the sense that there is a Creation. It has no Honor. It has no Community.
>
>   (Times have changed but in none of the respects mentioned.)

What interested Goodman most was youth's reaction—and in 1959 he saw, or thought he saw, signs everywhere of the gathering storm: resignation in the good little boys, anger in the juvenile delinquents, confusion at all levels. Goodman admitted that youth's excesses and gauntlets are a constant in human history, so in one sense the rebellion was nothing new. But he also had the good sense to point out that the burden of guilt lies with the society critiqued not with the beatnik or the delinquent. And he had the further good sense to perceive the direction from which meaningful revisions of American life would come: the young, the alienated, society's washouts and delinquents. He even perceived that Eros, when he arrived, would come dressed in rags and feathers radically different from those worn by himself, Marcuse, Whyte, all the aging forties and fifties liberals, all the Mr. Joneses of straight fifties culture.

> (Eros came, in fact, dressed as Thoreau. In the tenth grade *Walden* rocked me and a lot of my friends to sleep each night with weird visions of mystic transcendence and revolt. "Lying, flattering, voting, contracting yourself into a nutshell of civility, or dilating into an atmosphere of thin and vaporous generosity, that you may persuade your neighbor to let you make his shoes, or his hat, or his coat, or his carriage, or import his groceries for him; making yourselves sick, that you may lay up something against a sick day, something to be tucked away in an old chest, or in a stocking behind the plastering, or, more safely, in the brick bank; no matter where, no matter how much or how little." *Here* was the voice of the sixties and the wellspring of Goodman's critique and of all the critiques of the fifties fathers.)

There is a strong distrust of intellectualism in each of these books. One of the many paradoxes of the sixties is that its best artists opposed the idea of art, its best musicians consciously avoided professionalism of music, its thinkers even in thinking opposed pure thought. Seeds of this paradox can be seen in Goodman, Whyte, and Marcuse. Eros comes playing and singing, not studying and analyzing and reorganizing. Goodman invariably finds in the system a perverse logic, so that logic itself becomes suspect. When he weighs the relative values of, say, camps for thousands of potential delinquents and "one of the Park Commissioner's new highways to West Chester," he does so not with the rational, long-term, cost-value accounting we might have gotten from Robert McNamara but with a call for decency and humanism. Reason provides no real solution.

Yet logical analysis remained the major tool of these fifties critiques. It is ultimately this rationalism that separates Marcuse, Whyte, and Goodman from the sixties, no matter how much they may have been revered in that decade. Variegated as it was, the rebirth could not travel two paths concurrently. Either play had to be intellectualized (something along the line of Marcuse's reasoning—we dance and sing because of our awareness of its therapeutic value, because we can thereby reverse the effects of excessive organization and psychoanalysis, counter the influence of Orpheus and Narcissus, and reveal a new reality principle), or thinking had to become play, act, game, a suspect truth at best, a truth without the exclusive, sacrosanct status it had attained in the post-Hellenistic world.

The sixties took the latter route. Analysis became a game—a fun game to be played with dedication and boundless energy, but a game just the same. A truth but no special truth. The real fathers of 1968 were not thinkers but doers—legends, howlers, fakirs, high priests, kings of cool and bop with no pattern, no organization, no morals, no language, no literature. Characteristically they despised the printed page, although some found themselves tangled in its net as Marcuse and Goodman were backed almost reluctantly into an antirationalist corner.

The great-great-grandfathers of the counterculture, unintellectual and inarticulate Cro-Magnons, were the juvenile delinquents of the postwar years, the greasers, the hoodlums, the teenage gang members, and in England the teddy boys and their descendants the rockers. Goodman and Robert Lindner (author of *Rebel without a Cause*) saw them as rebels without a cause, indictments of society, indications that all was not well beneath the Eisenhower tranquility of the fifties. James T. Farrell saw them as "children without goals, confused, unwanted," desperate to be *men* and *women* instead of *big boys* and *big girls*, acting out mixed-up concepts of maturity.

They were the American dream gone berserk: violence, sadism, sex, meaningless consumption, irreverence, flagrant disregard for the person and property of anyone but the self. Robbery, murder, vandalism, hanging out and looking tough. The systematic destruction of a storefront. The murder of a randomly selected victim just to prove yourself "tough enough to wear the jacket of the Rebels." Razors in the toes of your shoes, gang bangs in the style of *A Clockwork Orange*. Aggression. Inarticulateness. The male of the frontier deposited absurdly in the heart of a twentieth-century city, carrying on his anachronistic war not against dehumanized Indians but against dehumanized organization men, their children, their institutions (the chickens have come home to roost), riding about not on a white (or a black) stallion but on a Harley-Davidson, leather jacket studded with steel, emblazoned with skull and crossed bones, looking for an excuse to shoot it out with the sheriff either to kill or to be killed, to carve another notch on the belt. Tough, Mindless. Frightening. England's teds modified the image by donning ridiculously archaic Edwardian clothing, but the difference was only cloth deep. They were mean blokes and could slash cinema seats, beat up old ladies, and knock off a random teenager on Clapham Common in July 1953. As English social critic George Melly observed, "They broke up the youth-clubs, bullied or beat up harmless intruders in their territories, and fucked anything that moved. The hard-core Teds were frightening and horrible, the dinosaurs of pop."

> "It is a thoroughly unoriginal contention of the writer that modern society provides amply for

those conditions which make for traumatization
of the personality along the specific lines which
lead to the evolution of the psychopathic type.
These conditions flourish, for the most part, in
cities or densely populated areas resembling cities
where personal and familial privacy (among other
factors) are absent."—Robert Lindner, *Rebel
without a Cause*

Delinquents came in several strains, some more virulent than others, so
they could be "understood," "reformed," or tossed in the slammer, depend-
ing. (In September 1955 *Science Digest* suggested treatment with the drug
chlorpromazine, which had "already won praise for its ability to quiet
greatly disturbed mental patients so that they can be given helpful psychi-
atric treatment.") But mostly delinquents were avoided: locked out of bars,
run out of town, hassled on the slightest excuse by police acting on the request of a straight society in'ent on taking care of business. Thus the delinquents' fears and suspicions were reinforced, and they indeed became a
persecuted minority as well as a symbol to critics of the system and to white
middle-class youth who understood their rebellion.

(One occasion for constant harassment was the
rock-n-roll concert, for on both sides of the Atlantic young rebels recognized this music as their
own. Teds lionized the embarrassingly straight
Bill Haley, destroying theaters in honor of "Rock
around the Clock." Rockers throughout the sixties
took their music loud, straight, and seriously.)

Rock also recognized its own and aided considerably in the trans-
mogrification of Cro-Magnons into—well, ultimately—lovable moptops.
("Leader of the Pack." "He's a Rebel." Lieber and Stoller's "He wore black
denim trousers and motorcycle boots," 1955, remember?) But rock-n-roll
had help, not only in the sociological and psychological treatises of Lindner
and Goodman, not only in the romanticized *West Side Story*, but in early
fifties movies as well, in the cults of Marlon Brando and James Dean.

In many respects Dean was a typical Hollywood actor: born in Marion
Indiana, of Middle American stock, a few years at UCLA, hunger as an
unemployed Hollywood hanger-on, the Actors' Studio, Broadway theater,
plus all the many nondramatic ways aspiring actors and dancers pay their
pipers. A country boy who was a little confused, but made it on the coasts,
and would return in off moments to the farm to help his cousin glue together a model car.

But Dean was also an image, *the* image of the lost generation of the postwar years. He came to embody the aimlessness, the restlessness, the old
fuck-the-system-even-though-it-will-take-care-of-you rebellion. Kicks for
the sake of kicks, alienation, angst, a suicidal antagonism toward authority.

The Brando sneer, greased hair, sunglasses, and a cigarette. Yet underneath the tough exterior, a vulnerability that made all the little girls and the big boys and even the mommies and the daddies want to take care of this mixed-up but basically decent kid whom the system had so abused.

Inarticulate, juvenile, an anti-hero, Dean (or the roles he played in *Rebel without a Cause* and *East of Eden*) was Goodman's youth trying to be a man in a world in which there was no honorable man's work. He was the leader of the pack, the rebel who's not a rebel to me, the high school hero in black denim trousers and motorcycle boots. He was the misunderstood, rejected, delinquent Christ eulogized by Phil Ochs in "James Dean of Indiana":

> His mother died when he was born,
> His father was a stranger.
> Marcus Winslow took him in;
> Nobody seemed to want him. . . .
> He never seemed to find a place
> With the flatlands and the farmers,
> So he had to leave one day,
> He said to be an actor.

Lies, all lies and myth. But who cared?

So James Dean died. All the good legends had to die. Is that not, when we get right down to it, the root of our ambivalence about Elvis Presley, Bob Dylan, and the Beatles—that they did not at the height of their powers self-destruct in a shower of sparks? Ought not every myth, really, to drink itself silly, blow its brains out with a shotgun, overdose in London or Paris, or drive a Porsche off a cliff or into a telephone pole just to remain true, to play the role out to its logical conclusion? That James Dean merely struck a Ford sedan driving in the wrong lane, that his final words were not an *Easy Rider* "Up yours" but a panicked cry—"This guy's got to stop!"—is irrelevant. The man was his myth. Dean was one of the true fathers, and with his death the generation of the sixties had its first martyr and an important myth. The cloak was there, lying on the ground for Bob Dylan to pick up half a decade later.

> (Dylan was well aware of his heritage. On a bootleg album he exulted, "Hey, man, you oughta see some pictures of me. I'm not kiddin'. Umm, I look like Marlon Brando, James Dean or somebody. You really oughta see me.")

The cloak was lying around for others to don, too. Somewhere between Paul Goodman and James Dean, but heir to the whole romanticized juvenile delinquent mystique, Caryl Chessman emerged in fifties consciousness. The Chessman case forked a lot of lightning at the close of the fifties and was partly responsible for the (temporary) abolition of the death penalty across these United States.

Arrested on January 23, 1948, for stealing a car and assaulting two women (with intent to commit fellatio, not rape or murder), consigned without public protest on July 3 of that same year to San Quentin's death row, Chessman wrote his way into being with his prison autobiography, *Cell 2455, Death Row*. The book, and other writing that grew out of his long struggle to avoid the gas chamber, set students rioting in Lisbon and attracted the attention of Albert Schweitzer, Dean Pike, Marlon Brando, Steve Allen, the Pope, and the American public.

> (At the other end of the decade George Jackson's prison writings—*Soledad Brother*—similarly converted Jean Genet to his cause: "When we read these letters from a young black in Soledad Prison . . . they perfectly articulate the road traveled by their author—first the rather clumsy letters to his mother and his brother, then letters to his lawyer which become something extraordinary, half-poem, half-essay, and then the last letters, of an extreme delicacy, to an unknown recipient. . . . George Jackson is a poet, then. But he faces the death penalty.")

Chessman's opponents, mostly middle-class Republicans, outraged by his candor and energy, demanded that he be dispatched posthaste, crying that the law is, after all, the law. His advocates, largely intellectuals and youth, saw in Chessman an existential anti-hero, not much different from James Dean, the nihilistic rebel without a cause, the punk, the hoodlum with the golden heart whose delinquency was more an indictment of society than a sign of depravity. Chessman's prolonged agony brought bubbling to the surface all those liberal clichés about good-hearted criminals and misunderstood kids and all the counterculture's vague deification of near psychopaths. "Chessman's schemes, his plans, his hopes, all expressed in the vigorous distortions of his own personality, were of a degree of vitality and daring beyond anything the parents could call upon," enthused Elizabeth Hardwick in the *Partisan Review*, 1960. His fondness for pilfered cars expressed "freedom, power, exhilaration, madness." He purposely rolled and crashed them, and he purposely got himself caught. The senseless determination of prison officials to prevent Chessman from writing—and thereby from self-discovery—became proof positive that jails do not encourage or even tolerate rehabilitation, which in turn was proof positive that society—not Chessman—was sick. And Chessman is executed not only for his crime but for his sexual predilections and for his stubborn, cocky, pugnacious, clever, I-will-not-kiss-your-ass fight for life.

> (Cf. *One Flew over the Cuckoo's Nest*)
> (Cf. *Cool Hand Luke*)

For twelve long years he stood his ground,
And he stood it like a man,
He said, "I am innocent of this crime,
My life is in your hands."
Oh, go down you murderers, go down.

His last appeal, it was turned down, ·
I'll never forget that day,
In the spring of nineteen-sixty,
They stole his life away.
Oh, go down you murderers, go down. . . .

We've laws to throw a man in jail,
And laws to take his life,
But none to end the miseries
That drive a man to crime.
Oh, go down you murderers, go down. . . .

Caryl Chessman went to the cyanide tank,
And what I say is true,
The law it was the murderer,
The judge and jury too.
Oh, go down you murderers, go down.

—Bill McAdoo, "The Ballad of Caryl Chessman"

Chessman might have been Kerouac's Dean Moriarty, hero of *On the Road*, whose specialty was stealing cars and gunning for high school girls. *On the Road*—that great mine of sixties consciousness, that ultimate statement of, by, and for the fifties counterculture, that great heroic and sweet book of the late forties, not to see the light of day until 1957, a statement against the postwar status quo and against every status quo that ever was.

On the road—the mystique is overpowering. It has been overpowering since time immemorial. Kerouac's invitation to adventure was nothing new, nothing peculiar to the time or the nation or even the man. Woody Guthrie had been on the road. Joyce's Ulysses had been on the road. Tom Jones was on the road. Chaucer's pilgrims were on the road six hundred years ago, · and Homer's Ulysses a few thousand before them.

Daddies of the fifties, however, were not on the road. They were hunkered down in their Levittown bungalows keeping a sharp eye on their kids and a sharper eye on the commies. So when Dean Moriarty (in true life Neal Cassady, who would in the sixties take to the road again with Ken Kesey and his Merry Pranksters in a school bus named "Furthur"—see Tom Wolfe's *Electric Kool-Aid Acid Test*) charged through bungalowville, soul strings resonated everywhere. And when the adventures of Dean and Jack hit the bookstores eight years later, it was hard times indeed keeping them down on the farm.

Kerouac's world was newly discovered and mud-luscious, the adventures were heroic, the country was great and groovy as only this great and groovy America was made to be great and groovy: cars (need not be a Porsche—in fact, a flatbed truck driven by two farmboys from Minnesota is quite as valuable as a genuine Cadillac, powered by Dean Moriarty himself, hauling ass through the Iowa night at 110 MPH); broads, usually blonde, always delicious and willing; booze and drugs (soft); music (jazz, Charlie Parker style); laughs, insanity, hot dogs, warm populist people of all ages, even the straights, apple pie with gobs of vanilla ice cream, youth, a genuine tenderness toward children and animals, a genuine distrust of cops, breadth, scope, good times, "trouble, ecstasy, and speed as ever."

On the Road has little plot. It is one eternal moment of being (or, more properly, of becoming). Paul Goodman took a count: "In three hundred pages these fellows cross America eight times." The total is as irrelevant as reducing the novel to seven (count 'em) "sociologically relevant" propositions, or complaining about the lack of writing, or observing that in the food consumed by Sal Paradise and his crowd "there is a lot of sugar for animal energy, but not much solid food to grow on." But Goodman and Kerouac speak different languages, and after a few years' standoff, Kerouac's came to prevail.

Kerouac's were the metaphysics of energy, exploding in all directions at once. Even contemplation (sixty-three days on a fire lookout in part one of *Desolation Angels*, contemplating "Hozomeen, Hozomeen, most beautiful mountain I ever seen") becomes a mode of action. There was some Buddhism in Kerouac (as well as in the sixties), both in its rejection of materialism and in its understanding of experience as a path to wisdom. To know more, one must do more. The essence of Buddhism, decides one of Kerouac's minor characters in *Desolation Angels*, is "knowing as many different people as you can."

It was the old longing for new experience, the romantic "as long as there is one street I have not walked, one pub I've not drunk in, one woman I've not slept beside." It's the natural reaction against system, analysis, paralysis, authority, niches, and laundered decency. The old James Dean rebellion.

> Then the old man'd get bored with that and say, "Goddammit, I wanta go to Maine!" And he'd get into his car and drive off a hundred miles an hour—great showers of chicken feathers followed his track for hundreds of miles. He'd stop his car in the middle of a Texas town just to get out and buy some whisky. Traffic would honk all around him and he'd come rushing out of the store, yelling. "Thet your goddam noith, you bunth of bathats!" He lisped.

Kerouac lived his myth, storming across the nation, the continent, the world, meeting people, getting bored and running off, knitting together a transcontinental community that included, among others, William Burroughs (*Naked Lunch*), Allen Ginsberg, Gregory Corso, Neal Cassady, Gary Snyder, Robert Duncan, and Peter Orlovsky.

Kerouac was also a musician, blowing out on his typewriter what Allen Ginsberg called "a spontaneous bop prosody," banging out *On the Road* in the space of several weeks, mostly on bennies, "an extraordinary project" designed to "discover the rhythm of the mind at work at high speed in prose."

What Kerouac was trying in prose, other beats were trying in poetry. The new style involved on the one hand a pumping out of a whole new pool of imagery. The style reintroduced sound into poetry, an acknowledgment of the Whitman I-hear-America-singing roots and a development of the William Carlos Williams "common speech rhythms." Above all else, the new style was a rejection of old forms of control. As Ginsberg said, "Analytically, *ex post facto*, it all begins with fucking around and intuition and without any idea of *what* you're doing, I think. Later, I have a tendency to explain it, . . . but anyway, what it boils down to is this, it's my *movement*."

"Howl" is Ginsberg's major monument, a poetic statement on the beat generation comparable to Kerouac's prose chronicles, written in the same spontaneous way suggested by Kerouac: "He sat me down with a typewriter and said, 'Just write a poem'" And so "Howl" was "typed out madly in one afternoon, a tragic custard-pie comedy of wild phrasings, meaningless images for the beauty of abstract poetry of the mind running along making awkward combinations like Charlie Chaplin's walk, long saxophone-like chorus lines I knew Kerouac would hear *sound* of—Taking off from his own inspired prose line really a new poetry."

"Howl" combines rhapsody, comedy, sympathy, and anger.

> I saw the best minds of my generation destroyed by madness, starving hysterical naked,
> dragging themselves through the negro streets at dawn looking for an angry fix,
> angelheaded hipsters burning for the ancient heavenly connection to the starry dynamo in the machinery of night,
> who poverty and tatters and hollow-eyed and high sat up smoking in the supernatural darkness of cold-water flats floating across the tops of cities contemplating jazz,
> who bared their brains to Heaven under the El and saw Mohammedan angels staggering on tenement roofs illuminated,
> who passed through universities with radiant cool eyes hallucinating Arkansas and Blake-light tragedy among the scholars of war,
> who were expelled from the academies for crazy & publishing obscene odes on the windows of the skull,
> who cowered in unshaven rooms in underwear, burning their money in wastebaskets and listening to the Terror through the wall . . .

Ginsberg raged, sustained by Blakean prophesy, humor, jazz rhythms, and a sordid vision that distressed poetical purists and conservative intellectuals both. Like Bob Dylan, his pupil and friend, Ginsberg seemed to the media-haunted public less a poet than a figure, a myth, a prophetic spokesman.

> (Although he never expected "Howl" to be published, Ginsberg beat *On the Road* into print. The poem, appearing in fall of 1956, created an instant outcry and a web of legal scenes that culminated in an obscenity trial that found "Howl" *not* without redemptive social value, and therefore *not* obscene, and therefore okay to sell.)

With Neal Cassady (but without Kerouac, who dropped out of the scene early in the sixties) Ginsberg became not only a father but also a part of the great decade. He continued to attack inequities and make poems and constitute a presence throughout the decade of the whirlwind: "War Profit Litany," "Grant Park: August 28, 1968," "Rising Over Night-Blackened Detroit Streets," "D.C. Mobilization," London's first psychedelic poetry reading in June 1965 at the Albert Hall ("Cosmic Poetry Visitation Accidentally Happening Carnally") visits to Ken Kesey and his acidhead Pranksters, the Human Be-in of January 1967.

Though certainly the most visible beats, Ginsberg and Kerouac were antedated by the older William Burroughs (*Naked Lunch*, 1959, also busted for obscenity), a shadowy father figure who had lived in Europe during the thirties and—the romantic myth passed along by Kerouac went—had sneaked a Hungarian countess off the continent by marrying her. Burroughs spent most of the fifties outside the United States, hating Truman, Dulles, materialism, bureacracy, and all the establishment ravens. He was a writer, a thinker, a quester after understanding and alternatives, first in characters and travel, then in drugs, ultimately in electronic supertechnology, which, he believed, might render the old cons—man, nature, speech—unnecessary. Ginsberg, looking back, described Burroughs as "a precise scientist investigating regions of consciousness forbidden to common understanding by the *Control* agencies." By 1960 Burroughs had become, in Jeff Nuttall's words, "the god of the underground, looming obscure and fabulous behind his high priests, Ginsberg, Kerouac, and Ferlinghetti." Also according to Nuttall, Burroughs attempted regularly to demythologize himself as the guru to his flock: "And now I have something to say to all you angle boys of the cosmos who thought you had an in with The Big Operator—'Suckers! Cunts! Marks!—I hate you all—And I never intended to cut you in or pay you off with anything but horse shit.'"

Of all the beats, Gregory Corso's rejection of the square world seems to be most understandable: he had led the life to which the others pretended. Corso's Italian immigrant mother returned to Milan shortly after his birth; he was orphaned at age one in Greenwich Village, spent time in a boys' home, three months in the Tombs, three years in the cooler (age seventeen, theft), at home with a remarried father and away from home in Los Angeles, San Francisco, Mexico, Europe, South America, Africa, months in the Village sleeping on rooftops, years at Harvard talking and reading and publishing in 1955 the gentle "Vestal Lady on Brattle."

> Full-bodied and randomly young she clings,
> peers down; hovers over a wine-filled vat
> and with outstretched arms like wings
> revels in the forming image of child below.

Other beat poets included Gary Snyder of San Francisco, protagonist of Kerouac's *Dharma Bums* (all the beats sooner or later wound up in one of Kerouac's novels), "a Buddhist monk" Kenneth Rexroth called him; Rexroth himself, who claimed to have invented the beat synthesis of jazz and poetry; and Ginsberg's companion, Peter Orlovsky. But we slide inexorably from individuals into the beat movement itself.

> "It seemed the protest songs were a natural development from beat poetry, which was very self-analytical."—Phil Ochs

Kerouac identified two kinds of beats: "COOL: bearded sitting without moving in cafes, with their unfriendly girls dressed in black, who say nothing; and HOT: crazy, talkative, mad shining eyes, running from bar to bar only to be ignored by the cool subterraneans." In the popular imagination the former stole the crown. But maybe the distinction is too nice: seen from the inside, the COOLS and the HOTS had more in common than either had with the STRAIGHTS. Beatdom was very much a community.

This sense of close community, built on principles of male friendship, more than anything else, differentiated the beats from other forms of fifties counterculture and anticipated an important element in the sixties mix: the impulse toward tribalism. The voices of Salinger, Mailer, and—way to the rear—Hemingway were individual voices. The central concern of social critics like Goodman and Whyte was the liberation of the individual from society's annihilating homogenization. The beat shared the straight critic's concern for defending the individual against the collectivizing pressures of the system and he, too, glorified the individual in his quest for new experiences. But the beat sought in a mystical fashion to communicate those experiences beyond words, to share them, to *feel* them with outsiders, to transcend experiences into Experience. So the outsiders with whom he shared became insiders, an in-group, a subclass, an elect. And you "made the scene" communally. The ethics of the beat subculture were ethics of the tribe.

> (And the ethics of the sixties, as in hippie tribes, the "participatory democracy" promoted by SDS, the feeling of community in a protest demonstra-

tion, a sit-in, a love-in, a be-in, a bed-in, a folk
festival, a rock concert, a festival of life, even—
ultimately—the shared experience of underground
press and FM radio.)

The most media-visible elements of beat counterculture, however, were
not its metaphysics but the accoutrements of the tribe: a copy of "Howl," a
sax or bongo drums, a cigarette dangling from the lips, in later phases a
beret (borrowed from the French existentialists), a goatee, a black
turtleneck. Also highly visible as characteristic beat behavior: free love and
sexual experimentation, often homosexual or interracial; liberal use of
drugs, both hard and soft (Burroughs, most famously, described in writing
his experiments and addictions, but also Michael McClure, Corso, and
Ginsberg, intelligently and extensively); a leave-me-alone-go-away aver-
sion to squares and an affinity with tramps, winos, hustlers, prostitutes,
jazz musicians, and ethnic minorities; and hip vocabulary, which outsiders
found unintelligible or thin and which thereby proved most effective in doing what it was supposed to do: keeping squares OUT and hipsters IN, until
it got absorbed via Madison Avenue and pop music into mainstream
speech: man, go, make it, cool, swinging, mad, bug, with it, geek, beat,
creep, dig, crazy, later, greatest, far out, gone! (Much of the language, like
jazz and the beat's ability to hang on while hanging out, was borrowed directly from blacks. The western home of beat was San Francisco; the eastern home was New York's Greenwich Village. Beat communities could also
be found in Boston, Philadelphia, Berkeley, New Orleans, and Denver—if
you went looking. Most people did not, including the news media, so despite the furor of underground countercultural activity, the plastic surface
of the fifties was plenty smooth. Mostly beats wanted privacy. When attention came, it always meant trouble (the hassle over "Howl") or uptight,
straight tourists. Both were a drag, uncool, not hip. The beat lacked the
messianic impulse of his sixties counterpart: not only did he not understand
how to *use* media for maximum exposure, but he didn't *want* to understand
either.

So looking at things from the top down, as it were, you couldn't see
much. A ripple over "Howl" or *On the Road* or *Naked Lunch*, Mailer's
piece in the *Voice* on "the White Negro," the magazine essays of Goodman,
a few light waves over juvenile delinquency, Caryl Chessman, *Rebel without a Cause*—but nothing, really nothing, to undermine domestic tranquility. Yet there were rumblings. First, and most seismic, there was rock-n-roll,
a real threat to sobriety, virginity, wholesomeness, structure, Republicanism; second, there was civil rights, the Little Rock confrontation, the
beginnings of the great crusade.

The system had ways of dealing with rock-n-roll and civil rights that
could make them *seem* unreal. The one was labeled another teenage fad, the
other was relegated to the South. Neither touched the heart and soul and

home of white, middle-class, working straights, so neither appeared to threaten the status quo, at least not until, as Malcolm X put it, the chickens came home to roost somewhere after 1960. Chessman was psychopathic, juvenile delinquents were losers, and beats were queer. The mainstream remained unshaken, even untouched.

Two minor components of late fifties culture, however, did touch the minds of middle-class whites, maybe giving them some cause for pause, maybe a moment's doubt.

The first was comedy, the kind of satire that bubbled occasionally out of the television set. Groucho Marx, on *You Bet Your Life*. And Sid Caesar ("the funniest man in America," claimed *Esquire*, and for a change they were right). And the crew Caesar gathered around him on *Your Show of Shows* and *Caesar's Hour*: Mel Brooks, Carl Reiner, Imogene Coca, Howie Morris, Woody Allen, Neil Simon. And the crew from the old *Tonight* show: Steve Allen, the intellectual who wrote pop songs and articles in the *Village Voice*, and Tom Poston and Louie Nye and Don Knotts. And Red Skelton, and Bob and Ray, and Ernie Kovacs, and Phil Silvers, and Stan Freberg. And later on Mort Sahl, Shelley Berman, Bob Newhart, and Lenny Bruce. In them American comedy thrived during the fifties. In retrospect, that decade seems a golden age of parody and satire.

In the satire of Kovacs and Caesar and Steve Allen, the white middle-class heard the only consistently audible voice of a counterculture, the only suggestion that there were alternatives, that perhaps something might be rotten in the republic. Here was something to balance the bland situation comedies that invariably outlasted and outearned the more innovative satirical programs. No matter that the safe and the sorry won the ratings bouts and—in the long run—knocked guys like Caesar and Allen off the air; new and stronger satirists took their place. Throughout the decade they kept the public exposed to a more or less steady stream of criticism mingled with laughter.

Satire functions best in a mildly repressive society with very strong ideas of what is and is not respectable—precisely the society of mainstream fifties America. Too much of the boot's hard heel, and you scare off both audience and satirist. Too free a society, and you open the door to high-minded reformers, who almost always lack a sense of humor. So the times were ripe for Sid Caesar.

Neil Simon remembers *Your Show of Shows*: "Other television shows would present situations with farcical characters; we would put real-life people into identifiable situations." Like Caesar playing Eddie Redneck in a parody of *This Is Your Life*. And Caesar and Coca in scenes out of *From Here to Obscurity*, *Strange*, and *Galapacci*, played not as they had been in romantic movies in which mom and dad and son and daughter all win the brass ring but as they invariably work out for normal, gummed up people. The waters of the Pacific splash over the lovers, as she calls him her knight in armor and he wonders whether she's brought a towel. Or the mechanical town clock from somewhere in southern Germany runs amuck—the mechanical blacksmith and helpers hammer each other on the head and douse each other with buckets of water. Or a domestic scene turns a tube of toothpaste into grounds for divorce. A constant, outrageous, funny, serious commentary on all the illusion and pretense that was the fifties, something to reassure you when your toothpaste tube didn't work and your marriage didn't either, when your life seemed somehow not to vibrate to the heartwarming television ideals of *Ozzie and Harriet, Father Knows Best,* or *I Remember Mama.*

Caesar's show was canceled in 1957, after a run of seven years. Steve Allen survived two years on late-night television, then did a much publicized stint going nose to nose against Ed Sullivan in a highly promoted ratings war, offering much of the same, crazy, serious, satirical, loose Sid Caesar stuff: man-in-the-street interviews with nervous Don Knotts and spacey Tom Poston and Louie "Hi, I'm Gordon Hathaway, and I live in the Bronx; hi ho, Stevarino" Nye. Television cameras would pan the streets of New York, seeing what the people were up to. Or Allen might do a satire of the Senate hearings on Jimmy Hoffa's union. Head stuff. Allen had the guts to cut the McCarthyites publicly and to suggest that maybe Stephen Decatur was on questionable moral ground when he sloganized "My country, right or wrong." Allen suggested that the proposition "God answers prayer" should be put to an empirical test. He once remarked, "All human history seems to show that man has expended vastly more energy combating progress than in furthering it. Even when a light has occasionally glowed . . . it has shone more brightly partly because the rest of our planet was in darkness." The important questions to Allen were not whether he drank or smoked, or did he worry about *Maverick's* ratings and Jayne's birthday, but what is the rating of individual men? He was an early supporter of civil rights, hung out with Norman Mailer, and even had the good sixties sense to regret that Brooks Brothers air of intellectualized liberalism that seemed to surround himself and other satirists of the fifties.

So the system gunned him down, too. But along came Mort Sahl as the fifties turned to the sixties, with more bite than Caesar and Allen and Kovacs put together (although not as funny). "Will Rogers with fangs," *Time* called him. You didn't see much of Sahl on television (his best material, even Allen had to admit, made him too controversial for the tube), but he had records and, late in the decade, attracted media attention. "You know, Kennedy had to have Lyndon Johnson on the ticket with him, because he can't get into Washington without an adult." "I'm for capital punishment—you've got to execute people. How else are they going to learn?" "I says to my girl, 'I don't think birth control is a very important issue,' and she says, 'None of you do.'" "I like Orval Faubus, but I wouldn't want him to marry my sister."

But with Sahl, the sixties were here. As the social and political criticism became more and more pointed, the humor began to drain. "I like fun," he told an audience in 1960, "but we don't have time for jokes. We have to overthrow the government." Out went the humor, in came the high seriousness. Out went the repression, in came the reformers.

> (Lenny Bruce, the ultimate extension of the Cae-sar-Allen-Sahl line, was pure sixties. After his death in 1966 he achieved an immortality he had not sought in life. His art was extreme, highly moral, self-conscious, peppered with obscenities (many in Yiddish), and incisive. No matter, Bruce, too, went down. The ultimate irony is that "tits and ass," for which Lenny was crucified, became in the seventies the title of a very catchy song in *Chorus Line*, a smash Broadway musical.)

The humorists pierced the crust during the fifties, especially late in the decade. Another thing that tended to grab white Americans was the protest against the Bomb. The protesters were adult whites, some of them establishment culture heroes; even Ike himself sounded a warning that, to the American apocalyptic vision, was sobering. Here was something worth thinking about—if only for a moment or two.

As *Time* magazine sourly observed, Ban the Bomb demonstrators crawled predictably out of their holes, regular as clockwork, before each series of announced U.S. nuclear tests—but *never* before, during, or after Soviet tests (perhaps because the Russians announced their dirty business either after the fact or not at all). Always someone was threatening to atomize himself by sitting on ground zero, chaining himself to the bomb tower, or sailing his ketch over whatever atoll was to be vaporized. These crazies would be hauled peacefully away by the police, the army, or the navy, to be noted in the *New York Times* and the *Christian Science Monitor* and forgotten until the next round of fireballs.

> (The appeals to conscience from Albert Schweitzer in *Saturday Review* on May 18, 1957, and from American nuclear scientists in the *Bulletin of the Atomic Scientists*, September 1957, were more embarrassing. They came from prominent establishment figures. But they could also be forgotten or ignored.)

Gradually the humanists and the intellectuals gathered themselves together and concocted by 1958 the grandfather of the Mobe (National Mobilization Committee to End the War in Vietnam), a motley bunch that packaged and repackaged themselves as occasion demanded: the Fight against Atomic Death in Germany; the Council against Atomic and Hydrogen

Bombs in Japan; the Campaign for Nuclear Disarmament; the Sane Nuclear Policy Committee; and the Non-Violent Action against Nuclear Weapons Committee in the United States. (The French, characteristically ignoring all the ruckus *and* a U.N. resolution, exploded their own bomb in the Sahara and entered the prestigious Nuke Club in early 1960.) The antibomb groups tried to increase the pressure by techniques now all too familiar: petitions, Gandhian civil disobedience, hunger strikes, legal suits (scientist Linus Pauling, socialist Norman Thomas, philosopher Bertrand Russell, and some Japanese fishermen versus the United States of America), and mass protest marches or rallies.

The marches were most effective, especially when the marchers were elderly Britons carrying pet kittens ("a symbol of the animals who have no voice in such matters") or a hundred East Side mothers with their kids.

The English, clustering around writer Philip Toynbee and philosopher Russell, were paradoxically the most radical and the most successful of the lot although, as we know only too well, nobody won anything of significance in this battle. Russell was willing, if pushed, to "surrender to the Russians" in order to "avert nuclear extermination"—a choice he was not likely to have confronted then, although nobody understood Soviet policy at the time. "Without people," he reasoned, "you have neither freedom nor the hope of freedom. I believe in both." Thousands of British subjects thought Russell was right and marched fifty-seven miles each Easter from 1958 to 1963 between the nuclear research center at Aldermaston and Trafalgar Square in London, demanding unilateral British disarmament or, at the very least, a moratorium on atmospheric testing.

> Don't you hear the H-bomb's thunder
> Echo like the crack of doom?
> While they rend the skies asunder
> Fall-out makes the earth a tomb.
> Do you want your homes to tumble,
> Rise in smoke towards the sky?
> Will you see your cities crumble?
> Will you see your children die?
>   Men and women, stand together
>   Do not heed the men of war
>   Make your minds up now or never
>   Ban the bomb forevermore.
>
> —John Brunner, "The H-Bomb's Thunder"

Year after year the numbers increased: 3,000 in 1958; 25,000 in 1959; 75,000 in 1960, making the march a voice of all Britain and "certainly giving Harold Macmillan something to think about this election year." The Labour party promised to lay off the nukes "if the superpowers would cease producing them," a nonpromise if ever there was one, but token recognition unmatched in America.

In the United States, protest zeroed in on the tests themselves. For example, before the Eniwetok atoll tests of 1958, Sane advertised in the *New York Times* urging readers to write President Eisenhower and Vice-President Nixon, to write their congressmen, and to organize community action groups. This approach was interesting but ineffective: Norman Cousins had seen *Mr. Smith Goes to Washington* once too often and had begun to believe it.

> (You can easily distinguish children of the fifties, sixties, and seventies by the way they deal with an obstacle. The child of the seventies will shrug his shoulders and put up with it. The child of the fifties will write his congressman or his better business bureau. The child of the sixties will demonstrate against it or blow it up.)

But by 1960 the men of Sane—Norman Cousins, Linus Pauling, Steve Allen, Paul Tillich, David Reisman, Martin Luther King, Jr.—could turn out Mrs. Roosevelt for a speech and Adlai Stevenson II for a message and seventeen thousand just plain folks for a rally in New York City.

Ban the Bomb was a cause both ahead of and behind the times. The crusade against Vietnam generated broad support not only because it was more compelling than Ban the Bomb, or because de-escalation of the arms race was less attractive than de-escalation in Nam, and not because the techniques used in the two campaigns were in any way different (Ban the Bomb gave the sixties both its strategies and its peace symbol), but because 1967 was simply more receptive to such ideas than 1957. The antibomb campaign was a decade too late as well as a decade too early: it was a lost game from square one. Not even the president of the United States could, had he been so inclined, stop the atomic express. Not that anyone cared, or even knew. Ban the Bomb advocates saw themselves as humanity's last stand against a government entirely out of control, against insanity, against ultimate annihilation.

> (They may yet prove to be right.)

But they lost, overwhelmingly though not unheroically. Quixotic, ragtag, predominately WASP, the ban the Bomb people were, even more than the civil rights crusaders, the true fathers of the quixotic, rag-tag, protesters of the sixties.

Every fifties countercultural rebellion was expressed in or allied with music of one type or another. Music was not the quintessence of rebellion that it became in the sixties, but it was more important to the champions of change than to the establishment. Not that there was *less* music to the latter but the coarse, yellow-grained discs of the underground were more vital than the Tin Pan Alley tunes of Jaye P. Morgan, Peggy Lee, Andy Williams, Dean Martin, and old Blue Eyes himself. More alive. Truer.

"The worst thing was that it all dragged on so long without changing. Most dance eras last a few years, a decade at most, but the war froze everything as it was, gave the big bands a second life; by the early fifties, the scene had come to a standstill." It was all show business, and, in the fifties, "mostly showbiz survived on habit."—Nik Cohn, *Rock from the Beginning*

Wherever the counterculture spread, music was there, an expression and a clue, if not a key. ("Don't you understand the enormity of your mistake," Mailer railed at Kennedy after the Cuban invasion of 1961; "you invade a country without understanding its music?") On the road between Aldermaston and London for the first Campaign for Nuclear Disarmament march: "Some young Cockneys in bowler hats rocked and rolled enthusiastically in front of the Albert Memorial when the march halted for a picnic lunch; they were there as fans of the jazz band [rock-n-roll was considered a mutant form of jazz even as late as 1960] that played the march through West London." Replay from one more sympathetic participant Jeff Nuttall, in *Bomb Culture*:

We thumb a lift ahead of the march. We file into the cheap cafe and we park the instruments and we order egg and chips and sit round the gas fire trying to dry out. I take off a shoe and a sock. Before I can take off the other a marshal comes in and says the march is approaching and they need some music in weather like this. So Dave Aspinwall picks up his trombone and I get my cornet and Mick Wright gets his banjo and we go and stand at the curb in the pissing rain. We play *Didn't He Ramble* and we play it again and again and the blood is trickling down Dave's lip and the girls bring out the egg and chips on plates and put them on the pavement by my one bare foot and the rain makes bubble patterns in the grease and we play *Didn't He Ramble* and the column disappears and what with the rain on the chips and one shoe off and one shoe on and the beautiful girls carrying food and Dave and Mick and me playing *Didn't He Ramble*, well, that was one of the good times, one of the really good moments if you know what I mean.

Music again on the road from McGuire Air Force Base to the United Nations, where Agnes Friedan concluded, "You can't really march without singing."

On the steps around Trafalgar Square, singing "The H-Bomb's Thunder" and "Hey, Little Man" and "The Family of Man" and "We're Marching to Trafalgar Square" and Alex Comfort's "First Things First":

Don't stand there kicking that ball.
If some bloody mutton should sit on the button
There'll be no more soccer at all.

And "Brother, Won't You Roll Down the Line" and "Strontium 90."

On the back roads of the South, in Mississippi and Alabama and Arkansas, where spirituals were secularized and an old hymn once used by CIO organizers to unionize food and tobacco workers in Monteagle, Tennessee, was remade into "We Shall Overcome." By the summer of 1960 Guy Carawan, a young folksinger with a master's degree in sociology from UCLA who had actually sung at the Moscow World Youth Festival in 1957, could recount his adventures of being jailed, threatened, used, and abused while singing at more than a hundred sit-ins, rallies, prayer vigils, and organizational meetings throughout the South: "They adapt everything. Blues, rock-and-roll songs, gospels, pop ballads, hillbilly songs, and spirituals were all used and freely adapted." "I Shall Not Be Moved." "This Little Light of Mine." "Keep Your Eyes on the Prize, Hold On."

Music on the back roads of America and in the beat corners of dark cities late at night, crossed and recrossed by Kerouac and the Holy Goof driving naked across Texas or racing Mad Buick to old Chi.

The girls came down and we started out on our big night, once more pushing the car down the street. "Wheeoo!! let's go!" cried Dean, and we jumped in the back seat and clanked to the little Harlem on Folsom Street.

Out we jumped in the warm, mad night, hearing a wild tenorman bawling horn across the way, going "EE-YAH! EE-YAH! EE-YAH!" and hands clapping to the beat and folks yelling "Go, go, go!" Dean was already racing across the street with his thumb in the air, yelling "Blow, man, blow!" A bunch of colored men in Saturday-night suits were whooping it up in front. It was a sawdust saloon with a small bandstand on which the fellows huddled with their hats on, blowing over people's heads, a crazy place; crazy floppy women wandered around sometimes in their bathrobes, bottles clanked in alleys. In back of the joint in a dark corridor beyond the splattered toilets scores of men and women stood against the wall drinking wine-spodiodi and spitting at the stars—wine and whisky. The behatted tenorman was blowing at the peak of a wonderfully satisfactory free idea, a rising and falling riff that went from "EE-yah!" to a crazier "EE-de-lee-yah!" and blasted along to the rolling crash of butt-scarred drums hammered by a big brutal Negro with a bullneck who didn't give a damn about anything but punishing his busted tubs, crash, rattle-ti-boom, crash. Uproars of music and the tenorman *had* it and everybody knew he had it. Dean was clutching his head in the crowd, and it was a mad crowd. They were all urging that tenorman to hold it and keep it with cries and wild eyes, and he was raising himself from a crouch and going down again with his horn, looping it up in a clear cry above the furor. A six-foot skinny Negro woman was rolling her bones at the man's hornbell, and he just jabbed at her, "Ee! ee! ee!"

Everybody was rocking and roaring.

Music was in the movies as well. In the ones we remember at least. And here is an interesting point: of the fistful of cinematic social critiques made during the fifties (*The Wild One*, 1953; *East of Eden, Rebel without a Cause,* and *Blackboard Jungle,* 1955) the one that sticks in my mind is decidedly the worst. *The Wild One* has terrific dialogue straight out of Paul Goodman: "What are you rebelling against, Johnny?" "What've ya got?" *East of Eden* builds on a Steinbeck novel, and *Rebel without a Cause* stars James Dean. All three boast good actors turning in good performances.

Blackboard Jungle is grade B all the way. A young, idealistic teacher, warned never to turn his back on his class and, above all, not to be a hero (the educational equivalent of *Waterfront* dockworker advice not to question or to answer questions) gets himself beaten up by a gang of school toughs after interrupting the rape of a female teacher. A nice piece of work but clichéd even in 1955. And no James Dean, his eyes "as empty as an animal's." So what made *Blackboard Jungle* stick in our heads? The song, of course, "Rock around the Clock," the song that sold fifteen million records, the song that in a movie titled after it would set audiences in America and Europe to rioting and to vandalism. The *New York Times* told us: "Teddy Boys rampaged through the South London streets for several hours, leaving a trail of broken windows and overturned cars." "37 youths held for new riots after Rock Around the Clock showing; Police eject 100 from Lewisham theater."

Again, what saved the inferior movie was its music. Hollywood caught on to this, of course, and soon every youth-oriented counterculture movie came heavily orchestrated. We were bombarded with Elvis Presley beach movies and the counterculture was no longer counter. In between, in 1956 and 1957, came movies about rock-n-roll: *Rock around the Clock, Jailhouse Rock, Don't Knock the Rock, The Girl Can't Help It.*

(I remember *The Girl Can't Help It* more vividly than any other picture I saw in the fifties because I saw it, along with *I Was A Teenage Werewolf,* one Saturday morning when I was supposed to be having my braces checked. It is an atrocious flick, which *Time, Newsweek,* and *Films in Review* all bombed, claiming it was designed to show off Jayne Mansfield's body. In fact, *Films in Review* spent most of its time in a [smirk] point by point comparison of Marilyn Monroe's and Jayne Mansfield's figures—not, however, without pummeling the movie first: "This film merits the attention of *Films in Review* even though it is a showcase for leading purveyors of the jungle caterwauling known as rock 'n' roll, and is thereby a cultural debilitator our descendants won't forgive us for [let us hope]." Funny thing, I do not recall the

> body at all. All I know is that my friends and I sneaked off to see *The Girl Can't Help It* because it featured Little Richard, Little Anthony and the Imperials, the Platters, Eddie Cochran, Gene Vincent, and a bunch of other far-out rock-n-rollers.)

And there was music in the Village, music in the cafés at night and revolution in the air. First there was jazz, for beats and for much of the straight population as well. The *Voice* commented religiously each week on jazz recordings (as well as on classical releases and FM radio programming but *not* on rock-n-roll), and in its pages you could read Ginsberg enthusing over Kerouac's bop prosody or Kenneth Rexroth extolling the virtues of poetry and jazz combined.

> Jazz Poetry gets poetry out of the classroom and into contact with the large audience. . . . Jazz gives to poetry, too, the rhythms of itself, so expressive of the world we live in, and it gives it the inspiration of the jazz world, with its hard simple morality and its direct honesty—especially its erotic honesty. Fish or cut bait. Poetry gives jazz a verbal content infinitely superior to the silly fantasies of the typical Tin Pan Alley lyric.

In San Francisco Ferlinghetti explained his *Oral Messages* (bound with *A Coney Island of the Mind*, 1958): "These seven poems were conceived specifically for jazz accompaniment and as such should be considered as spontaneously spoken 'oral messages' rather than as poems written for the printed page. As a result of continued experimental reading with jazz, they are still in a state of change. 'Autobiography' and 'Junkman's Obbligato' are available on the Fantasy LP recording No. 7002."

> (The poetry-music synthesis of the beats never materialized. It was by rubbing against folk music, especially protest music, that pop would, in the words of Ralph Gleason, take song lyrics out of the hands of hacks and give them to poets. But beat poetry affected such rock poets as Phil Ochs, Donovan Leitch, and Bob Dylan. Donovan recalled in 1968, "At school I wrote long poems full of sex frustration. Then I read about the American Beats. I wrote long things that sounded beat. I just liked the idea of moving.")

The other music of the Village, the slighted sister, was folk, a tradition of long standing by virtue of its early affiliation with socialism, communism, unionism, and radicalism. Folksingers had been giving unlicensed Sunday afternoon concerts for years in New York's Washington Square when Park Commissioner Morris tried to shut them down. There had been hassles as early as 1956 with the city administration but never anything like this. It was "the unsavory appearance of the singers," the commissioner said, thereby provoking a "riot" of three thousand hipsters, thereby causing Mayor Wagner to change Morris's mind.

And there was also Izzy Young's Folklore Center on MacDougal Street, and there was *Sing Out!*, the "folk song magazine" edited by Irwin Silber, a steady quarterly or bimonthly throughout the fifties. *Sing Out!* attracted the talent of Pete Seeger (a regular columnist), kept in touch with Alan Lomax, Woody Guthrie, and Aunt Molly Jackson, and had an international following. It took a typically Village intellectual approach toward folk music. Many of the contributors—not Seeger, who knew better, or Silber— argued endlessly over whether folk authenticity requires oral transmission, anonymous or communal authorship, and a setting somewhere outside of twentieth-century urban centers.

Sing Out! published new or newly discovered or traditionally popular folk songs, noted new releases (few indeed) from Folkways Records, chronicled the singing engagements and appearances before the House Un-American Activities Committee of staff members and friends. It recorded in short, simply written essays the infusion of folk music into the ban the Bomb and civil rights movements and, in the early sixties, into mainstream musical consciousness. Like folk concerts in Washington Square, *Sing Out!* was there in the fifties, nice to have around but not really central to what was happening. Something of an atavistic expression of the postwar socialist left.

When folk music began to eclipse jazz somewhere around 1961 (by the time major record companies started signing up poets and jazz groups for LP records called *Beat Scene*, you knew that both poetry and the beat movement were dead), many Village residents raised the "neighborhood is going to hell" banner. "We're starting to ruin the coffee houses with too much music, poetry, and the like," the owner of Manzini explained in the *Village Voice*. "They're losing their European atmosphere," he complained. The owners' solution was a slight cover charge to "keep the riff-raff element out." Beats were bad enough, but the scruffy, second generation, guitar-totin' beat-folkies were clearly the end of civilization as the Village had known it: a nineteen to six majority of the informal Village Board voted on April 20, 1961, to support the Morris ban on folksinging, complaining of "indecency and disorderliness."

> (Bob Dylan's long poem on the jacket of Peter, Paul, and Mary's *In the Wind* recalls the "old Village" as a place of blessed and honest poverty, people huddled together for warmth and each other in the snows that lay on MacDougal Street, nightly busts, everybody including the cook defending the Gaslight against cops and the bullies with chairs and brooms and swords that hung on

the wall, but now Peter's grown some, and Paul and Mary and all of us and the Village, too—and the neighborhood is gone to hell. The answer to Dylan and his romantic reminiscence is to be found in Stephen Stills' "Old Times Good Times": "New York City was so damned cold/ Had to get out of that town before I got old." And in Dylan's own "Talkin' New York" and "Hard Times in New York Town.")

Still, the music was there, and as Leonard Cohen noted, "The music on Clinton Street always came through." Despite the Village's provinciality and conservatism, the emigrant hordes, itinerant beats, and roving entertainers kept the scene reasonably current. It is doubtful, however, whether anyone took to heart the advice of Jean Shepherd, writing in the *Voice*, to give ear to that other great (musical) America out there.

Some night when the espresso tastes flat and you tire of hearing third rate poets shout above fourth rate jazz groups, and you happen to be near a radio, I would suggest that you dig a few sounds that are truly closer to the pulse of America than anything today. . . . Move radio away from N.Y.C. and to Tennessee, the Carolinas, Michigan, and Minnesota. Everywhere. I listened for three hours one night to a station in Hattiesburg, Mississippi, and after a while I had the feeling that I was truly eavesdropping on something I shouldn't have heard.
    Man, dig the folk.

New Yorkers *never* tune their radios away from the Big Apple. But people in other parts of the country do. And what they'd been hearing brought to the counterculture rock-n-roll, its most characteristic—although its most unrecognized—expression.

Got a gal, named Daisy,
She almost drive me crazy.
Got a gal, named Daisy,
She almost drive me crazy.
She knows how to love me, yes, indeed,
Boy you don' know what cha doin' to me.
Tutti Frutti o rutti,
Tutti Frutti o rutti,
Tutti Frutti o rutti,
Tutti Frutti o rutti,
Tutti Frutti o rutti,
A-wop-bob-a-loom-op-a-lop-bam-boom!
    —Little Richard, "Tutti Frutti"

The story is now familiar, but it's worth retelling just to make a point. How Alan Freed, a run-of-the-mill disc jockey in Cleveland, happened to be in the record shop of his friend Leo Mintz in the spring of 1951; and how

Mintz happened to remark to Freed on the curious phenomenon of white teenagers buying black ("race" or "sepia" soon to become "rhythm and blues") records at his store; and how Freed got himself a late-night radio program on WJW (Cleveland), the *Moondog Show*, in July 1951, which he devoted exclusively to r&b; and how on March 22, 1952, some twenty-five thousand fans, mostly white, showed up at the Arena (capacity ten thousand) for the Moondog Coronation Ball, a dance featuring live performances by Freed's r&b artists; and how there was a riot and Freed was famous and rock-n-roll was born. And how Freed moved to WINS in New York and then to WABC, bringing rock-n-roll with him, promoting his artists up and down the east coast with the same results he'd gotten in Cleveland and the same shows, even acting in rock-n-roll movies, making a lot of money and a lot of enemies, spreading the gospel, driving the establishment to ban his shows and issue warrants for his arrest (on charges of inciting to riot, Boston, May 1958).

The point is that the audience was there before Freed, before "Rock around the Clock," before Elvis. The audience was that as yet undefined mass of disaffected youth who would become angry young men, beats, teds, greasers, juvenile delinquents, "early resigned" and "early disaffected," rebels without a cause, all the various counters of the fifties. They were looking everywhere for something different, for something moving, and—having poked around French existentialism, jazz, Zen, poetry, Hemingway macho, the road—they were bound sooner or later to poke around the places something different was to be found: those two subcultures most suppressed from white middle-class consciousness, the black and the poor southern. Maybe books led them there. Maybe movies. Maybe idle twirling of radio dials. Anyway, they had short-circuited the literary transmitters and gone directly to go: those faraway stations that, usually late at night or early in the A.M., filled the American air waves with wild, weird, and wonderful sounds, the sounds of black and backwoods.

Alan Freed bent over and picked them up. And they made him rich and famous.

Rock-n-roll was, by genetic inheritance, completely outside of, and somehow threatening to, mainstream American culture. That simple fact explains, I suspect, why most discussion of fifties rock-n-roll is sociological, whereas most discussion of sixties rock is paraliterary. It explains the almost pathological, often contradictory responses from all elements of the establishment, which took time off from their mutual antagonisms to unite against this virus from outside. And it may explain why such critics as Paul Goodman, Village intellectuals, and aging socialists, standing with their left foot forward and their right foot behind, simply could not come to grips with bopping at the hop. Here was a whole new world that transcended liberalism and radicalism, argument and dialectic, even reason itself—naturally, without trying.

> (It is interesting that postwar socialists spoke and wrote endlessly about proletarian music as the logical vehicle for proletarian propaganda and devoted their lives to resurrecting the dead horse of prewar unionist folk music and then failed completely to recognize rock-n-roll, which was *precisely* the music they were looking for.)

We tend to forget the Puritan fervor with which the forces of decency attacked the new music. A few hours spent browsing through old newspapers and magazines can be instructive.

Psychologist Francis Braceland called rock-n-roll a "communicable disease," "cannibalistic and tribalistic" music, "another sign of adolescent rebellion" along the order of ducktail haircuts and zoot suits. (The younger generation would have agreed on all points but disliked Braceland's tone.) Psychiatrists compared rock-n-roll to medieval types of spontaneous lunacy and St. Vitus's dance and urged a comprehensive, federally funded study of this phenomenon.

Asa Carter, executive secretary of the North Alabama White Citizen Council, charged that the NAACP was "infiltrating" white youth with rock-n-roll music and announced that he would ask jukebox operators to throw out "immoral" records. (Operators claimed that that meant most of their hits.) The NAACP issued a statement shrugging off the charge; what they did not say was that blacks, used to seeing rhythm and blues hits covered by white singers (that is, bowdlerized and toned down—play Little Richard's "Tutti Frutti" back to back with Pat Boone's "Tutti Frutti" to grasp what "cover" really means) and to seeing the white versions sell millions and the black versions get no air play, were beginning to think rock-n-roll was a rip-off. (Which it was.)

Jersey City and Newport banned Bill Haley and the Comets, and—following rioting in the streets—Birmingham, England, banned Bill Haley's movie *Rock around the Clock*, as did Iraq, Cuba, Iran, and Spain. (In Indonesia, students kidnapped the film censor to warn her against taking such harsh and discriminatory action.)

Moscow claimed that American capitalists reaped huge profits from rock-n-roll and called for "better jazz from Eastern Europe to combat rock-n-roll." British teachers of ballroom dancing complained that Princess Margaret's endorsement of rock-n-roll hurt their business.

St. Louis radio station KWK promised in January 1958 to destroy all its rock-n-roll records. Billy Graham, who admitted to never having met Elvis and not knowing much about him, said, "From what I've heard, I'm not so sure I'd want my children to see him." Harold Stassen, perennial Republican presidential hopeful, pointed out that rock-n-roll riots were overwhelmingly counterbalanced by constructive youth activities.

"If the establishment knew what today's popular music really is saying, not what the words are saying, but what the music itself is saying, then they wouldn't just turn thumbs down on it. They'd ban it, they'd smash all the records and they'd arrest anyone who tried to play it."—Alfred Aronowitz, 1963.

The American reaction to rock-n-roll in 1958 was *precisely* the reaction of Rumania to the music of Blood, Sweat, and Tears in 1970: "We must play more jazz—'jazz meter.' We must play less rhythm." Because in their minds the rhythm, the strong, heavy rhythm, was inciting kids to riot. Not the fact that they'd been repressed for so long that when they saw a glimpse of anything free, they just busted loose. It was also the reaction of the twenties to jazz (Bolshevik-inspired, lewd, licentious, capable of causing death, disease, insanity, and loss of virginity)—right down to a congressional investigation into the correlation between rock-n-roll and juvenile delinquency. And the forces of decency tended to get their targets: Chuck Berry was busted under the Mann Act, Alan Freed for payola; Elvis was drafted; Jerry Lee Lewis was drummed out of the big time for marrying his thirteen-year-old cousin ("Hell, we all knowed about her," one of the locals announced. "And besides, she was only twelve."). More subtly, they drowned rock-n-roll in a flood of drippy music that Charlie Gillett labeled "stupid rock": Neal Sedaka, Gene Pitney, Pat Boone, Frankie Avalon, Fabian, Paul Anka, Connie Stevens, Connie Francis, Brenda Lee, Dion, Ricky Nelson, Brian Hyland, Bobby Vinton, Bobby Vee, Tommy Sands.

The process was not helped by the auctioning off of talent discovered and nurtured by independent producers to the very record companies (the majors) responsible for the fifties shlock against which rock-n-roll (and the independents themselves) had revolted; by the eagerness of the independents to exploit quickly a new talent or a new sound; and by the tendency of rock-n-rollers to die young (Chuck Willis, the Big Bopper, Buddy Holly, Eddie Cochran) or to get religion (Little Richard threw his jewelry into the river at Sydney, Australia, and enrolled in Oakwood Bible College) or to go back to the less controversial r&b or c&w music whence they had strayed into rock-n-roll (Carl Perkins, Marty Robbins, Jerry Lee Lewis).

The question that pops up is, what was this rock-n-roll about which everyone got so punched out of shape?

Charlie Gillett, in *The Sound of the City*, took a classification and division approach. For what it's worth, he came up with this list:

western swing (Bob Willis)
northern band rock-n-roll (Bill Haley and the Comets)
New Orleans dance blues (Little Richard, Fats Domino)
Memphis country rock (Elvis Presley, Carl Perkins)

gospel style harmony groups (the Dominoes)
late ballad blues (Ray Charles)
Chicago r&b (Chuck Berry, Bo Diddley)
Louisiana country rock (Jerry Lee Lewis)
frantic combo rock (Little Richard)
frantic country rock (Gene Vincent)
intense gospel style (Hank Ballard)
Arkansas western rock (Johnny Cash)
up-tempo c&w (Marty Robbins)
twist (Chubby Checker)

There were others. And Gillett did not categorize British forms such as skiffle (remember "On the Bedpost over Night" and Lonnie Donegan?).

You can work toward definition from a list of fifties rock-n-roll classics:

"Love Me Tender," "Hound Dog," "Jailhouse Rock" (Elvis Presley)
"Blueberry Hill" (Fats Domino)
"The Great Pretender" (Platters)
"Blue Suede Shoes" (Carl Perkins)
"Why Do Fools Fall in Love?" (Frankie Lymon and the Teenagers)
"See You Later, Alligator" (Bill Haley and the Comets)
"Be-Bop-a-Lula" (Gene Vincent)
"Long Tall Sally" (Little Richard)
"Searchin'" (Coasters)
"Bye Bye, Love" (Everly Brothers)
"Party Doll" (Buddy Knox)
"Rock and Roll Music" (Chuck Berry)
"C. C. Rider" (Chuck Willis)

(During these same years, Dean Martin released "Memories Are Made of This," Perry Como released "Hot Diggity," Debbie Reynolds released "Tammy,"Jimmy Dorsey released "So Rare," and Gogi Grant released "The Wayward Wind," all of which ranked higher on pop charts than any rock-n-roll songs except Presley tunes. Which is a good indication of where America's head was at.)

So what separates rock-n-roll from pop shlock? And how is it possible to determine, as everyone has, that by 1958 rock-n-roll was soft in the head and by 1961 virtually dead?

The easy response is that you know it when you hear it, when your feet move of their own volition and you bounce right out of the chair and are compelled to dance or to pound your fists into the wall, and when it's done you yell, "Jezuz, they don't make songs like that any more!" And you play the record again and again and again. What happens with the Crystals' Phil Spector–produced "Then He Kissed Me" that does not happen with the Kiss version thereof, what happened to the kids in London and Boston and New

York and Fayetteville and Glasgow who left windows smashed, cars over-turned, seats ripped, and in Boston one sailor stabbed and a dozen other people roughed up. What happened to Kerouac when the big tenorman blew his horn? A physical reaction, some foot stompin'. St. Vitus's dance, spontaneous lunacy, maybe even cannibalism.

> Everybody young and old
> Learns how to rock-n-roll
> Listen you somethin' new
> Everybody sure can do
> Foot stompin' foot stompin'
> All the time.
>
> No wonderin' man or guest
> No need to take a rest
> Listen to the junky beat
> Shake your head and stomp your feet
> Foot stompin' foot stompin'
> All the time.
>
> Even just the other day
> Taught it to my sister May
> At last Mr. Blue
> Can do the foot stompin' too
> Foot stompin' foot stompin'
> All the time.
>
> —The Flares, "Foot Stompin'—Part 1"

Any number of things distinguish rock-n-roll from commercial shlock. Most obviously, it is rougher, simpler, more homemade, less professional. In a lot of cases, it's just plain off-key. Listen to the Shirelles' backup work or the "da-ooo" behind Bobby Day on "Over and Over." Folk music had this same sound in the forties and early fifties and then again in the early sixties. In each case it provided welcome relief from big-time, slick, formulaic, *produced*, and generally bogus music. Roughness is the quality of music slightly out of control, eager, impatient, urgent, setting out, young. What Presley had in 1955 that he had to press for in 1958 and had lost by 1960.

> (It is difficult to find a simpler, thinner, less pro-fessional piece than "Love Me Tender," Elvis's first number-one ballad: lean, acoustic guitar accom-paniment, tenth-grade barbershop harmony, voice coming at you as through a long tunnel, delivery accentuating the jog trot meter of pure doggerel: "Love me tender, love me true, / Never let me go. / You have made my life complete, / And I love you so." A complete embarrassment; next to "Aura Lee," from which it stole its tune, an abomination. The perfect example of rock-n-roll's

rejection of prettiness, overrefinement, academic orchestration and lyrics, smoothness, even subtlety. And for that reason, very big in 1956.)

Rock-n-roll sounded homemade because in most cases it was. The majors had their stables full of big names and salaried songwriters, but rock-n-roll came from the independents: the legendary Sun Records in Memphis, King in Cincinnati, Chess in Chicago, Specialty in Los Angeles. Also Ace, Aladdin, Imperial, Gee, Atco, Argo, Roulette, Josie, Brunswick, and, my own favorite, the S.P.Q.R. label, which recorded Jimmy Soul's "If You Want to Be Happy." Many of the independents—need it be said?—were as short-lived as the "artists" whose hits flashed like shooting stars across the late fifties skies. And the more independent the studio, the more primitive the facilities and the more homemade the sound.

Furthermore, the standard rock-n-roll musician was not the studio dropout who his sixties counterpart often was (although let it not be forgotten that Artur Rubenstein in 1956 singled out Neil Sedaka as New York City's best high school pianist and sent him off to Julliard on a scholarship, which may explain why Sedaka sounds so un-rock-n-rollish). Rock-n-rollers had no formal training. Some even lacked the background in gospel, ballroom, or barroom singing that did serve as musical education for so many r&r people. Some really were picked up on a street corner. "You used to go down to Jefferson High on 49th & Broadway and could get sixteen groups," recalled Phil Spector in 1969. Or maybe they'd just wander into Sun studio to cut a demo and get famous. Such casualness was not conducive to subtle harmony or complex arrangement; what it did foster was a strong feeling of regionalism, an airing of local accents homogenized by voice instructors and actually encouraged because of the independent company's sense of the local market. Hearing rock-n-roll was like overhearing a part of America you'd never quite picked up on before.

(Frankie Lymon, thirteen, has been dumped by his girl and is despondent. He mopes around a few days trying to talk himself out of love, and a phrase keeps recycling through his brain: "Why do Fools Fall in Love?" Little Frankie turns that phrase into a song.

Scene two finds Frankie and the gang rehearsing this little ditty in front of the local soda shop, when along comes Richard Barrett, lead singer for the Valentines.

Scene three finds Frankie and pals in the Gee Records recording studio, and scene four finds Frankie Lymon and the Teenagers with a smash hit, rich and famous.

Scene five, a decade later, finds Frankie dead of an overdose.)

Also characteristically, rock-n-roll was loud. There were ballads, but they were not really characteristic. Rock-n-rollers grasped very early the therapeutic value of noise, and r&r was neither offended nor embarrassed by "a-wop-bob-a-loom-op-a-lop-bam-boom!" or "ah-ummm" or "da-doo-run-run-run, da-doo-run-run." Voices were more expressive than they were in shlock music: Little Richard and Elvis Presley emoted circles around Johnnie Ray and Frank Sinatra, the big weepers and feelers of the big time.

When rock-n-roll lost its roughness and its regionalism, when arrangements became smoothed and complicated by production people at the majors (as would inevitably happen), when songs were written *for* instead of *by* artists, when—in short—rock-n-roll became mass-produced, it lost its energy and its uniqueness and ceased to be a driving social force. The process of absorption, at which Western technological society is so terrifyingly adept, we shall examine later; the point for now is that as this inevitable process occurred, the rock-n-roll artist had three choices. He could allow himself to be buoyed up by the bucks, the mansions, the women, and the golden Cadillacs, in which case he most certainly knew he'd become the central figure in technology's almost painless rite of castration. He could throw himself against the machine, staying visible and potent, in which case he either killed himself or got himself "removed." Or he could take his winnings and go home, back to the smaller stakes and the friendlier audiences and companies of either r&b or c&w, allowing himself to be replaced on the pop charts by South Philly lads more responsive to the pressures of the big-time music biz and the genial Dick Clark.

> (Chuck Berry and Dick Clark crossed at least once in the fifties, when Berry objected to the lip-synch thing on *American Bandstand*. Berry expected Leonard Chess to back him up, but Leonard didn't. "There are some things you gotta do in this business that you don't want to do," he told Berry. "He had a lot of power," Chuck adds of Clark, "and, of course, he also had a lot of money.")

The same process of absorption enervated rock-n-roll lyrics. It is a commonplace of rock-n-roll that when it came to words there weren't any—they didn't mean anything, who cared, it was the music that counted. That is a fiction perpetrated by the poetry professionals on the one hand (who found rock-n-roll's lyrics painfully banal and its adolescent subjects too narrow by 90%) and the good-beat-you-can-dance-to-it boys on the other (who figured—correctly—that the rock-n-roll revolution was in its sound and therefore nonintellective and assumed that words must therefore be irrelevant). One tended to come at rock-n-roll from the adult mainstream, the cultural heritage of two millennia of Western civilization, which was bound to overwhelm everything, including twentieth-century establishment culture. The other tended to come from swing, blues, or r&b backgrounds, which was bound to make the revolution of rock-n-roll seem tame indeed. White kids of the fifties were coming from neither direction. They had little exposure to Western civilization except high school English literature textbooks that dry-cleaned Shakespeare, Chaucer, and the Greek dramatists. And they had only the bits and snatches of r&b and c&w they may have picked up on late-night radio. When "Blue Suede Shoes" broke upon them it sounded just as poetically compelling as Poe's "Raven" or Sandburg's "Fog" and as musically and sociologically revolutionary as Bo Diddley's gutty, suggestive, bump-and-grind.

Rock-n-roll presents a fairly succinct and radical critique of fifties life, along with an equally coherent alternative. "Rock around the Clock" was a potent song in 1955, although it seems innocuous now. It is saying that we're gonna rock-n-roll. And we're gonna do it all night long. And we're gonna drive this thing right out front of us because *we're* in charge now and we're gonna have fun (the one thing money can't buy). So what if dancing is a cheap revolution; so what if all the standard r&b sexual overtones of *rock* are underplayed if not submerged entirely? To a middle-class teenager stuck inside the fifties, "Rock around the Clock" was a declaration of independence. In words as well as in music.

Take sex. Now the grown-ups obviously had been screwing around for a lot of years: they had kids, they had us. It was not, however, part of young middle-class experience that men and women make love. Inside or outside marriage. I mean, you did not see it on television. You did not see it in the movies. You didn't see it in your parents, you had no *Playboy* magazine to help you along with it, and nobody talked much about it. Memories, Dean Martin sang, were made of one girl, one boy, some grief, some joy, a blessing from above, and a kiss.

The conspiracy of silence was unbroken.

In this kind of world it was a revolution to be able to say with Elvis in a very tame ballad, "I want you, I need you, I love you with all my heart." It was even more revolutionary to realize not so much that there is a way of making it without the formalities but that there is a way of making it, period. That guys could and did cut in on other folks' girls, and "Speedo" was a nickname you could wear with pride on account of havin' made a lot of pretty women change their minds. That people held each other in the still of the night (the Five Satins). That people rock-n-rolled sixty minutes (the Dominoes) or all night long and then boasted about it. That you could look at "Young Blood" with fire in your eyes and lust in your heart ("What crazy stuff, she looked so tough I had to follow her all the way home"). Or "Chantilly Lace," with the Big Bopper moaning "Oh, baby, that's what I *like!*" That you could sing, "Come along and be my party doll and I'll make love to you." That you were allowed to just walk out of a bad situation warning cockily, "You're gonna miss the best man you ever had, you're gonna miss me early in the morning one of these days."

Little Richard was a revelation in this respect, what with the gal named Sue who knew just what to do ("Knows how to love me, yessireee," sang the boy from Macon in "Tutti Frutti," a cleaned up version of a piece of scurrility he'd launched into in the studio one day), and "Good Golly, Miss Molly" ("sure like to ball"), and "Long Tall Sally."

> Gonna tell Aunt Mary
> 'bout Uncle John
> Claims he has the mis'ry
> but he's havin' lot of fun
>
> Oh, Baby
> Yes, Baby
> Whoooo Baby
> Havin' me some fun tonight
>
> Well, long tall Sally
> She's built for speed
> She got everything that
> Uncle John need . . .
>
> (chorus)
>
> Well, I saw Uncle John
> With bald-head Sally
> Saw Aunt Mary comin'
> And he ducked back in the alley
> Oh, Baby
> Yes, Baby
> Whoooo Baby
> Havin' me some fun tonight

There were even references, for those sharp enough to catch them, to the taboo subject of VD: "You'll be scratchin' like a hound the minute you start to mess around with Poison Ivy." And a piece of infidelity in "But I've got news for you: I was untrue! I found another love, be on your way."

And to hear a female voice sing, "I'm available and willing," or "Oh, Johnny, how you can love," or "and when I sleep I always dream of Bill." Or maybe, "I feel so good when you're home" (the answer to which is, "Come on, baby, rock me all night long"). Not quite as revolutionary as the earlier and more direct r&b "Work with Me Annie" from Hank Ballard and the Midnighters ("Please don't cheat, give me all my meat"—plus the sequels "Annie Had a Baby" and "Roll with Me Henry" and "Annie's Answer" and "Annie Pulled a Humbug" and "Annie's Aunt Fannie"), but still a revolution by middle-class standards.

How much of this revolution struck home is a moot question. I was always more comfortable with the bespectacled Buddy Holly than with the sex symbol Elvis Presley, and not until college could I really *deal* with the nitty-gritty grind of hard-core rhythm and blues. Most often I felt more in the camp of Travis and Bob, plaintively, hopefully, fearfully, desperately praying, "Tell him no-oh-a-oh-oh, tell him no-oh-a-oh-oh, /If he offers his ring tell him no."

But rock-n-roll spoke out on matters other than sex. Like school. It lined up directly behind Paul Goodman: school was the agent of repression or at least of resignation to the social straightjacket, complete boredom and futility. "Scarcely," as the Who would put it in the jacket notes to *Quadrophenia*, "worth mentioning." When it was mentioned, school was a drag. "School is out at last," rejoiced Gary (U.S.) Bonds, and I'm so glad I passed and no books and studying in the summer and let's celebrate. Celebration amounted to "doin' the things I want to do," which in turn meant rootin' for the Yankees from the bleachers, stayin' out late with the guys ("Rock around the Clock"), takin' the girl out for a night with Daddy G. This was 1961. The scene was virtually unchanged from 1959, when the Coasters had cased the joint in "Charlie Brown" and thrown in their lot with the proto-beatnik, spitball-throwing, goofballing Charlie, who shoots craps in the gym, writes on walls, smokes in the auditorium (Lawdy, Miss Clawdy, did they freak out whenever they smelled smoke during assembly!), and refers to the English teacher as Daddy-O. *That* is alienation.

> "One thing you may always count on in Springfield is the fine appearance and good conduct of your classmates. Any time we make a field trip, have visitors in our assembly programs, or go before the public in any fashion, the boys wear coats and ties and the girls "dress-up" a little more than usual. As a representative of Springfield High School, you must at all times keep your best foot forward both in and out of school."—*Springfield (Pennsylvania) High School Student Handbook*, 1957

And the scene was unchanged from 1957–1958, when Chuck Berry had surveyed it in "Anthony Boy" and "School Days."

> Soon as three o'clock rolls around
> You finally lay your burden down
> Close up your books and get out of your seat
> Down the halls and into the street.

And right down to the juke joint, where you could purge your head with some good, hard rock-n-roll. "The feeling is there, body and soul." This alienation, naturally, has been lost on the Fonz who becomes a grade school mascot in the seventies. (And it was lost in 1963, when, with rock-n-roll soft in the head, Brian Wilson wrote "Be True to Your School.")

> "Students in good health are expected to be in homeroom before the tardy bell rings in the morn-

ing. Most students arrive about 8:00 o'clock to allow time for locker use. If a student is absent, the
school will attempt to reach the home by phone.
In the event that this is impossible, a note is required before the student may attend classes when
he returns. Illegal absence from school results in a
three-day suspension and a loss of 9 points on all
subject grades for the report period."

Rock-n-roll did criticize social institutions. You have been told that
"Maybellene" is a car-woman, sex-and-driving song. Read it another way:
Maybellene off with some hot, new lover in a big-assed Cadillac, po' boy
Chuck lights out after them in his working-class, overheated Ford V-8. And
doesn't the jalopy bust on past the thievin' Coupe de Ville like it was stand-
in' still and catch the two-timin' Maybellene at the top of the hill. Class conflict. And, while we're at it, Chuck Berry's other great car song, "Jaguar and
the Thunderbird," is not so much about drag racing as about beating the
sheriff to the county line.

Or take the Coasters, complaining in "Along Came Jones" about the
same old television melodrama one channel to the next and parodying the
whole business with smooth talkin', cool walkin' Jones.

Or "Tobacco Road," 1960: gonna split this place, get a job, pile up the
dollars. And then take all that dough and come back here with dynamite
and a crane and level this slum.

Or the rose in Spanish Harlem, with her black and soulful eyes and the
fire burning out of control. Or the Duke of Earl, an almost pathetic subli-
mation of suffering into dreams and aspirations that singer, writer, listener,
and everybody knows can never be realized.

Or Chuck Berry's distillation of fifties alienation into the angry point-
lessness of "No Particular Place to Go."

Or the fondness of rock-n-roll for anti-heroes. It's a simplistic, romantic
view of prisons indeed that emerges from a song like "Jailhouse Rock" and a
simpering sentimentalism that underlies "He's a Rebel" and "Leader of the
Pack," but all three reflect a very genuine affection in rock-n-roll for the
• other side of the tracks (the old stomping ground, as it were). And none is a
more outrageous misrepresentation of reality than what the folks at *Partisan Review* did for/to Caryl Chessman. "Alley-Oop," a novelty record,
gives a good clue to the emerging type of the anti-hero: "The cats don't bug
him, 'cause they know better; he's a mean motorscooter and a bad go-
getter." With Jerry Lee Lewis's version of "Drinkin' Wine Spo-Dee-O-Dee"
the connections are much more real and presentation less bogus. Such also
is the case with Sam Cooke's presentation of the men working on the chain
gang! "You hear them moaning their lives away." Basically, rock-n-roll was
incurably hoodlum; it died when it was plucked from Long Tall Sally's
alley, scrubbed up, and decked out in clean clothes.

The most general and profound criticism of the American mainstream is to be found in two classic rock-n-roll singles and the collected works of r&r's greatest singer-composer, Chuck Berry. "Get a Job" could have been lifted directly from any of the prose critiques of meaningless or nonexistent employment in the promised land. "Yakety-Yak" is about a lot more than paying your dues so you can get out of the house on a Friday night; it's about the unproductive or trivial work a society invents ("Bring in the dog and put out the cat") to make sure that people do not do what they feel like doing—in this case rocking and rolling and going for a ride with "your hoodlum friend outside." (Anybody you didn't like or understand in the fifties was either a communist or a hoodlum. "Hoodlum" was the more middle-class of the two epithets, and my mother used it a lot.)

> "If I was 23 years old and you was 22, I bet nobody'd try to run our lives the way they do."
> —Chuck Berry

Chuck Berry was a very sharp thinker and perhaps the only real poet among fifties rock-n-rollers. He returned again and again to the theme of meaninglessness in his songs. In "Too Much Monkey Business," the great-grandfather of Dylan's "Subterranean Homesick Blues," Berry catalogued middle-class blandishments.

> Runnin' to and fro
> Hard workin' at the mill,
> Never fail in the mail
> Here come a rotten bill.
> Too much monkey business,
> Too much monkey business,
> Too much monkey business
> For me to be involved in.
>
> Salesman talkin' to me,
> Try an' run me up a creek,
> Say "You can buy it,
> Go ahead and try it,
> You can pay me next week."
> Ah, too much monkey business. . . .
>
> Blonde hair, good lookin',
> Try an' get me hooked,
> Want me to marry, get a home,
> Settle down and write a book.
> Ah, too much monkey business
> For me to be involved in.

The same aridity reappears in "No Particular Place to Go," with Chuck cruisin' through town, listenin' to his radio, doin' nothin' (there bein' nothin' worth doin'); in "School Days," where the only option is to wait it all out and then escape; in "Come On" ("Some stupid jerk tryin' to reach another number"); and in "Almost Grown," which presents the most universal of Berry's heroes. More common in real life than the hot-rodders in their V-8s, the brown eyed handsome men and the Johnny B. Goodes, were the guys who, never really daring to cut the rope, played it cool and waited. And waited and waited, until their youth evaporated and they were left frustrated, having played by the rules, and feeling angry and cheated.

> Yeah, I'm doing all right in school,
> They ain't said I've broke no rule,
> I ain't never been in Dutch,
> I don't browse around too much;
> Don't bother me, leave me alone,
> Anyway I'm almost grown.
>
> I don't run around with no mob,
> I got myself a little job,
> I'm gonna buy myself a little car,
> I'll drive my girl in the park;
> Don't bother me, leave me alone,
> Anyway I'm almost grown.
>
> I got my eye on a little girl,
> Ah, she's really out of this world,
> When I take her out to a dance,
> She's gotta talk about romance;
> Don't bother me, leave me alone,
> Anyway I'm almost grown.
>
> You know I'm still livin' in town,
> But I done married and settled down,
> Now I really have a ball,
> So I don't browse around at all;
> Don't bother me, leave me alone,
> Anyway I'm almost grown.

Against this ruin, Chuck offers all the consolations of the counterculture: speed, youth, sex, music: "Anything you want, we got it in the U.S.A." His heroes take what they can get as fast and as greedily as they can and eat the ice cream before it melts. "Sweet Little Sixteen" dances her tight little ass off before she turns into a pumpkin again next Monday in the classroom. "Johnny B. Goode" hits the marquees and the Hollywood films. The "Brown Eyed Handsome Man" rocks and reels through the wives of doctors, lawyers, and Indian chiefs and is off before you can catch him. In "No Money Down," Chuck trades in that old, broken-down, ragged Ford for a big, shiny Cadillac with every option he can think of, including a telephone to call his baby on. Everybody boogies. You gotta grab it before you're too pooped to pop, too old to stroll. You gotta light out for the promised land, call the folks back home, and tell them you've made it, before it's time to leave. "The Promised Land" is, in fact, Berry's affirmation of life in America, a flurry of dust and chicken feathers as the po' boy hauls it off to California, Greyhound, midnight flier, and finally first-class air ticket, his silk suit and luggage acquired along the way. The greatness is in the going and the getting there, in the action.

Kerouac would have understood: "Hey, M.F., I'm out here in fucking *California*, baby!" "Hey, baby, far out! What you gonna do now?" "I'm gonna go to fuckin' New York."

Children of the sixties will understand perfectly.

October, 1968, Tommie Smith (center) and Juan Carlos (right), Olympic medalists in the 200 meter run, give the Black Power salute during the playing of the Star Spangled Banner. Both were dismissed from the squad and send home. *Wide World Photos. Used by permission.*

Oxford, Mississippi, 1962: Major Gen. Edwin Walker, who in October of 1957 had led federal troops in Little Rock to support integration, is removed by young soldiers from the courthouse, where he had appeared to support Governor Ross Barnett, 1962. *United Press International Photo. Used by permission.*

Shock troops of the new and old orders confront each other outside the Pentagon in 1967. *United Press International Photo. Used by permission.*

Cassius Clay (Muhammad Ali) leaves U.S. Induction Center on April 8, 1967, after refusing induction into the Army. He would lose his world heavyweight title and the three best years of his fighting career and dramatize to youth of all races that you could say "No." *United Press International Photo. Used by permission.*

Phil Ochs — "The reward is the act of struggle itself, not what you win ... That's morality, that's religion. That's art. That's life." *Photo by Alice Ochs. Used by permission.*

Moratorium Day in Washington, D.C. A huge crowd protested the Vietnam war, November 15, 1969. *United Press International Photo. Used by permission.*

Georgia rock festival. Two signs of the distressing times. *United Press International Photo. Used by permission.*

Buffy Sainte-Marie at the Alcatraz rally for the Indians. *Photo by Alice Ochs. Used by permission.*

Ray Davies and the Kinks. *Photo by Chuck Pulin. Used by permission.*

Bob Dylan in 1963, just arrived in New York City from Hibbing, Minnesota. *United Press International Photo. Used by permission.*

The British Invasion, first wave, arrive in America. *United Press International Photo. Used by permission.* "Do you hope to take anything home with you?" "The Rockefeller Center."—Beatles at New York City press conference, February 7, 1964.

John, Ringo, Paul, and George. *Photo courtesy of Michael Ochs Archives. Used by permission.*

Frank Zappa and The Mothers of Invention. *Photo by Alice Ochs. Used by permission.*

Abbie Hoffman is arrested in Washington, D.C., in 1968 for wearing the American flag. *United Press International Photo. Used by permission.*

The San Francisco Mime Troupe performing "Ripping Off Ma Bell—S as in Sabotage." *Photo courtesy of Ramparts magazine. Used by permission.*

Arlo Guthrie and friends.

The Fugs, Allen Ginsberg (in Uncle Sam hat), Peter Orlovsky, and about fifteen thousand other antiwar demonstrators in New York City, 1966. *United Press International Photo. Used by permission.*

|2| The Angry No

"Eighteen years of American dream . . .
Did you see him?"—Neil Young, "Broken Arrow"

The sixties will be remembered as the Age of the Great Rejection. Racism, militarism, Big Brotherism, censorship, commercialism, sexism, organization, inhibition, liberalism, conservatism, Mr. Chipsism, poverty, pollution, bureaucracy, reason, progress, deliberation, efficiency, domestic tranquility (the indictment read in the fifties by Paul Goodman and Herbert Marcuse)—even the virtues that *are* really virtues, like consideration and patience and humility—the sixties exploded Western civilization, clearing the way for pioneers and exploration.

This wholesale negation, this angry no, was much misunderstood by America's elders and by establishment apologists, who took it to be simple nihilism. It was exactly the opposite. First, it represented a great opening of the mind and spirit, a rejection of stultifying conventions and a demand for meaningful choices. Second, the angry no grew directly out of a fervent affirmation of American ideals. As sixties people saw it, the real negativism, the real leveling, the real sellout was to be found in the America they had known as adolescents: a betrayal of the ideals of freedom, justice, and equality as articulated in the Constitution, the Declaration of Independence, and Memorial Day speeches. Whatever Spiro Agnew might have said at the close of the decade about "nabobs of negativism," sixties people saw in him—as in Lyndon Johnson, Richard Nixon, Billy Graham, Lawrence Welk, Bob Hope, Clark Kerr, Robert McNamara, many of their teachers, most of their entertainers, and all businessmen, politicians, and generals—the real denial of American tradition. Their elders' easy accommodation to injustice, corruption, and patent lunacy maddened children of the sixties, whose no was a no *to* a no: a yes. It is in this context of denial as affirmation that the decade must be viewed. Only by grasping this yes in the no can the high moral seriousness of sixties protest be understood.

("This is a land full of Power and Glory," celebrated Phil Ochs in what he once called "the greatest song I'll ever write." This was the same Phil Ochs who, in "The War Is Over," suggested, "Just before the end even treason might be worth a try." Ochs contained a lot of Guthrie.)

51

For in one corner of their schizophrenic souls, children of the sixties took themselves and others very seriously. They all believed in things like ethics, equality, and justice—everything they'd been taught in eighth-grade civics class and seen in Frank Capra movies. They expected, especially in America, *everybody* to get a fair deal. And they could see that *nobody* was getting a fair deal. You can always recognize a bad check by the way it bounces, a phony politician by the hollow sound when you knock on his head, a rotting corpse in Mississippi or Indochina by the evil odor that seeps out from under the locked closet door.

Moreover, thanks largely to sputnik and the Protestant temper of the fifties, they were a very motivated bunch of kids who felt personally guilty and individually responsible for the gap between reality and possibility. If their neighbor was unloved, it was up to them to love him. If people were being killed—and there are in the twentieth century so many ways to kill a man—it was their responsibility to save them. If the system was a fraud, it was up to them to fix it. And by action more direct and more effective than mere voting and letter writing, immediately.

> What is the price-current of an honest man and patriot to-day? They hesitate, and they regret, and sometimes they petition; but they do nothing in earnest and with effect. They will wait, well disposed, for others to remedy the evil, that they may no longer have it to regret. At most, they give only a cheap vote, and a feeble countenance and God-speed, to the right, as it goes by them. . . . Even voting *for the right* is *doing* nothing for it. It is only expressing to men feebly your desire that it should prevail. . . . Under a government which imprisons any unjustly, the true place for a just man is also a prison.
> —Henry David Thoreau on liberals in "Civil Disobedience"

A less aware or educated generation or one distracted by a war or a depression might have ignored the injustices and irritations that so troubled the sleep of sixties children. It would have slumbered blissfully and ignorantly and quite comfortably. A more cynical generation would have been less obsessed, less righteously angry. It could maybe have laughed or shrugged its shoulders. A less motivated generation would have despaired and retreated to the safety of distances.

Undistracted, innocent, and responsible, children of the sixties brashly attacked injustice, irritation, and idiocy head on. The undertaking was, though quixotic and naive, supremely heroic.

And it was massive.

Between September 16 and October 15, 1968—one month of one year of the decade—over two hundred separate incidents of protest were reported in the *New York Times* and the *Washington Post*. How many hundreds, how many thousands of marches, rallies, and demonstrations in Carbondale, Illinois, or Wapakoneta, Ohio, or Tallahassee, Florida, escaped the media (and thereby the consciousness of the nation)? How many

American boys, convinced they could not participate in an immoral and stupid war, slipped quietly across the Canadian border that month? How many hundreds of thousands of friends and family were lost because of the rigid moral stands young Americans took?

> "If you decide to burn your draft card then burn your birth certificate at the same time. From that moment I have no son."—Victor Lundberg, "An Open Letter to My Teenage Son"

Moral and ethical considerations weighed heavily on all Americans during the sixties. It was a time when you could not, in good conscience, carry a card that assimilated you, however peripherally, into the U.S. Army; when you would refuse to buy fruit sold by exploitive California growers or plastic wrap manufactured by the makers of napalm; when you gave more than your cheap vote and a feeble countenance and Godspeed to the right, lest it pass you by. When protest was a condition of daily life. When people sat in, marched, seized, and occupied almost as casually as they rolled joints or turned on their favorite FM station. And if protest meant going down, then that was okay because you were going down in a good cause and that was the kind of commitment you were making.

> Oh, what'll you do now, my blue-eyed son?
> Oh, what'll you do now, my darling young one?
> I'm a-goin' back out 'fore the rain starts a-fallin',
> I'll walk to the depths of the deepest black forest,
> Where the people are many and their hands are all empty,
> Where the pellets of poison are flooding their waters,
> Where the home in the valley meets the damp dirty prison,
> Where the executioner's face is always well hidden,
> Where hunger is ugly, where souls are forgotten,
> Where black is the color, where none is the number,
> And I'll tell it and think it and speak it and breathe it,
> And reflect it from the mountain so all souls can see it,
> Then I'll stand on the ocean until I start sinkin',
> But I'll know my song well before I start singin',
> And it's a hard, it's a hard, it's a hard, it's a hard,
> It's a hard rain's a-gonna fall.
> —Bob Dylan, "A Hard Rain's A-Gonna Fall" 1963

Public dissent took many forms during the sixties. Each act was as much a reflection of individual circumstance as of personal philosophy. In the summer of 1961, Freedom Riders protested segregation in southern bus terminals by the simple act of taking a bus ride. In 1963, Martin Luther King registered a very moving protest by delivering a speech to fifteen U.S. senators and two hundred thousand other folk gathered before the Lincoln Memorial. In May 1965, Columbia University students registered their protest against militarism by throwing lemon meringue pies during the NROTC officer awards ceremony. In August 1965, blacks in Watts ghetto protested racism by setting Los Angeles ablaze. In 1968 the Poor People's Campaign protested poverty by constructing Resurrection City of plywood shacks in Washington and moving in for the spring. At Amherst College, students protested by smashing dining hall dinner plates that depicted Lord Amherst killing an Indian. Cassius Clay protested by refusing induction into the army, thereby losing the best three years of his fighting career and becoming a myth to millions of young people. At the 1968 Olympics, Tommie Smith and John Carlos, gold and bronze medals around their necks, protested American racism with black gloves and clenched fists raised high. Late in the decade it was customary to protest the war in Vietnam with a general strike on Moratorium Day. Faculties and students studied the war; the names of war dead were read in public ceremonies, hurled against the White House and the vastnesses of America; and speeches by the thousands reminded everybody that still a hard rain was falling.

Amid the chaos of causes, organizations, and styles, it is possible to distinguish four strains of sixties rejection, each with characteristic music: the nonviolent protest of the pacifists; the violent protest of the radicals and the anarchists; the holy goofs, who parodied corruption and injustice in weird carnival nightmares; and the artists, who moved on from attacking the topical and the specific to challenging the human condition. In the popular imagination and with much help from the news media, these strains tended to be associated with individuals like Martin Luther King, Jr., Tom Hayden, Malcolm X, Ken Kesey, and Abbie Hoffman. But the archetypes were probably not as pure as they were drawn, and most people of the sixties resonated to anything that moved—which was all four.

The nonviolent approach that characterized ban the Bomb marches, early stages of the civil rights and anti–Vietnam War movements, and almost all environmental protest was borne of Gandhi's nonviolent civil disobedience—orthodox Christianity, with a pinch of Tolstoy and a dash of Thoreau. It sought to confront injustice directly, but it was assiduously nonviolent. In many cases it acted by not acting, by simply refusing to become an accomplice to the crime, or by behaving as if discrimination, trespassing laws, and organized power structures simply did not exist. It accepted its role as victim and applied, to reverse the cliché, the subminimal force necessary to get a job done.

It lost. It marched in the teeth of dogs and the barrels of guns with flowers and smiles. When beaten, it went limp, got hauled off to court, and then chose jail over bond or fine, thereby making itself an embarrassment to injustice. It expected to lose battles in order to win the war. And it lost plenty of battles.

> You may choose to face physical assault without protecting yourself, hands at the sides, unclenched; or you may choose to protect yourself making plain you do not intend to hit back. If you choose to pro-

tect yourself, you practice positions such as these: To protect the skull, fold hands over the head. To prevent disfigurement of the face, bring the elbows together in front of the eyes. For girls, to prevent internal injury from kicks, lie on the side and bring the knees upward to the chin; for boys, kneel down and arch over with skull and face protected.—Southern Christian Leadership Conference instructions at Orangeburg, South Carolina, 1960

This type of protest continues in "No Nukes" and "Save the Whale/Seal," identified by its peaceful and orderly demonstrations, usually with proper permits and along predetermined routes (often with police escorts), by its polite but firm refusal to comply, and by its assumption that ends are inseparable from means (as the popular slogan went, killing for peace is like fucking for virginity). The nonviolent protester assumes that laws and institutions grow directly out of prejudices and that once you change hearts and minds by pointing out injustices again and again, institutions will take care of themselves. But you take your time, and always you turn the other cheek. As much as you hope for change, you accept the fruits of your protest as inevitable, if unjust: privation, pain, jail, even death. They are the necessary costs of changing society, of living the moral life. The cost of freedom, as Stephen Stills observed retrospectively in 1972, lies buried in the ground. (Besides, television and the other news media may record your death and spread the record of your suffering all across the country, and you just might discover—as so often was the case in the sixties—that you win by losing.)

popular archetype: Martin Luther King and the NAACP
moment: Birmingham, Alabama, May 1963, and the high point of nonviolent civil rights protest. Police Chief Bull Connor meets five hundred black children with high-powered fire hoses. Then police wade in with clubs and German Shepherds, arrest all the kids, and pack them off in school buses become paddy wagons. The world looks on dumbfounded at a spectacle that, Wayne Morse tells the Senate, would disgrace the Union of South Africa.
slogan: "We Shall Overcome" (someday)
song: Bob Dylan's "Blowin' in the Wind"

Musically as well as sociologically, nonviolent protest predominated throughout the sixties, especially early in the decade, when the folk music revival brought both the acoustic guitar and sharp public protest out of Greenwich Village coffeehouses and onto college campuses across America. The decade's most poignant protests were almost all folk-based songs.

Hints of the folk rebellion to come reached America in the hits of the Highwaymen ("Cotton Fields," 1962), Brook Benton ("Boll Weevil Song," 1961), Sam Cooke ("That's the sound of the men workin' on the chain gang," 1960), the Kingston Trio, and the Brothers Four. Other indications of what was going on down underground could be found in media coverage of civil rights or ban the Bomb activity or—on the west coast—of anti-HUAC demonstrations:

> A friend of mine telephoned me about three weeks ago, it was the day after we read in our newspapers up here what was going on in Birmingham with the dogs, and he said, "Pete, you have to see it to believe it. They have a little dance down there, I don't even know the name of it (I found out since it's called the wooble), but they do a song with it, they start with a twist and then a step back and then a step forward and a hesitation somewhere, but they all sing, "I ain't afraid of your jail because I want my freedom, I want my freedom, I want my freedom; I ain't afraid of your jail because I want my freedom, I want my freedom now.'"
>
> He says you have to see it, though, to see how it works. There's the Reverend King giving them a lecture in church, he says, "This is to be a silent demonstration today, no songs, no slogans, and if any obscenities are shouted at you from the sidelines, you don't reply to them. You keep right along the line of march . . . until you are arrested. Then the singing can begin." So they all file out of church, just as solemn as deacons and quiet as mice, down the street, a couple hundred of them. Along comes a policeman, "You're all under arrest. . . ." "I ain't afraid of your jail, because I want my freedom."
>
> —Pete Seeger, recounting the scene in Birmingham, Alabama, May 1963

Many of the songs of protest that filled civil rights rallies in 1961 and 1962 were spirituals a century old; many of the folk songs that filled Village coffeehouses were protests against men and events buried long before. At first the folk flowering represented a reaching back to the tradition of hand-crafted American music and thirties and forties radicalism. The hip owned a tall stack of Weavers records, and Vanguard Records was truly hip because they recorded the Weavers (and Joan Baez). The image of Woody Guthrie loomed large in the minds of men.

As did the old stories spun by Guthrie and Seeger and Aunt Molly Jackson, stories of Joe Hill and Casey Jones and Pretty Boy Floyd, the battle between striking Colorado miners and Rockefeller scabs at Ludlow in 1914. And the genuine folk songs, protests against work and bosses and hard times, like "Drill Ye Tarriers" and "All My Trials" and "The House of the Rising Sun." Songs of the dust bowl and the depression and even old war songs (well, actually a Woody Guthrie song about the war) like "The Sinking of the Reuben James," with its pointed remark that the worst of men must fight and the best of men must die. The folk scene in 1960 was dominated by the past: the collections of Alan Lomax and other pioneers, the songs of Guthrie, Seeger, the scattered Weavers, traditional folk material of all countries and races. In fact, folk purists made a point out of tradition: a *real* folk song cannot have a known author.

This argument, of course, is foolishness. What was significant was that protest singers of the early sixties were grounding themselves musically and sociologically in the past: in Gandhi and Thoreau and Tolstoy and Guthrie and Joe Hill and the IWW.

And sixties protest was learning from the past. While Peter, Paul, and Mary, Joan Baez, the Chad Mitchell and Kingston trios, even Ramblin' Jack Elliott, Phil Ochs, and Bob Dylan were reviving, impersonating the past, many of them were learning from their elders techniques that would allow them to make new songs of their own. They were learning how to take an old song, change a few words, and turn—for example—a fairly stiff, white, European hymn "I Will Overcome" into a relatively loose, black, American hymn, which could with minimal alteration be turned into a powerful civil rights protest song. They were learning how to take an old tune, change a few notes here and there, make it go up where it used to go down, add a chord that wasn't there before (as Woody Guthrie once advised the young Bob Dylan), and come up with a song of their own. They were learning how to write their own "Ludlow Massacre" and "Reuben James."

So that Phil Ochs would cop a tune from Guthrie's "Tom Joad," which Guthrie had copped from Leadbelly's "John Hardy," and set to it his lyrics about Joe Hill, the martyred labor organizer and one of the wellsprings of early sixties protest. Later, Ochs would take his own 1964 "Here's to the State of Mississippi" and, by changing a word or two here and there, come out with "Here's to the State of Richard Nixon."

Very quickly it became apparent that sixties folk protesters were not just resurrecting a buried past. They were constructing a new protest of contemporary social and political conditions.

I still have a dream. It is a dream deeply rooted in the American dream. I have a dream that one day this nation will rise up and live out the true meaning of its creed: "We hold these truths to be self-evident; that all men are created equal."

I have a dream that one day on the red hills of Georgia the sons of former slaves and the sons of former slaveowners will be able to sit down together at the table of brotherhood; I have a dream—

That one day even the state of Mississippi, a state sweltering with the heat of injustice, sweltering with the heat of oppression, will be transformed into an oasis of freedom and justice; I have a dream—

That my four little children will one day live in a nation where they will not be judged by the color of their skin but by the content of their character; I have a dream today. . . .

Let freedom ring from every hill and mole hill of Mississippi. From every mountainside, let freedom ring, and when this happens, when we allow freedom to ring, when we let it ring from every village and every hamlet, from every state and every city, we will be able to speed up that day when all of God's children, black men and white men, Jews and Gentiles, Protestants and Catholics, will be able to join hands and sing in the words of the old Negro spiritual, "Free at last! Free at last! Thank God almighty, we are free at last!"—Martin Luther King, Jr., August 28, 1963

And the songs were printed in *Broadside* and *Sing Out!* and they were sung in the streets and coffeehouses of New York and Boston and Philadelphia and across the South and finally on records and on FM stations, and they have thus found their way into American consciousness, a permanent record of early sixties protest.

The most popular song to come out of the Village in the early sixties, and the anthem of the protest movement throughout the decade, was Bob Dylan's "Blowin' in the Wind." Written in 1962 and sung onto the top forty in 1963 by Peter, Paul, and Mary, "Blowin' in the Wind" is a classic statement of nonviolent protest. Two concerns dominate the song, and they are the two causes that dominated early sixties protest: racism and militarism, men who are not allowed to be men and the white dove of peace rocked by cannon balls. As the decade unfolded and people of the sixties began to understand just how immense the task would be, "Blowin' in the Wind" gathered a wealth of associations no other song of the sixties could match. Versatile enough to lend itself to any cause, as timeless as "We Shall Overcome," Dylan's simple statement of 1962 carried many through the decade.

There were others as well. "If I Had a Hammer" was a Pete Seeger–Lee Hayes song folksingers had known for years: Peter, Paul, and Mary sang it into national consciousness in 1962. It, too, made a general statement: freedom, justice, love between brothers and sisters all over the land. If the hammer hinted vaguely at barrel-of-a-gun protest, the bell and the song made clear the nonviolent predilections of Seeger and everybody else who sang along: the revolution was love, the means was music.

> (Woody Guthrie had written on his banjo, "This machine kills fascists." Seeger, perhaps in imitation, had written on his, "This machine surrounds hate and forces it to surrender.")

As folk music flowered and as sixties protest began to define for itself causes and issues other than racism and militarism, folksinger-writers increased both their range and their output: Malvina Reynolds ("Little Boxes," "What Have They Done to the Rain," and "It Isn't Nice"—to block doorways and go to jail), Pete Seeger, Phil Ochs, Tom Paxton. Paxton's classic "That's What I Learned in School" (1962) is remarkably comprehensive in its jabs at education, militarism, racism, capital punishment, politicians, and policemen.

> "How did you get to be such puppets? You *perform*. But when do you think? Dutifully and obediently you follow, as a herd of grade-worshiping

> sheep. . . . But whether you are strong or weak
> you perform like trained seals, and like sheep you
> follow."—Bradley Cleveland, "A Letter to Under-
> graduates," Berkeley, California, 1964

A great deal of the folk flowering, however, was not as universal as "Blowin' in the Wind" or even "That's What I Learned in School." The air was full of topical songs, throwaway broadsides in which the folksinger turned himself into a radical newspaper, bringing to his audience, in the words of Phil Ochs's first album, "all the news that's fit to sing." It was a trick the youngsters had learned from their elders, a trick as old as Joe Hill and union organization early in the century, a trick Guthrie had learned, and Seeger and Hayes after him. In March 1963 Phil Ochs had written for *Broadside* a combination explanation of his art and call for more topical songs. In this article, "The Need for Topical Music," Ochs argued that every newspaper headline is a potential song and that one "good song with a message" would speak "more deeply to more people than a thousand rallies." At the Newport Folk Festival of that same year, he and Dylan and the Freedom Singers held a workshop that turned the topical protest song into *the* musical genre of the next few years. Langston Hughes, writing the jacket notes to *Joan Baez 2* (1964), observed, "In a worried period, the folk singers, many of them, particularly the city folk singers, are taking the troubles of our times and wrapping them up in songs—documentary songs, musings songs, angry protest songs."

> "I think in '63 especially, at the Civil Rights apex,
> musical esthetics came together with politics, and
> it was good to be involved with both."—Phil
> Ochs, interview with Izzy Young at the Folklore
> Center, September 4, 1968

And so they came, topical protests about every person and event imaginable, most now lost with the memory of the persons and events they memorialized. Richard Fariña wrote and Joan Baez recorded "Birmingham Sunday," the story of the black children killed in the church bombing of September 15, 1963. After the missile crisis of late October 1962 Phil Ochs wrote "Talking Cuban Crisis," and in 1964 he wrote "Talking Vietnam" (yes, as early as 1964 some Americans were concerned about the war in Vietnam—but only a handful), and before, during, and after he wrote songs like "Oxford, Mississippi," "The Thresher" (on the nuclear submarine lost while being tested), "Lou Marsh" (on a priest killed in trying to stop a gang war), and "The Ballad of William Worthy" (on an American newspaperman whose passport was revoked after he visited Cuba illegally). When Medgar Evers was assassinated in June 1963, not hours after President Kennedy had called for a revolution in race relations that would be "peaceful and constructive for all," Ochs wrote "Too Many Martyrs," an ironically prophetic song, as things would turn out, and a plea for nonviolence.

> The killer waited by his home hidden by the night
> As Evers stepped out from his car into the rifle sight.
> He slowly squeezed the trigger; the bullet left his side.
> It struck the heart of every man when Evers fell and died.

> Too many martyrs and too many dead,
> Too many lives, too many empty words were said
> Too many times for too many angry men;
> Oh, let it never be again.

"The country gained a killer and the country lost a man," Phil noted at the end of his nearly journalistic recounting of the event, a characteristically aphoristic conclusion that would plant this song (he hoped) firmly in people's hearts and minds and help make of Medgar Evers a political battle cry. This was what most topical protest songs of the early sixties attempted to do, although virtually all of them failed to carry their causes or themselves further than a decade or so.

Meanwhile, Bob Dylan had been pumping out topical songs of his own. "I don't sit around with the newspapers, like a lot of people do," Dylan once said in an obvious dig at Ochs, "spread out newspapers around and pick something out to write about." But a glance at some of Dylan's early albums shows that Dylan was as much into the topical protest bag as anyone else: "The Death of Emmett Till," "Ballad of Donald White," "Oxford Town," "The Lonesome Death of Hattie Carroll," "The Ballad of Hollis Brown." And when Medgar Evers went down, Dylan wrote for him—or for his killer—"Only a Pawn in Their Game":

> A South politician preaches to the poor white man,
> "You got more than the blacks, don't complain.
> You're better than them, you been born with white skin," they ex-
>   plain.
> And the Negro's name
> Is used it is plain
> For the politician's gain
> As he rises to fame
> And the poor white remains
> On the caboose of the train
> But it ain't him to blame
> He's only a pawn in their game.

Today these songs have a quaintness to them, like old copies of *Life* magazine. A line or two—the rhetorical snapper hammered home in each refrain—live today, but mostly these songs remind us that there once was a time when, if singers didn't spread newspapers in front of themselves, they at least functioned as a kind of newspaper, bringing to their audiences not only the latest atrocities but important editorial commentary as well.

By the middle of the decade, the topical protest song had lost much of its appeal although the genre persisted long after Dylan left it (and folk music) with *Bringing It All Back Home* in 1965. Ochs included a number of topical protests in *I Ain't Marching Any More*, among them his popular "Draft Dodger Rag" ("Sarge, I'm only sixteen, I got a ruptured spleen, and I always carry a purse"). When the United States invaded Santo Domingo, Phil got right on it with "Santo Domingo," and as he committed himself more and more to campus demonstrations against the war he ground out increasing numbers of songs against both U.S. militarism and the heavy hands of college administrators and local police in repressing campus unrest. In 1965 Tom Paxton released *Ain't That News*, which is full of topical protests, including "Lyndon Johnson Told the Nation," an anticipation by two or three years of the president's unpopularity because of the war. Seeger carried Ochs and Paxton and himself from campus to campus, the only places he was allowed to find an audience (because of the old HUAC blacklist), bringing his musical newspaper to the people who didn't bother to read newspapers. Buffy Sainte-Marie, a Cree Indian, took up her people's cause with an album in March 1964 titled *It's My Way*, which introduced her soon to become popular "Now That the Buffalo's Gone" and the antiwar "Universal Soldier," popularized in 1966 by Donovan Leitch during his Bob Dylan period. Buffy followed with "My Country 'Tis of Thy People You're Dying" in 1966, and the Indians had an eloquent voice. Paul Simon and Art Garfunkel included her song "He Was My Brother" on their first album. Protest was still the order of the day in folk music.

In 1964–1966, however, folk music protest was changing in several respects. Most obviously, the genre was broadening its subject matter. Phil Ochs had complained in 1963 that only civil rights and the antiwar crusade seemed to spur people to action or song; by 1965 the movement, both social and musical, was considerably broader. More important, a tone of anxiety, almost of desperation, had crept into the music—and the movement. The old, naive optimism was burning low as martyr piled upon martyr, as civil rights turned violent, and as the election of "peace candidate" Lyndon Johnson brought bombing to North Vietnam (begun in February 1965) and raised the U.S. troop commitment from 23,000 men at the end of 1964 to 165,000 men at the end of 1965 to 375,000 men at the end of 1966. It was becoming clear to everyone that America was in for a long and bitter struggle in the quest to "live out the true meaning of its creed" of social equality, and the outcome was very much in doubt. Barry McGuire's "Eve of Destruction" (1965) has been often criticized as Chicken Little "sky is falling" all-purpose apocalypse, "a vague philosophical point that can be taken any way by anybody" as Phil Ochs said, the end of responsible protest singing, pure commercialism. But it reflects the growing uneasiness of 1965, when things seemed to be coming slightly unglued. Many folksingers moved left and toward violent protest.

The drift of mid-decade events was obscured, however, by the British invasion of America, led by the Beatles and the Rolling Stones in 1964, and by Beatlemania, which prevailed in 1964–1965. Commercial, faddish, cute, flip, and in the early stages plenty innocuous (despite the hair), the Beatle phenomenon might have provided hope for anxious politicians—and cause for alarm among those who believed pop music could yield songs with art and message. Certainly, beside "Blowin' in the Wind," "I Want to Hold Your Hand" sounds like pure pop fluff. But in a matter of years lovable John Lennon would go over to the peaceniks, "All we are saying is give peace a chance."

Which is the way rock music went, and the way it was heading even in 1965, when the Beatles released *Rubber Soul*, Dylan released *Bringing It All Back Home*, and the Byrds brought the social statements of folk music to the popular medium of rock-n-roll to create the "folk rock" that would give protest a new dimension. Far from being a distraction, the Beatles and the Stones and Dylan and an explosion of their followers gave protest a much broader audience than it had ever had before, and a range of techniques infinitely more sophisticated and more suited to the times than Seeger had ever dreamt possible. In fact, had rock not become a vehicle for intelligent social statement, it's quite possible that protest would *never* have achieved the sophistication it needed to address increasingly complex causes and audiences. (Conversely, of course, it may have been exactly the increased sophistication of sixties people, both musical and social-political, that created the new music.) Either way, what the mid-sixties heard were protest songs like "Think for Yourself," "Nowhere Man," "Dr. Robert," and "Taxman" from the Beatles; "Like a Rolling Stone" and "Desolation Row" from Dylan; the Rolling Stones' 1965 blockbuster, "I Can't Get No Satisfaction" (*and* "Get Off My Cloud," "19th Nervous Breakdown," and "Paint It Black," all protests in the general sense of the word); and the Kinks' light "Well-Respected Man about Town" and Simon and Garfunkel's heavy "Sounds of Silence." And Otis Redding's "Respect," and Langston Hughes and Nina Simone's "Backlash Blues" ("Whatta ya think I got to lose? I'm gonna leave you with the Backlash Blues"). Even a new, nontopical breed of Phil Ochs song: "Pleasures of the Harbor," "Miranda," "Crucifixion."

These songs are qualitatively different from those that preceded them. They are generally angrier, as a comparison of "Backlash Blues" (1966) and, say, Sam Cooke's magnificent "A Change Is Gonna Come" (1964), or "Get Off My Cloud" (1965), or maybe the Drifters' "Up on the Roof" (1964) will make immediately clear. More important, however, the scope of causes had grown: taxes in the Beatles song, alienation and lack of communication in the Paul Simon song, the intrusions of an unwanted and obnoxious commercialism in the Stones' "Get Off My Cloud." But most important, the thought in these songs is considerably more sophisticated than the thought behind almost all folk protest lyrics except those written by Bob Dylan.

Dylan was ahead of the pack. More than the others, he had been able almost from the start to see beyond black and white moral distinctions to shades of gray and to "the them in us." And he had been sensitive to the self-righteousness of nonviolent protest. In this respect he was whole marches ahead of the others, often to his following's frustration and uncomprehending anger. Like his speech in accepting the Thomas Paine Award from the Emergency Civil Liberties Committee in 1963, when he found himself identifying with (horror of horrors) Lee Harvey Oswald.

> When I got up to make my speech, I couldn't say anything by that time but what was passing through my mind. They'd been talking about Kennedy being killed, and Bill Moore and Medgar Evers and the Buddhist monks in Vietnam being killed. I had to say something about Lee Oswald. I told them I'd read a lot of his feelings in the papers, and I knew he was up tight. Said I'd been up tight too, and I'd got a lot of his feelings. I saw a lot of myself in Oswald, I said, and I saw in him a lot of the times we're all living in. And, you know, they started booing. They looked at me like I was an animal. They actually thought I was saying it was a good thing Kennedy had been killed. That's how far out they are. I was talking about Oswald.

As for topical protest, Dylan told his friend Ochs, "The stuff you're writing is bullshit, because politics is bullshit. It's all unreal. The world is, well, it's just absurd." On the Bomb, Dylan observed, "What's wrong goes much deeper than the bomb. What's wrong is how few people are free." So the real issue for Bob Dylan had become how people are or are not free, which in turn became the subject for the new kind of protest songs he was writing in 1965. In "Subterranean Homesick Blues," Dylan explored in short, staccato lines, jangling rhymes, and machine gun rhythms the incredible unfreedom of America in the mid-sixties.

> Maggie comes fleet foot
> Face full of black soot
> Talkin' that the heat put
> Plants in the bed but
> The phone's tapped anyway
> Maggie says that many say
> They must bust in early May
> Orders from the D.A.
> Look out kid
> Don't matter what you did
> Walk on your tip toes
> Don't try "No Doz"
> Better stay away from those

That carry around a fire hose
Keep a clean nose
Watch the plain clothes
You don't need a weather man
To know which way the wind blows.

The scene is repainted more darkly in other Dylan lyrics of this period. "It's Alright, Ma (I'm Only Bleeding)," a marathon recitation of social ills, both greater and lesser (advertising, education, war and war toys, authority, irrelevant jobs, religion, hypocrisy), begins with the frank admission that there's no sense trying and ends with the fatalistic "it's life." "Highway 61 Revisited" is nearly unique in Dylan's poetry in that the highway—usually an escape and therefore uncontaminated—is poisoned by Louie the King and Mack the Finger and the roving gambler's hired promoter who's trying to stage the next world war.

"Everybody must get stoned," Dylan warned. There's no exit.

Other Dylan songs of the middle sixties are slightly more optimistic. "Maggie's Farm," for example, offers a world no saner than that of "Subterranean Homesick Blues" but suggests what all Americans always want, something that can be done.

I ain't gonna work on Maggie's farm no more.
No, I ain't gonna work on Maggie's farm no more.
Well, I try my best
To be just like I am,
But everybody wants you
To be just like them.
They say sing while you slave and I just get bored.
I ain't gonna work on Maggie's farm no more.

(Dylan himself worked for a very big Maggie's Farm, Columbia Records—and he, like the rest of us, could not escape all that easily. But the myth was heartening, to think that you just might tell them all to take this job and shove it and they would dissolve like the wicked witch of the west.)

The problems of America, as Dylan saw them, were interconnected and largely internal. The solutions were internal as well: everything might be solved once you were out on your own, no direction home, a rolling stone. Or, as the Beatles put it about the same time (December 1965), "Say the word and you'll be free."

This new music reflected a new maturity in the children of the sixties. They had been, this generation of renegade middle-class whites, to college; some of them, to graduate school. And they'd been doing some heavy thinking about social and moral problems and some reading and a lot of talking. Blacks in CORE and SNCC had become increasingly adamant about black leadership of civil rights activities not so much to achieve effective organization as to enhance black self-image. Self-image was becoming more important than immediate material gains. The real problems *were* internal.

And Selective Service, the way it drafted the poor and the black and sent them off to die, while waving the white sons of middle-class Americans safely by into college and 2-S deferments, and the way the 2-S hung over your head once you got into school—burn your draft card and you lose it; thumb your nose at the dean and get expelled from school and you lose it; and then it's straight to boot camp and straight to San Diego and straight to Nam and home in a wooden box. So they really *had* you, and it *was* all connected, just as you had always suspected.

> "The point is that the problems we're up against, and those include environmental crime, race crime, political, total, obnoxious corruption, and international crime, which is war—all of those problems, man, relate to a power structure that is running this country. . . . I'm trying to explain to people that it isn't the President, it isn't Congress, it isn't the governors. It seems like it, but as far as I can tell, it's an inter-locking whole socio-economic systems group."—David Crosby, *Rolling Stone*, 1970

And the way those in authority reacted to student protest, black protest, antiwar protest—wasn't it all the same, and wasn't it all part of a hopelessly corrupt American consciousness, an obsession with violence and repression? At antiwar teach-ins, increasingly common after spring 1965, you could rap into the early morning about causes and connections and the great web of entanglements. From graduate students and hardened radicals you could borrow a copy of Herbert Marcuse's *One-Dimensional Man* (1964) or James Baldwin's prophetic *Fire Next Time* (1963) or *Ramparts* magazine. At SDS meetings (the organization had grown by leaps and bounds following the free speech disturbances at Berkeley in the fall of 1964) you could catch up on neo-Marxism. Words and ideas and fragments of arguments filtered through media straights reached sixties people all across the country, and heads were churning. Nothing was decided, nothing was clear except that *something* was very definitely happening here, and the straights had no idea what it was.

As the sixties rocked to their climax in 1968, nothing became any clearer. Indeed, the onrush of events, the organization of the New Left, the emergence of an underground press, the growth of the National Mobilization Committee to End the War in Vietnam (organized in September 1966), the increased attention paid to dissent and protest by all media, the great awakening of counterculture, the flowering of rock music in which so much of the sixties was concentrated—all merely intensified the confusion: more causes, more songs, more ideas. In the late sixties protest became such a natural condition of so many people's lives (pushed from below by the war in Vietnam, pulled from above by media attention) that numbers no longer meant anything. Everyone was protesting everything in every way imaginable. Conservatives, hard hats, and know-nothings of the right were counterprotesting. And some sixties heads who were very far along the metaphysical march were hinting that maybe the angry no might be transcended into a yes, that this was not the way to put an end to war.

A new and more strident voice was now being raised in discussions and in music, the voice of violent revolution, of anarchy, of fighting in the streets. The move from pacifism to violence was justified, in some minds, by establishment response to nonviolent protest. The war in Vietnam was exploding, white response to civil rights initiatives was largely what Martin Luther King had warned against in 1963: "Those who hope that the Negro needed to blow off steam and will now be content will have a rude awakening if the nation returns to business as usual." The bombed church at Birmingham in 1963, the murder of Medgar Evers in 1963 and of fifteen more civil rights workers during the so-called freedom summer of 1964, the explosion of Selma in March 1965 and of Watts in August—these things Lyndon Johnson could use to prod Congress into guaranteeing voting rights and antipoverty programs, even highway beautification and Medicare programs besides, but the congressional victories were soon overshadowed by the war, the incessant war, the omnipresent war, and the bodies decaying in the closet. Anyone could tell that America was in trouble even before the climactic year of 1968, when King went down and Columbia went up and police clubbed/gassed/pounded demonstrators while Hubert Humphrey was receiving Richard Daley's blessing in Chicago.

> "We'd like to do a song about this guy who was a friend of ours. And just by way of mentionin' it, he was shot down in the street. And as a matter of strict fact he was shot down in the street by a very professional kind of outfit. Don't it make you sort of wonder? The Warren Report ain't the truth, that's plain to anybody. And it happened in your country. Don't you wonder why? Don't you wonder?"—David Crosby, introducing "He Was a Friend of Mine," Rolling Stone

Pacifism, many believed, was not working.

The major problem with nonviolent protest is that it hurts. You have to put up with getting arrested, teargassed, spat and shat upon, bitten by police dogs, beaten on the head, shot at, maybe even killed and dumped in an earthen dam near Philadelphia, Mississippi. People who studied protest during the sixties, most notably the National Advisory Commission on Civil Disorders (1968) and the *Walker Report* on Chicago (1968) and the *Skolnik Report* on protest (1969)—both reports made for the National Commission on the Causes and Prevention of Violence—concluded that "the weight of violence was overwhelmingly on the side of the police" (Walker), that "nearly all the violence that has occurred in mass demonstrations has resulted not from the demonstrators' conscious choice of tactics, but from the measures chosen by public authorities to disperse and punish them" (Skolnik). These were American investigations, of course, but nonviolent protest met with substantially similar reactions in Germany, Japan, France, and to a lesser extent England and Holland. Police brutality is not the American frontier spirit come home to haunt but a frightened reaction to nonviolent protest. Pacifists always get whacked.

Radical protesters therefore rejected nonviolence as naive, impractical, holy, ineffective, and slightly suicidal. Why should *our* heads ache? Why should fifteen good people be murdered during the freedom summer of 1964, Medgar Evers in 1963, King in 1968, and four Kent State students in 1970, and all the rest while Bull Connors becomes a national hero, Lester Maddox gets himself elected governor, and George Wallace runs for president of the United States? Besides, the advocates of violence argued, *your* broken bones and bombed homes will never cause *them* any discomfort, will never force *them* to change. Beat their heads, take a few shots at them, blow up their offices and cars, then you will see some action. Bring the Irish cause from working-class Belfast to chic London; bring the anger of the ghetto from Watts and Harlem to the suburbs; bring your demands for free speech directly to the dean's office, then you will get remediation (or at least you will get even). "Revolution is never based on begging somebody for an integrated cup of coffee," Malcolm X wrote in 1962. "Revolutions are never fought by turning the other cheek. . . . And revolutions are never waged singing 'We Shall Overcome.' Revolutions are based on bloodshed." Power comes out of the barrel of a gun, and in this great and good and blessed country of ours, it is possible for every man to wield power.

> "If somebody points a gun at me, I'll do my best to point one back."—Paul Kantner of the Jefferson Airplane

"We'll only use the tactics that the oppressor makes us use; if they could change peacefully, then good, but they can't and they won't," explained a radical bomb-maker to the *East Village Other* in 1968. And up they went: the Bank of America, the CIA, army recruiting stations, ROTC buildings, anything remotely connected with the establishment. (Which, for black Americans, meant everything. They torched whole neighborhoods—usually, ironically, their own: Birmingham in 1963, not three days after the triumph of nonviolence mentioned above; Watts in 1965; Newark and Detroit in 1967; a hundred towns and cities in the days after King's assassination in 1968.)

There was something awesome in this wholesale leveling. And something characteristically American as well. For all their religiosity, Americans seldom turn the other cheek. They speak loudly and carry big sticks. If a foreign government doesn't suit us, we send the CIA to get us one that does. We intervene wherever we see fit to defend our "interests." And we come with guns and tanks and planes. The violent revolution of sixties radicals was as American as the CIA.

> *popular archetype:* Mark Rudd and the Weathermen (as in Bob Dylan's line "You don't need a weather man to know which the way the wind blows")
>
> *moment:* October 1968 Weathermen bomb the CIA building in Ann Arbor, a U.S. Army recruiting station, the school board building of Michigan's Macomb County, another building in nearby Roseville, and the 10th and 13th precinct stations in Detroit—the 13th twice!
>
> *slogan:* "Up against the Wall, Motherfucker!"
>
> *song:* "Volunteers," by the Jefferson Airplane ("We're all outlaws in the eyes of America")

> (Violent protest, however, was never the threat it was made out to be by the FBI–CIA–U.S. Army Intelligence–local police authorities. Not the Black Muslims in 1959 or the Black Panthers in 1969 or the Weathermen or any of the Maoist splinter groups. Most protesters *were* on the side of life against death and lacked the heart for serious killing. Whether on the campuses of Jackson State and Berkeley; in the slums of Philadelphia, New York, and Detroit; in the swamps of Georgia or the parks of Chicago and Los Angeles—when the official estimates were in, the guys in uniform always outnumbered the students, Black Panthers, Weathermen, civil rights workers, hippies, and Yippies at least five to one. Malcolm X, the Kennedys, King, and dozens more were shot; Nixon, Hoover, Helms, Agnew, and Daley were not.)

Phil Ochs, on the cutting edge, was growing impatient. He had put in his time politically and musically and could see that not much was happening. Late in 1964 he wrote "I Ain't Marching Any More." Then he used the song to title his next album. A note of explanation on the jacket reads, "Borders between pacifism and treason, combining the best qualities of both. The fact that you won't be hearing this song over the radio is more than enough justification for the writing of it."

> "There was a definite flowering-out of positive feelings when John Kennedy became President. The Civil Rights movement was giving off positive vibrations. There was a great feeling of reform, that things could be changed, that an innovator could come in. . . . Things looked incredibly promising.
> Then came the Bay of Pigs, the beginnings of Vietnam and the assassination was the big thing. It ruined the dream. November 22, 1963, was a mortal wound the country has not yet been able to recover from."—Phil Ochs

By winter 1965 Phil was celebrating "Rhythms of Revolution" in a vindictive but purely imaginary triumph over the power elite. "You're supporting Chiang-Kai-Shek while I'm supporting Mao," he sang in the guise of a student to his tweedy professor and noted "other countries where the students . . . helped to overthrow the leaders of the land." His *In Concert* album arrived in 1966 with poems by Mao Tse-tung and the caption "Is This the Enemy?" Ochs was at the front of those moving left and toward violence. "Love me, love me, love me, I'm a liberal," he sneered. Students and militant blacks applauded. Parents, university administrators, and liberal politicians (including Lyndon Johnson) flushed and wondered what to do. No longer could they take comfort in the impotence of the demonstrators, in the small numbers or the quiescent pacifism. It became increasingly difficult to support even the lunatic fringe explanation with which the establishment so frequently dismisses anything it cannot or will not understand.

In "The War Is Over" (1968) Ochs hinted as broadly as he decently could that the time was ripe for something stronger than marching and carrying signs.

So, do your duty boys and join with pride;
Serve your country in her suicide;
Find a flag so you can wave good-bye.
But just before the end even treason might be worth a try—
This country is too young to die.

It was tough to be pacifist. Like the Little Rascals, on tour of the South with Dick Clark, split off from the rest of the tour in Fort Pierce, Florida, their equipment in a broken-down van somewhere along the road. And in the local diner, a scene right out of *Easy Rider*: "I'm trying to figure out whether you're a boy or a damn girl." "Where we come from, we chew on people like you." "Let me see your draft card."

So the Rascals split the diner for their trailer, only to be met by "50 or 60 motorcycles waiting for us. On each of the motorcycles there was at least one person. Some of them had as much as three. They were going to kill us, evidently. They definitely wouldn't just hurt us" (*Rolling Stone*, 1979). So the Rascals cleared out and wrote "People Got to Be Free," an innocuous enough song. But their hearts were elsewhere: "Eddie swore he was going back in there and clean the town out with a machine gun."

> (Behind every radical with a gun protesting against the injustices of America stand John Wayne and the long cowboy-Indian film tradition. "He shoots first, he shoots later," Phil Ochs sang. It's the American way.)

That's the way violent radicals got made, and by 1968 many thousands had been radicalized. "We'd rather die on our feet than keep living on our knees," sang James Brown in "Say It Loud—I'm Black and I'm Proud" (1968). The fires in the street were alluded to in Arthur Brown's "Fire" and Sly and the Family Stone's *There's a Riot Goin' On* and the Rolling Stones' "Street Fighting Man." "Summer's here and the time is right for fighting in the streets," Jagger announced in 1968, parodying Martha and the Vandellas' 1964 hit "Dancing in the Street" and tying rock and revolution together. The group United States of America officially acknowledged the inclusion of violent revolutionaries into the sixties pantheon with "Love Song for the Dead Ché." And John Sinclair brought his White Panthers to the nation via the rock house band the MC5.

Kick Out the Jams is not an album to rattle the memories of most sixties heads, but it rattled plenty of music systems in 1968 and 1969. And not just because of the "motherfucker" that came through loud and clear until it was changed in mid-run to "brothers and sisters." And not just because of the ultra high-energy rock that blasted from the speakers. The MC5—in the Sinclair days, at least—was a revolutionary group.

> I want to hear some revolution out there, brothers! I want to hear a little revolution. . . . The time has come for you to decide whether you are gonna be the problem or you are gonna be the solution.

> (The career of the MC5 was short and tragic. The group quarreled with a well-known record store chain, suggested in Detroit's underground newspaper that fans level the joints, and then sent the bill for their underground ad to Elektra Records. Which finished the MC5 at Elektra. When Atlantic picked them up, they split from Sinclair and his Panthers and settled docilely into what Mike Jahn termed "life at the high school" songs. That made

it with nobody, and the MC5 disappeared after only 3 LP records, only one of them at all significant.)

The most radical album of the sixties, however, was the Jefferson Airplane's *Volunteers* (1969), with the group chanting in obvious delight, "Look what's happening out in the streets, got a revolution, got to revolution." Complete with a chorus or two of "Up against the wall, motherfucker, tear down the wall." And intimations that we should all be together, volunteer outlaws in America, and suggestions from Gracie Slick that we either go away or go *all* the way. It was a very heavy album, very in tune with a segment of the late sixties, and an album not aired on AM radio.

Naturally *Volunteers* got the Airplane in plenty of trouble with RCA Records because among the many revolutions it brought home was the right to free speech. Curiously RCA made little attempt to censor content (not even when the Airplane-Starship eulogized Weatherman Diana Oughton, killed in the explosion of a homemade bomb, with two other Weathermen, in New York in 1970). Censorship meant no dirty words. Perhaps, as everyone suspected, the real revolution was in language and dress; everything else was mere window dressing.

Ultimately it was language that made an outlaw of Country Joe McDonald, whose "Superbird" and "Fixin' to Die Rag" ("An' it's one, two, three, what're we fightin' for?") should really have been the main issues.

Wooster, Mass.
November 21, 1969
I would like to explain to you exactly what it is that we are being charged with doing, because people have a tendency to be really tripped out about a specific thing that we do as a regular part of our act, and we have done it for almost two years now. At a certain point in this set, usually towards the end of the show, we do a song which is a protest against the war in Vietnam. It's a very popular song amongst the Underground. Almost everyone in the Underground knows the song, and before we do it we spell a word. We used to spell FISH—we used to say "Give me an 'F' "—the audience would say "F"; "Give me an 'I' "—the audience would say "I"; "Give me an 'S' "—the audience would say "S," and give me an "H"—the audience would say "H," and then someone would yell, "What does that spell?"—and they would say *"FISH,"* and then we would play the song, which is called "I Feel Like I'm Fixin' to Die Rag."

We got tired of spelling FISH, and at one point we started spelling out another four-letter word which begins with "F." And the audience seemed to enjoy it even more than saying "FISH." As a matter of fact, the thing caught on so much that at several performances we would spell "FISH" but the audience would respond with the contested four-letter word, which begins with "F."

The absurdity of the paranoia of the Establishment has been carried so far that right after our last Wooster, Massachusetts, date (for which we have been charged with being obscene), we were met in Boston by one police captain, three lieutenants, 75 uniformed patrolmen with clubs, guns and mace, police squad cars, 25 plain clothes detectives and a paddy wagon, and we were informed that we couldn't do that thing which we had done in Wooster, but no one would articulate what it was we had done because I imagine they were just waiting for us to do it again.

It is really an infringement upon the Constitutional rights of the audience to have the police decide what we can and cannot hear, particularly when this is such a very small issue; it is generally the tendency of the Establishment to treat young people as if they were second-class citizens, as if they were not capable of making rational decisions which would lead to moral conduct. The kids are finding out that the real obscenities and the real immoral acts are committed by the Establishment—the adult community which choses [sic] to manifest its hangups in poisoning the rivers and the oceans, and the food we eat, by smoking themselves into alcoholic stupors and by forcing their own children to go off into a foreign country and murder for them.

You will understand how it was that Country Joe McDonald and the Fish dedicated a record album to Bobby Hutton, the eighteen-year-old Black Panther murdered by Oakland police in 1968. And how the band got itself into trouble that same year at the seige of Chicago and thereby became part of the heroic and absurd trial of the Chicago Eight. And how it brought the revolution in free speech home to America. And how life went for millions of sixties heads at the close of the decade.

Pacifist and violent protesters, for all their differences, shared several fundamental characteristics. The first was high seriousness. The second was commitment to if not *the* system then *a* system. Only the pure anarchists freed themselves from organization, and many leftists who accepted violence as a legitimate and necessary escalation of the fight to free America developed codes of behavior far more rigid than those of the establishment against which they warred: the Black Muslims, Black and White Panthers, Weathermen. Finally—and most important—violent and nonviolent protesters shared an implicit acceptance of the game. Pacifists played expecting to lose; their more violent comrades played to win. Both played and thereby reinforced the sanctity of the game.

Not all sixties people, however, saw the game as either desirable or necessary. To many it appeared a lose-lose proposition. If you played and lost, your body ached and you wasted your time, energy, youth, and maybe your life. If you played and won, you were also screwed: the prizes (money, power, and ego gratification) were hopelessly corrupt to begin with, and the things you had to do to win them were dehumanizing; so you still wasted your time, energy, youth, and maybe your life. Furthermore, it was impossible, really, to play the game without accepting tacitly the value of the prizes. At best you might replace one system with another, but the prizes remained, and power corrupts, over and thus out.

"Meet the new boss, same as the old boss," as the Who put it, looking over their shoulders in 1971.

Or, as the Buffalo Springfield said in 1967, "Perhaps you have just been bought."

So what you do is step *outside* the game and freak the whole thing out. Quit buying and start stealing. Fold, spindle, and mutilate. Stop working and start playing. Do it in the road. Kiss a cop. Nominate a pig for president of the United States and then serve him for dinner. Haul ass down the road at 90 MPH with your clothes off and the windows open. *Steal This Book.*

> "Fun was what adolescent revolt had to be about —inebriated affluence versus the hangover of the work ethic."—Robert Christgau on Chuck Berry and the late fifties

"There's only one thing that's gonna do any good at all . . . and that's everybody's just got to look at it, look at the war, and turn your backs and say 'Fuck it.'"—Ken Kesey on Vietnam and protest

> "A militant Lower East Side group, the Black Mask, once staged a mill-in at Macy's during the Christmas rush. Demonstrators flooded the store disguised as shoppers, floor-walkers, and counter assistants. Stock was either spoiled, stolen, swapped around or given away. Half-starved dogs and cats were let loose in the food department. A berserk buzzard flew around the crockery section, smashing china and terrorizing sales girls."—Richard Neville, *Playpower*

Not playing the game was, in sixties America, the greatest sin of all. Although the grown-ups were accustomed to a certain amount of horseplay from their children (especially from their sons, away at college and pledged to a fraternity and all), there existed a line not to be overstepped, especially in serious matters like the U.S. Army, courts of law, trade and commerce, and free elections. Especially not by unwashed, long-haired hippies with an absurdist vision. Holy goofs who flaunted their fuck it style had a tough time; this country does not tolerate disrespect. Besides, the goof cut straight to the heart of the matter: was the whole business worth a damn or was it all just too surrealistic, too corrupt, too impossibly gone to care about? Here was a matter too overwhelming for most Americans to ponder.

So the goof seemed even more threatening than the apostle of violent protest. The Mafia—which played an essentially American game by essentially American rules and was as American as the Colt .45—could flourish, but hippies and yippies got whacked. And there was no halo around their mangy heads to make people feel sorry.

popular archetype: Abbie Hoffman, throwing money on the floor of the New York Stock Exchange in 1966

moment: the attempt during the 1967 march on Washington to raise the Pentagon three hundred feet in the air and exorcise its demons (to the music of the Fugs).

slogan: "Yippie!"

song: Mrs. Miller's version of "Chim Chim Cheree." (Talk about freaking out the whole music industry! She couldn't carry a tune in a bucket, no personality, no looks, no nothing. A complete musical goof.)

> (This protest, in a curiously mutated form, has endured whereas massive, nonviolent protest demonstrations and outright guerrilla warfare against the system have largely disappeared. Nobody is blowing up the Bank of America. Literally millions of Americans have, however, decided that no, the whole business isn't worth a damn. And while we've lost our sense of joy, absurdity, and ingenuity, we are—many of us—busy folding, spindling, mutilating, ripping off, ignoring, and generally fouling up the system.)

As the sixties unraveled, holy goof protest gained momentum, fueled by the rediscovery of Joseph Heller's *Catch-22*, Dylan's experiments in absurdist vision, and constantly increasing evidence that this world was totally fucked up, inside *and* out, and what else could you do with it except goof the whole thing? For some, goof was the endpoint of escalation.

Jerry Rubin began his journey into the absurd by organizing the 1965 Berkeley Vietnam Day teach-in. He moved on to more direct protest, less passive and less pacifist, including attempts to stop trains bringing troops to embarkation points for Vietnam, Laos, Cambodia, and the fabled East. It was all too bizarre and yet too earnest for Rubin, so with Abbie Hoffman and Paul Krassner he "got very stoned so we could look at the problem *logically*" and came up with the Youth International Party, the Yippies. And holy goof protest was by 1967 institutionalized.

> (Light years earlier, Hoffman, it will be recalled, had participated in quiet, nonviolent protest at the sit-in against the execution of Caryl Chessman.)

The Chicago Festival of Life, conceived as a protest against the war and the war's candidate, and the conspiracy trial of 1969–1970 were historically the high point of holy goof protest. Media attention was crucial to effective goof; Tuli Kupferberg and the Fugs, who had goofed for something like nine hundred performances in a row in some of the coffeehouses along the Village's MacDougal Street with "Kill for Peace" and "Group Grope" and "Coca-Cola Douche" (all pre-1968), never got much media attention and could not therefore be effective media marauding holy goofs.

Lunacy with a cause seeped into sixties music. On the more serious side were songs like Dylan's "Tombstone Blues" and the Procol Harum's "Whiter Shade of Pale" (August 1967), with its mishmash of musical and verbal allusions to Chaucer, Bach, vestal virgins, you name it. The crazy scenes, humor, rhythms, and rhymes could not entirely conceal a serious declaration of insanity lurking just below the surface. Nor could the light rhymes and tripping meter of the Buffalo Springfield's "Mr. Soul" (December 1967) hide the fact that Neil Young was registering a protest and making an important statement about insane times.

> In a while will the smile on my face
> Turn to plaster?
> Stick around while the clown who is sick
> Does the trick of disaster.
> For the race of my head and my face
> Is moving much faster.
> Is it strange I should change? I don't know,
> Why don't you ask her?
> Is it strange I should change? I don't know,
> Why don't you ask her?
> Is it strange I should change? I don't know,
> Why don't you ask her?

Somewhere between joke and earnestness came the Airplane's "Doesn't Mean Shit to a Tree" ("It doesn't," Paul Kantner once remarked. "Don't get serious about it at all. 'Cause it's not serious. . . . We didn't even know what we were doing when we started doing it."). Country Joe McDonald goofed protest with his campaign to clean up America by sending out the Fantastic Four and Doctor Strange to round up Lyndon Johnson in "Superbird."

> So come out Lyndon with your hands held high
> Drop your guns baby, and reach for the sky
> We got you surrounded and you ain't got a chance
> Gonna send you back to Texas—make you work on your ranch

Madness, pure fun, and high-spirited lunacy. And the lovable Beatles had a bit of goof in their random.

> "There's a lot of random in our songs . . . writing, thinking, letting others think of bits—then bang, you have the jigsaw puzzle."—Paul McCartney

On the lowest level were trashy songs that made no pretense of being art *or* novelty *or* pop shlock *or* anything except trash: Mrs. Miller in 1967, Tiny Tim in 1968.

Amid the swirl of nonviolent protest, violent protest, and holy goofing (and the counterrevolution, embodied in songs like "The Ballad of the Green Berets" and "Okie from Muskogee") the suspicion developed that perhaps protest itself was not where it was at. Amid the shouts and cries came warnings and whispered reservations. People dropped out, quietly or flamboyantly. Dylan, of course, quit the marches in 1964 with "My Back Pages" ("I was so much older then," he explained, "I'm younger than that now"), and he quit the protest movement in its broadest sense with *John Wesley Harding* in 1968. He was a man ahead of his time, but by the close of the sixties he had company. In 1967 Stephen Stills cautioned against protest-fed paranoia in "For What It's Worth." That same year Phil Ochs lamented the way protest bred dissension bred anger bred lack of love and lack of communication: "Walk away both knowing they are right. Still nobody's buying flowers from the flower lady." A year later he declined participation in black-white protest games, arriving somewhat belatedly at Dylan's position in the Tom Paine Award speech: "One is guilty and the other gets to point the blame. Pardon me if I refrain." The Beatles opted out late in 1968 with "Revolution": "But when you talk about destruction, don't you know that you can count me out."

"Think," Aretha Franklin warned in 1968: in trying to make other people lose their minds, be careful you don't lose yours. You were risking more than your mind, Country Joe pointed out in "Playing with Fire."

> Dynamite Charlie was a loser,
> Buildin' bombs in his bath;
> Filled up his head with too many words,
> You know where that's at.
> One day when he was workin'
> He made a bad mistake.
> He was playin' with fire,
> But it was too late.

Even if you didn't lose your mind or blow yourself up, you might freak out on the paranoia or the heat and have to split.

> I hopped on a plane, Oakland–New York, New York to Marseilles,
> I hopped on a plane, Oakland–New York–Marseilles;
> Pigs on my trail, I gotta make my get-away.
> When the man holler, you sure got to jump, sure got to jump bail;
> When the man holler, you sure got to jump bail;
> First you stand trial and then they put you in jail.

> (In "Air Algiers," Country Joe might just have been talking about promising novelist-turned-

counterculture-superhero—and holy goof protest-er—Ken Kesey, who, after a couple of pot busts and in the teeth of a stiff jail term, hopped in a car for south of the California border in January 1966. But the song fit so many in the closing years of the sixties.)

In 1969, Phil Ochs opted out, publicly at least, with *Rehearsals for Retirement*. There was his tombstone on the jacket with his own epitaph.

Phil Ochs
(American)
Born: El Paso, Texas, 1940
Died: Chicago, Illinois, 1968

The title cut is a bitter farewell to the movement and to the country.

The days grow shorter
For smaller prizes;
I feel a stranger
To all surprises.
You can have them,
I don't want them.
I wear a different kind of garment
In my rehearsals for retirement.

The lights are cold again,
They dance below me.
I turn to old friends,
They do not know me.
All but the beggar
He remembers.
I put a penny down for payment
In my rehearsals for retirement.

Might have known the end would end in laughter;
Still I tell my daughter that it doesn't matter.

The stage is tainted
With empty voices;
The ladies painted,
They have no choices.
I take my colors from the stable;
They lie in tatters by the tournament
In my rehearsals for retirement.

Where are the armies
Who killed a country
And turned a strong man
Into a baby?
Now come the rebels,

They are welcomed.
I wait in anger and amusement
In my rehearsals for retirement.

Might have known the end would end in laughter;
Still I tell my daughter that it doesn't matter.

Farewell my own true love,
Farewell my fancy.
Ah, you still own me, love,
Though you failed me.
But one last gesture, for your pleasure
I'll paint your memory on the monument
In my rehearsals for retirement.

One option open to Ochs that he declined to take although he had dabbled in the area throughout the later sixties was the art lyric. From its lowly birth in reduced circumstances to disreputable parents on both sides, rock-n-roll had come a long way in a very short time and aspired, in the middle to later sixties, to fine art. Whether rock ever managed to become fine art or not, it did in fact become a legitimate form of pop art, and like art it took to making big statements, many of which constituted a form of protest against the human condition, against immorality and insanity, against insensitivity and lack of communication. As a form of protest, the art lyric was very much alive in popular music of the sixties.

The American artist's relationship with his audience historically has been neither clear nor happy. On the one hand Americans are notoriously disrespectful of art since it lacks obvious utilitarian value and defies easy packaging and marketing. On the other they are *too* respectful of Culture with a capital C, of Shakespeare and Russian ballet and French impressionists. Most Americans see art as a moral tonic, a decoration, or a business investment. A tiny minority, mostly artists, turn it into a secular religion, complete with vows of poverty, if not also of chastity and obedience.

Art, of course, is none of the above. What the artist does is speak to the heart of the human condition as she understands it, realizing that institutions *do* derive ultimately from moral and philosophical presuppositions (just as the nonviolent protesters always suspected) and that once hearts and minds have been straightened out, systems are bound to follow. Thus, artists place themselves in, but at some remove from, society. They see the world around them through the glasses of metaphysics.

> "A people's artist sings about the life and deeds and joys and sorrows of the people. If that is politics, so much the better."—Mike Gold, *Daily Worker*

Here artists face two problems. If they speak directly to social or political issues, their expertise will be questioned. "What the hell does Norman

Mailer know about Vietnam? He's a writer." ("What does Bob Dylan know about civil rights? He's a folk singer.") Americans are not accustomed to the Russian notion, embodied in a writer like Solzhenitsyn, that artists are responsible for the moral health of their society, for its politics and economics and social structure. If Robert Lowell has the impudence to refuse an invitation to President Johnson's garden party and lectures him on the Vietnam war in the process, the American public is likely to send Lowell back to writing poems. Let Paul Newman forget Eugene McCarthy and get back to acting. Let Bob Dylan write songs and let Joan Baez sing them and let both of them quit telling America how to run its business, and if she won't pay her taxes, then throw her in jail.

On the other hand, if artists do not speak directly to the issues, if they insulate themselves from social and political realities, they run the risk of being too esoteric and thus misunderstood, in which case they are both ineffective and elitist. As protest became increasingly subtle and increasingly artistic during the sixties, it did lose contact with much of its audience: artiness was vitiating the movement in the later sixties.

This dilemma, which confronts every artist in America, was made somewhat less thorny by the generally politicized atmosphere of the sixties. Audiences were unusually receptive to moral and ethical statements of all varieties, and the times literally demanded such statements from artists. The sixties nudged both audiences and artists toward a more natural state of affairs: audiences became responsive, artists became responsible.

> (One of the more significant aspects of Norman Mailer's *Armies of the Night* is the author's frank admission that he was reluctant to participate in the demonstration in Washington, the recounting of which experience nevertheless won him a Pulitzer Prize. His reluctance stemmed from a commitment to overly refined art. "When was everyone going to cut out the nonsense and get to work, do their own real work?" he challenged at the outset of *Armies of the Night*. "One's own literary work was the only answer to the war in Vietnam." Three hundred pages later Mailer speaks a new aesthetic and has a book far more important than the work he left behind when he went to Washington.)

And so the sixties, like other periods of social and political unrest, were also a time of great artistic flowering. In print, in theater, in film, art flourished, but most of all in music, the chosen medium of the decade. The Beatles, the Stones, the Who, the Doors, Bob Dylan, Paul Simon and a dozen other artists (both popular and fine) turned folk music, rock, rhythm and blues, even country music into a form of protest more refined than the topical ballads of the protest singers, infinitely more to the moral and social point than the cotton candy of Tin Pan Alley or *American Bandstand.* This protest has weathered the intervening years much better than the songs that tied themselves more closely to civil rights or the war. Art always does. In fact, some of it speaks as much to the seventies as it did to the sixties, both the fine art and the pop art.

The most important work in the latter category is unquestionably the Beatles' *Sgt. Pepper's Lonely Hearts Club Band,* released in June 1967 (and resurrected eleven years later as a purely shlock piece of nostalgia). This album was in many respects the most remarkable of the decade: in its production, instrumentation, lyrics, and conceptualization it was a musical revolution. It virtually created the concept album. It introduced multitrack recording technique. It turned rock into art, completing a process begun with Bob Dylan's *Bringing It All Back Home* and the Beatles' own *Rubber Soul* (both 1965). It was a terrific head album and did much to promote the use of dope by giving heads something rich and complex to listen to while stoned. It contained one great song after another, so that whether you picked up on the words or not (and many folks didn't although the lyrics were printed on the back of the album jacket—a pretty good indication that the Beatles were trying to tell us something), the album tended to get inside you.

And it made a remarkably coherent statement on modern society and on the pervasive emptiness of all our lives and on the assorted methods we use to cope with that emptiness.

On the album, the Beatles pose as Sgt. Pepper's Band, his *lonely* hearts club band, performing a concert for us. The loneliness is right out front, from the very introduction of the band, which follows the dubbed in warm-up sounds at the beginning of the record. "We'd love to take you home," the band hints, but nobody takes them up on their offer and the concert proceeds with the introduction of lead singer Billy Shears (Ringo Starr, the puppy dog, lonely one). He's uptight, insecure, afraid the audience will walk out on him or laugh in his face. (The laughter is there, all right, although it does not appear until side two, just after the band's most direct appeal to love and to be loved, "Within You and without You").

The songs are filled with lonely characters. There is the girl (*and* her parents) of "She's Leaving Home." Both sides of the generation gap live in exile, and both are or will become painfully aware of their isolation. The parents now know that money will not buy fun or love; she must soon realize that fun and freedom are the most cruel illusions of all. There is the recluse of "Fixing a Hole," who shuts the world out and himself in. There is the anxious mail-order suitor of "When I'm Sixty-four," who looks forward to a cottage on the Isle of Wight and scrimping and saving. There's the vacuous hustler of "Lovely Rita," who turns his slick seduction into a grotesque parody of a scene from the fifties: "I nearly made it/sitting on the sofa with a sister or two." Emptiest of all is the stud who cruises town in "Good Morning," full of boredom and clichés, casing the old school, hustling a skirt, nothing to say because there is nothing in his head.

In "Within You and without You," the band—and the Beatles—speak directly to their audience—and to us—and explain the whole album in unmistakable, clear, frightening prose: "We were talking—about the space between us all" and about the illusions and the love that's gone cold. The audience in the concert recorded on the album is unable to deal with this kind of direct statement. They laugh. And the band progresses to more holes and more illusions and more defeated attempts to discover love and sublimate loneliness, until it's back for the big finish with a reprise of the "Sgt. Pepper's Lonely Hearts Club Band" theme song. There is no mistaking the point now: Sgt. Pepper's lonely.

We're all lonely and depressed. And then, outside the context of the band's performance, the Beatles turn the mirror on us and on modern civilization in "A Day in the Life."

> I read the news today oh boy
> About a lucky man who made the grade
> And though the news was rather sad
> Well I just had to laugh
> I saw the photograph
> He blew his mind out in a car
> He didn't notice that the lights had changed
> A crowd of people stood and stared
> They'd seen his face before
> Nobody was really sure
> If he was from the House of Lords
> I saw a film today oh boy
> The English army had just won the war
> The crowd of people turned away
> But I just had to look
> Having read the book
> I'd love to turn you on
> Woke up fell out of bed
> Dragged a comb across my head
> Found my way down stairs and drank a cup
> And looking up I noticed I was late
> Found my coat and grabbed my hat
> Made a bus in seconds flat
> Found my way upstairs and had a smoke
> And somebody spoke and I went into a dream
> I read the news today oh boy
> Four thousand holes in Blackburn Lancashire
> And though the holes were rather small

They had to count them all
Now they know how many holes it takes to fill the Albert Hall
I'd love to turn you on

A lot of sixties heads grooved on gossip in this song (and on this album—the games you could play with the cover!): who was the man from the House of Lords? Did smoke mean dope? What were the holes in Blackburn supposed to represent? But those who understood about the space between us all, and the illusion, and the lost love knew that the holes were sitting right there in Albert Hall in front of the band. It was the holes that laughed at the end of "Within You and without You." It was the holes that were listening to the album.

And it still is. Having transcended self-righteousness, we recognize ourselves as Nowhere Man and fear that we may one day become Eleanor Rigby or Father McKenzie.

"and we are all together. . . . I am the walrus."

It's hard to respond to the kind of criticisms leveled by the Beatles in *Sgt. Pepper*. Clearly, liberal reform, escalated protest, and tinkering one way or another with the system were out. Attractive options were all escapist: withdraw into the self or loop through time-space to some future world, past world, or remote corner of the present world. At the time of *Sgt. Pepper* the Beatles were busy largely with exploring remote corners of the physical, spiritual, and musical worlds of the twentieth century in *Magical Mystery Tour*, their white album, and *Abbey Road*. Others in England and America would exercise different options—if they found any exit at all.

The Kinks, an important British group that (unfortunately, in light of many of the groups that did) never achieved widespread popularity in the United States, found their resolution in the past. Ray Davies and his group first made the pop charts with a series of heavy British r&b singles, then turned to light satire in the tradition of the Rolling Stones: "Well-Respected Man about Town," "Dedicated Follower of Fashion," and "Dandy." But Davies's vision gradually expanded—like that of the Beatles, unlike that of the Stones, who never did manage a comprehensive statement unless it is their collected works. In 1969 the group offered the *Village Green Preservation Society* and *Arthur, or the Decline and Fall of the British Empire*. *Village Green* is interesting in its typically British feeling for warm anachronism and its attempt to preserve in the midst of anarchy Donald Duck, vaudeville, variety shows, draft beer, Old Mother Riley, Moriarty, Tudor houses, "the George Cross and all those who were awarded them."

(The American version of *Preservation Society* is the Band's album *The Band*, fondly looking backward in "The Night They Drove Old Dixie Down" and "Up on Cripple Creek.")

Arthur represents the Kinks' major critique of modern society. Like the Beatles' *Magical Mystery Tour, Arthur* was the soundtrack for a television film; like the Beatles' *Sgt. Pepper,* it is a complex statement, as applicable to the United States as to the United Kingdom. *Arthur* tells the story of one Arthur Morgan, who lives in a suburban London home indistinguishable from any other on the block. He calls it Shangri-la. The album opens with an unabashedly sentimental lament for Victorian England and the empire, the time when everyone worked hard and knew his place and there was order and dignity of a sort. This is followed by a real authority piece called "Yes Sir, No Sir," which suggests on the one hand the price Victorian Englishmen paid and on the other the reward they reaped. This nineteenth-century stability Arthur still values, although he has spent, as his grandson points out, his entire life "on his knees, laying carpets." Arthur's brother was killed in the battle of the Somme and his son was killed in Korea. Still, he has not learned any lessons. His pleasures are few and pathetic: driving in the country, eating gooseberry tarts, and drinking beer (the Beatles' cottage on the Isle of Wight). Arthur is not so much angry as puzzled. His world is crumbling, has crumbled. This he understands. But he has not figured out why. Neither has his surviving son, who is leaving England for Australia, the land of opportunity. But the grandson knows the score and explains it in "Brainwashed": the aristocrats and bureaucrats have combined to grind Arthur down. They kick and push him around until he can't take any more.

> "You men should remember how you used to fight."—The Who

Standard Marxist analysis.

Arthur is filled with obvious contempt for the creeping socialism of bureaucracies (what Charles A. Reich called "consciousness two" in *The Greening of America*): trade unions, social security, tax-savings benefits. And *Arthur* reflects a similar contempt for look-alike houses made of ticky-tacky and look-alike people made of ticky-tacky, for a land of no opportunity and a conditioned citizenry. It also shows a genuine nostalgia for the old days of handcrafted values, of order and stability, for a social order that seems in retrospect more open than it really was. The Kinks' anger is externally directed: it's not Arthur who's daft, it's the world that's passed him by. Maybe the world is wrong, maybe Arthur is wrong, nobody can say. But surely something is very, very screwy.

Unlike the Kinks, England's Who were, in the sixties at least, mod, mod ultra mod, without a shred of fondness for the old. New clothes, new music, new instruments (had to—they were busted after every performance), all gilt and flash and consumption. Youth. Kineticism. Pinball. Flashing lights. Mmmmy Generation. The anti-heroes of tomorrow here today.

"A group with built-in aggression," they called themselves, mean motor-scooters and very bad gogetters. "Pretentious," some people called them in 1968. "Living social criticisms of modern British society." "Artists." "A fraud." Whatever, the debate virtually disappeared after *Tommy*. After all, you can't quarrel with success, and the Who had played the Met. Besides, *Tommy* is good music, fair theater, and a sound critique of both English society in the sixties and the human condition in the twentieth century.

Most of all *Tommy* is a plea for seeing, feeling, loving, understanding, a plea from one of society's rejects-become-idols. It is the story of one who does unto others as has been done unto him and then receives from his fans-turned-disciples exactly what he has passed on to them: disdain, abuse, hate. He ends as he began: despised and rejected. Underneath its mod flash-iness *Tommy* teaches a hard lesson: Tommy is warped by the same forces that warp everyone in the twentieth century—lack of love, absence of com-munication.

As a very young child Tommy sees his father kill his mother's lover. Tommy is told he didn't see or hear the murder, and Tommy believes his parents and does not see, feel, hear, or speak. (Jackson Browne returned to the same theme of self-imposed blindness as a modern defense mechanism in "Dr. My Eyes.") Then Tommy is abused by queer Uncle Ernie, Cousin Kevin the bully, and the freaked out Acid Queen. So that when Tommy learns to play pinball and thereby makes himself into a semireligious sensa-tion, Tommy has learned a lot of abuse and a lot of hatred. And, having lost temproarily his physical blindness and deafness, he is still *morally* blind, deaf, and dumb.

The situation comes to a head in the song "Sally Simpson," in which the Who cast Tommy as a rock star, Sally as an average fan, and the human relationship in star-fan terms. Sally, drawn by Tommy's words and person-ality (he is "preaching" on the text "Come unto me"), rushes onstage, only to be pitched by guards back into the audience, receiving a gash that re-quires her to be hospitalized. Tommy is entirely unaware of what has hap-pened. He remembers fondly the day when the fans went wild. Later, when Tommy opens his summer holiday camp, he retains Uncle Ernie to help him train recruits. They will learn as he learned: by suffering. And they turn out as he turned out and forsake him and rape him and there is Tommy, love-less and sightless again.

Here is a statement nearly as bleak as that in *Sgt. Pepper*, a glimpse into the darkness of the soul, the hypocrisy, the sexual repression, the violence, and the terrible isolation that are ours in the twentieth century. Here is a protest against the lonely crowd, against the lack of community (doubly de-bilitating, as the Who knew only too well, for rock stars), against the empti-ness of modern society. The noise and lights and flash of mod society, like the irrepressibly high spirits of the Beatles' music in *Sgt. Pepper*, serve only to make the protest more morose.

(The Who did not leave us comfortless, however.
They went from *Tommy* to *Quadrophenia*, a 1973
retrospective on the sixties and on mod, with its final affirmation "Love, Reign o'er Me." Just the
way the Beatles moved from *Pepper's* to "Hey
Jude," who made it better. Just the way Dylan
moved from "you'd know what a drag it is to see
you" to "love is all there is.")

It didn't always take an entire album to create a work of art that registered in some small way a protest against the human situation. The Beatles
had warmed up for *Sgt. Pepper* with singles like "Eleanor Rigby," and they
returned to the subject in songs like George Harrison's remarkable lament
for modern mankind, "While My Guitar Gently Weeps." Either is in minia-
ture nearly everything that the album is. The Who, for their part, had "Pictures of Lily" and "My Generation" to their credit when they produced
Tommy. The first is a masturbation song and thus more or less directly a
statement on sexual repression; the second, the anthem of mod England, is a
vague but defiant protest comparable to "Get Off My Cloud" or Chuck Berry's "Almost Grown."

Other singer-composers offered equally impressive miniatures. Like
Leonard Cohen's "Story of Isaac," in which the poet-folksinger turned to a
biblical theme for an allegory of the sixties. Cohen set a story of suffering
victim and inscrutable divine purpose against the less holy victims of the
late sixties and their less holy butchers.

You who build these altars now
To sacrifice these children
You must not do it any more.
A scheme is not a vision
And you never have been tempted
By a demon or a god.
You who stand above them now
Your hatchets blunt and bloody,
You were not there before.
When I lay upon a mountain
And my father's hand was trembling
With the beauty of the word.

"A scheme is not a vision," Cohen asserted, speaking through the mouth of
Isaac. Terrific, practically a slogan. Bumper sticker material at least—I
wonder that it was never paraded around the White House along with "Hell
no, we won't go" and "Fuck the war" and "Peace now." Except that it so
transcended the specific context of 1967 and the LBJ mentality: as a subsequent stanza makes clear, Cohen regarded the modern victim as equally
suspect. Do we not all have our schemes? We are each victim *and* criminal,
and we will all kill if we can or must. Beware the sin of holy pride. "The

peacock spreads his fan." The new revolutionaries were caught in mid-punch and dropped their arms because they no longer knew where to swing.

> "Of course it's a revolution," Cohen said in 1968, surveying the carnage. "But I want to see the *real* revolution. I don't want it siphoned off by the mobilization people. . . . Revolutionaries, in their heart of hearts, are excited by the tyranny they wield. I'm afraid that when the Pentagon is finally stormed and taken, it will be by guys wearing uniforms very much like the ones worn by the guys defending it."

Another jewel of art protest was Paul Simon's "America." It came in a collection of statements and testimony, *Bookends* (1968), one of the important art albums of the sixties, which included "Punky's Dilemma" "Mrs. Robinson," "A Hazy Shade of Winter," and "Save the Life of My Child." Each is a very fine song, each a clear statement on the human condition, end of the sixties. Each shows a compassion toward and an awareness of others that was then relatively new to Simon's writing. He had told the *New Yorker* in September 1967:

> I write about the things I know and observe. I can look into people and see scars in them. These are the people I grew up with. For the most part, older people. These people are sensitive, and there's a desperate quality to them—everything is beating them down, and they become more aware of it as they become older. I get a sense they're thirty-three, with an awareness that "Here I am thirty-three!" and they probably spend a lot of afternoons wondering how they got there so fast. They're educated, but they're losing, very gradually. Not realizing, except for just an occasional glimpse. They're successful, but not happy, and I feel that pain. They've got me hooked because they are people in pain. I'm drawn to these people, and driven to write about them. In this country, it's painful for people to grow old. When sexual attractiveness is focused on a seventeen-year-old girl, you must feel it slipping away if you're a thirty-three-year-old woman. So you say, "I'm going to stop smoking. I'm going to get a suntan. I'm going on a diet. I'm going to play tennis." What's intriguing is that they are just not *quite* in control of their destiny. Nobody is paying any attention to these people, because they're not crying very loud.

Out of this awareness came the protest of *Bookends*. And out of *Bookends* came "America."

It is a young song—Paul and Kathy rolling by Greyhound bus from Saginaw, Michigan, down the lower peninsula, across the flatlands of Indiana and Ohio, through the Appalachians around Pittsburgh, and up the New

Jersey Turnpike, inexorably drawn to the heart of modern American neurosis, New York City. But their age does not insulate them from the sense of isolation felt by everyone else on *Bookends*, and the song ends up being a delicate protest against isolation and lack of communication. After a long epic of pies and cigarettes and the headlights of cars all come to look for America, there is only the emptiness and the spaces between the lights, between the cities, between Paul and Kathy and a thousand, a million individuals, locked each behind her own set of headlights, all out looking on their own.

"I'm empty and aching and I don't know why."

> ("America" is important also in the way it turned Greyhound and Mrs. Wagner's pies and even the Jersey Turnpike into art objects set in lines of nearly perfect tetrameter. "America" *is* an art song.)

The times were full of such gems. In a Rolling Stones album, for example, in a song like "Ruby Tuesday" in a phrase like "cash your dreams before they slip away." Or in the Mamas and Papas' "California Dreamin'," in which what might be is contrasted to what is, with religion (in the person of the preacher) interposed between, preventing one from becoming the other. Or in the Who's "Substitute," a song that really hit the nail on the head, a lyric of accepting what you can get in place of what you want, of plastic substituted for silver, Coke for gin, phony love for real love, phony girls for real. Or in the Doors' "Twentieth Century Fox," with its accusations of plastic girls, plastic lives, plastic worlds. And—on FM radio only, because AM would not play him—Phil Ochs's art lyrics, wherein the crucifixion became an allegory of the Kennedy assassination and "Miranda" became a symbol for the whole new sociopolitical reality.

Bob Dylan started out, like all of us I think, with folk music and nonviolent protest. He matured and he raged, nearly insane. He filled himself up with hate, for some years with a white passion: the masters of war, his friends, his self. And in the end he loved. He wrote songs of protest and songs of love, public songs and personal songs, topical songs and art lyrics. And, earlier than anyone else in the movement, he transcended his rage and his protest entered into a new dimension. Most of us who lived through the sixties have of necessity made the same journey. Dylan's is the story of the generation.

John Wesley Harding is an album second in importance only to *Sgt. Pepper* in terms of long-range influence on sixties style, thought, and behavior. The album is a concept album and a pilgrimage. The pilgrimage takes us from protest to transcendence, from nightmare absurdity to sanity, from rock to country, from despair to hope, from guilt to salvation. It is the pilgrimage of one man's soul and of America's soul, a twentieth-century allegory complete with anagogical, tropological, typological, and moral levels of interpretation.

Dylan begins with "John Wesley Harding," a song set in the heart of American mythology: the good outlaw and the bad sheriff. How old is this motif? Older than Woody Guthrie, who before Dylan was born was singing of Pretty Boy Floyd, the outlaw who paid many a farmers' mortgage and "saved their little home." Like Robin Hood and Billy the Kid (a movie that Dylan was to lend a hand with later), Harding was "always known to lend a helping hand," to straighten things out, dispense justice, rob the rich and feed the poor, and—most important of all—never ever to make a foolish move. Harding is Dylan on square one. He is your average American and also your standard sixties head: we're good, they're bad, and we're all outlaws on the side of justice.

This kind of cliché, however, serves Dylan only as a point of departure. In the next song this comfortable myth is inverted. Tom Paine and narrator Bob Dylan, both good guys for sure, are transformed into the twin forces of enslavement of the fairest damsel that ever did walk in chains. As she clutches Dylan, begging him to free her and take her south, the paranoid singer yells to be unhanded. Tom Paine apologizes for the whole ugly scene. And off she goes to bondage again. There is no room for holiness here—nor in "I Dreamed I Saw St. Augustine," in which Dylan finds himself among the crowd that put the saint to death. The song involves a Kafka-like recognition of guilt, which terrifies the speaker and reduces him to tears of remorse. The "Ballad of Frankie Lee and Judas Priest" then extends this confusion of good and evil, innocence and guilt into the eternal. As Judas Priest claims Frankie's soul, the stage is set for Dylan's redemption.

The last two songs of the first side of *John Wesley Harding* bring Dylan (and us) to the eye of the hurricane, the moment of judgment. As usual, the moment of fiercest wind heralds an instant of calm and then grace. "All along the Watchtower," demonic, apocalyptic, terrified and terrifying, magnificently biblical (and slightly New Testament, like many other songs on this album), is the moment of Dylan's crucifixion. Joker and thief converse from their respective crosses, complaining of confusion and misunderstanding and the bad joke that is life. On the watchtower people wait expectantly. In the distance, a wildcat growls. Two riders approach. The wind howls. The song ends and we await the judgment.

It comes, disreputably and even comically, in "Drifter's Escape." The song begins with an admission of guilt and inadequacy that would have been inconceivable from the Bob Dylan who sang "Go away from my window" and "Positively 4th Street." Who kicked Baby Blue onto the street. Who used and abused and whenever things got tense just walked out and left. Who was free and tough and brutalized Ochs and Baez and everyone else who tried to touch him. Who was traveling not a few songs ago with guns in both hands, never making a foolish move. "Help me in my weakness." Meet the new Bob Dylan. It is exactly the admission of weakness and guilt that brings Dylan's release. In what can be called only the classic deus ex machina, a bolt of lightning strikes the courthouse in which drifter Bob is being tried, and while everybody sinks to his knees, the drifter slips free. The moment of confession is the moment of rebirth. The end of protest is grace.

Side two of *John Wesley Harding* provides further insight into the reborn Dylan, praying for his landlord's soul, pitying the poor immigrant back there on square one, returning like the Ancient Mariner, like Lazarus raised from the dead to warn his brothers and sisters, the kind ladies and kind gentlemen, that they must avoid petty jealousy, keep their judgments to themselves, and learn to love each other. Finally, Dylan encapsulates his past self into "The Wicked Messenger," sent from Eli with a flattering tongue and a mind that multiplies trivia. In an intensely personal song, Bob Dylan explains both his old self and his new mission.

> Oh, the leaves began to fallin'
> And the seas began to part,
> And the people that confronted him were many.
> And he was told but these few words,
> Which opened up his heart,
> "If ye cannot bring good news, then don't bring any."

Good news follows immediately, in "Down along the Cove" and "I'll Be Your Baby Tonight." (And in *Nashville Skyline, New Morning, Self-Portrait,* all the mellow Dylan of the early seventies in all the country songs he found to be an appropriate musical and lyrical analogue to the simple, clean, pure life he wanted to live.)

John Wesley Harding is a remarkable album in the way it extends the angry no from myth to myth, from position to position, and then finally manages to break through the barriers of metaphysics to a new reality. It is protest cast in the broadest of terms, protest against the human condition, against the propensity to do what we do not want to do and leave undone what we should be doing. Interestingly, the album ends with a simple, clichéd statement of love—exactly where the Beatles found themselves after their own confrontation with the waste land in *Sgt. Pepper*. Exactly where the Who found themselves after *Tommy*. Exactly where so many sixties activists ended up. On the other side of the sixties looking glass, the neoromantic, radiant, transcendent yes.

Top right: Logo designed for antiwar group Another Mother for Peace. Below: Phil Ochs and Greenwich Village friend, 1966. "In such an ugly time the true protest is beauty"—Phil Ochs. *Photo by Alice Ochs. Used by permission.*

From working-class Liverpool, the Quarrymen became the Silver Beatles became the Beatles. *Photo courtesy of Retna. Used by permission.*

Bob Dylan and Joan Baez. *United Press International Photo. Used by permission.*

Poet Allen Ginsberg walks home through the streets of his Lower East Side neighborhood, New York City, 1966. *United Press International Photo. Used by permission.*

The Great Crusade. Eugene McCarthy for President, 1968. *United Press International Photo. Used by permission.*

The Reverend Martin Luther King, Jr. (right), and the Reverend Ralph Abernethy (at his side) lead a march in Birmingham, Alabama, 1963. *United Press International Photo. Used by permission.*

John F. Kennedy, youngest president since Teddy Roosevelt, gave sixties politics a refreshing and much needed injection of humor and idealism. *United Press International Photo. Used by permission.*

A close look at Wood-
stock. *Photo by Burk Uzzle,
Magnum. Used by permission.*

The Woodstock nation
gathers in upstate New
York, August 1969. *Wide
World Photos. Used by permission.*

3 | The Transcendent Yes

"I came into this world, not chiefly to make this a good place to live in, but to live in it."—Henry David Thoreau

The Woodstock Music and Art Fair has become in retrospect "the greatest event in counter-cultural history" (historian William O'Neill in *Coming Apart in the Sixties*, but anyone could have said it). Half a million people in the steady rain to hear major and soon to become major musical talents, to share their food and the limited toilets and a lot of dope and love and comfort, to become briefly the third largest city in the state and to survive without violence or crime, if only for a few days.

We remember Woodstock as the golden moment of the decade. Three deaths, four births. No riots, no disasters, no hassles despite the traffic jams that extended dozens of miles in all directions, despite the hundreds of thousands of celebrants who overwhelmed inadequate preparations, despite the bad acid, despite the pouring rain. Here was conclusive proof that the love generation could survive and even flourish under the most adverse circumstances if left to its own devices. Conclusive proof that a new consciousness was being born. That it *had been* born and was alive and growing. That the transcendent yes could survive the compromises of the world around it.

Police were impressed. So were friends and neighbors and even the old folks. And the news media. Here was incontrovertible evidence of the moral superiority of the new order.

Sheriff Rather called them "the best kids I ever met in the world." A police aid described them as "the most courteous, considerate, and well behaved group of kids I have ever been in contact with in my twenty-four years of police work."

For a moment, with nothing more than some dope and some goodwill, half a million ordinary freaks had greened America. Bombers were turning into butterflies, the Age of Aquarius had found a home in Bethel, New York. Flower children had their paradise regained.

By the time we got to Woodstock
We were half a million strong
And everywhere was song and celebration

91

And I dreamed I saw the bombers
Riding shotgun in the sky
And they were turning into butterflies
Above our nation
   We are stardust
   We are golden
   And we've got to get ourselves
   Back to the garden
—Joni Mitchell, "Woodstock"

Politics and protest, racism and the war in Vietnam existed only in another dimension, a hundred million light-years away.

If part of the sixties mind could sacrifice itself on the altar of the military-industrial-educational complex, discipline itself to tedious hours of close analysis and careful planning, make a firm and long-term commitment to social reform, another part of the sixties mind did not much care. It demonstrated because doing something was better than doing nothing. It joined the Peace Corps as an excuse to travel. It turned militant so it could carry a gun and strike a pose. It supported Gene McCarthy (a religious man who wrote poetry, who was never going to become his party's candidate, let alone president) because he was pure and would take them all down heroically. It joined CORE as a quest. It was hopelessly disorganized, inconstant and inconsistent.

It was not political, not practical.

The sixties generation confounded Johnson and Humphrey and liberals, but terrified conservatives.

The yes of the sixties, very different in almost every particular from the angry no, was just as compelling. Rooted in idealism, this affirmation could overlap and encompass both protest marches and liberal politics; yet it also transcended politics and social reform and economics to the point that the blueprints and the programs and the votes and the angry shouting didn't really matter.

The yes of the sixties was a romantic yes, and children of the sixties were a wildly romantic generation. They adored youth, novelty, excess, the eccentric and the exotic. They struggled, quixotically, unnecessarily, heroically, hopelessly. They quested—after the past and the future and an infinity of alternative presents. After personal fulfillment, after freedom, after America and the world. After social justice and nirvana. After a higher high and a louder rock album. They felt sorry for the poor, the outcasts, and the good outlaws. They preferred losing to winning, outlaws to sheriffs, poverty to wealth, because losing and outlaws and poverty are all somehow more pure. They believed in little people and in big people masquerading as little people. They elevated feeling to a station equal to or higher than that of thought. So they loved. They believed the impossible dream, and they also believed that it is impossible. However, they believed in the Horatio Alger myth of America, land of opportunity; they pulled Elvis out of his truck, Little Richard away from the sink of a Greyhound bus station restaurant, Chuck Berry from his cosmetics shop, and the Beatles from working-class Liverpool and made them big stars overnight. They were almost totally disorganized and lacked staying power: they flitted from project to project, leaving things half done. They were idealistic beyond all hope. They preferred imagination to practicality, tending to think broad thoughts and leave details fuzzy. They would do anything just for the sake of doing it, for the sake of gathering more evidence, for the sake of having a new experience, for the sake of pressing Furthur along. The generation was religious in the broadest sense. It was keen on dogs, children, and old folks. And on its own sweet self. It suffered. It loved. It hated. It was full of silliness and madness and all the colors that ever were.

> (The increasing romanticism of the sixties can be measured in the heroes it fashioned to replace the organization men of the late fifties: Eldridge Cleaver and Bobby Seale and the Black Panthers (1968) for Martin Luther King, Jr. [whose popularity among the young crested in 1963]; Gene McCarthy for Hubert Humphrey; Ché Guevara for John Foster Dulles; Mario Savio and free speech for Clark Kerr and the so-called multiversity; activist priests Dan and Phil Berrigan and the Maharishi for Billy Graham and Norman Vincent Peale; long-haired Bill Kunstler for Joe Welsh; Abbie Hoffman and Lenny Bruce for J. Paul Getty and Steve Allen; Timothy Leary for Benjamin Spock; Mao Tse-tung for Dwight Eisenhower. Ho Chi Minh became an American cult hero.)

The yes of the sixties, like all other expressions of the romantic spirit, was essentially private: not so much a social movement, organized and programmed and charted, as a groundswell of developing individual psyches. A hundred million people discovered their separate consciousnesses in a hundred million different ways, mostly quiet and unnewsworthy, like a flower uncurling into blossom. Before the decade was out, however, whole slums were in bloom, and the public mind was ever so slightly aware of a meteor shower of exploding consciousnesses, a great kaleidoscope of romanticism. The sixties yes was a magic yes, a hidden reality that might break out (or through) in any circumstance, extraordinary in its ordinariness, lunacy, spontaneity, freedom, magic.

The yes can be described but it cannot be charted. It can be tasted today in the remembered savor of public moments like Woodstock and of exquisitely private moments. It can be caught in recreations of the great kaleidoscope (the histories faithful in spirit as well as fact to the decade) and in the fragments of the sixties from which those recreations must be made.

Like the Beatles' *Magical Mystery Tour*, for example, a film tucked away in the vaults of many American libraries, an album tucked away in the collections of most children of the sixties, magnificently amateur and incoherent, affirmative, as faithful a reflection of the transcendent yes as Woodstock. A real mystery trip, you know, a little Boxing Day puzzle put together for the BBC viewers by the wizards from Liverpool.

"AWAY IN THE SKY, beyond the clouds, live 4 or 5 Magicians. [Who is the fifth, who walks always beside us? When I count, there are only four Beatles. Mystery number one.] By casting WONDERFUL SPELLS they turn the Most Ordinary Coach Trip into a MAGICAL MYSTERY TOUR. If you let yourself go, the Magicians will take you away to marvelous places."

So off go the Beatles, and a coach full of ordinary folks besides (Ringo and his aunt Jessie, in foul temper both, always quarreling), on this magical bus tour (roll up for the mystery trip), a big yellow and blue bus with courier Jolly Jimmy Johnson and hostess Wendy Winters. And before you know it Mr. Buster Bloodvessel has fallen in love with Aunt Jessie (love is all you need), the bus is flying, and the world is tripped out in a swirl of colors, and everybody is having a wonderful time. (Did you ever listen closely to "Magical Mystery Tour," to the bus that roars out of one speaker and into the other? Or to "I Am the Walrus," all those words at the end? Why is Paul wearing a black carnation while the other three wear red? Who is the walrus?)

So the bus trip and the day and the movie and the album unravel, a delight of satires and scenes and even a strip show—with the Bonzo Dog (Doo Dah) Band—and by the time the bus returns from wherever it is that it is returning from, they're all there, Mr. Bloodvessel and Aunt Jessie and George and Ringo and John and Paul, having a wonderful time doing the most ordinary thing you can imagine, singing corny old show tunes to an accordian. "BUT I WILL TELL YOU IT IS MAGIC!"

(Out we go to "Let's all get up and dance to a song that was a hit before your Mother was born.")

The point is, of course, that mystery, love and excitement are all around us and life is groovy even if you're not at Woodstock or Big Sur and you never quite know when you're going to stumble into a magical mystery tour.

> "Maybe YOU'VE been on a MAGICAL MYS-
> TERY TOUR without even realising it."

The most obvious aspect of sixties romanticism was the great value it placed on youth. Like all other romantics of the last two centuries, sixties heads pretty much assumed that age is equivalent with senility and is scarcely so well qualified a teacher as youth. It's straight downhill after twenty-one, and after thirty you might just as well be dead. This assumption would cause big problems as the generation passed traumatically to the north of thirty. But during the golden decade it offered a justification.

> "Hope I die before I'm old."—the Who

> "I have lived some thirty years on this planet, and I have yet to hear the first syllable of valuable or even earnest advice from my seniors. They have told me nothing, and probably cannot tell me anything to the purpose."—Henry David Thoreau

Kiddierock:
Pete Seeger: "Beans in My Ears"
Peter, Paul, and Mary: "Puff, the Magic Dragon"
Rolling Stones: "Dandelion"
Tom Paxton: "We're All Going to the Zoo"
Beatles: "Yellow Submarine"
Buffalo Springfield: "I Am a Child"
Jefferson Airplane: "Lather"
Beatles: "Dear Prudence, won't you come out and play?"
Airplane: "White Rabbit"
Beatles: "Lucy in the Sky with Diamonds"
Beatles: "I Am the Walrus"
Johnny Thunder: "Here we go loop de loop,"
John Sebastian: "I Had a Dream"
Kenny Loggins: "The House at Pooh Corner"
Paul Kantner: "The Ballad of You and Me and Pooneil"

Romantics—and the sixties—also tend toward a mystical religiosity. In fact, all romantics are highly religious in an offbeat way: you find them professing agnosticism and hanging around ruined Gothic cathedrals. Or drawing soft pictures of a soft and loving Jesus. Singing "Jesus is just all right with me" or spirituals or folk songs full of secondhand religion. Meditating with the Maharishi. Studying Zen.

A major complaint of the sixties against the fifties was the loss of spiritual values: the sellout of the virtues taught in Sunday school, the loss of what Paul Goodman called in borrowed theological terminology "Justification" and "vocation." Sixties people sought both, and they sought religious affirmation in the broadest sense by rejecting the rules and superstitions and rigidities of orthodox religion.

Some got themselves right down to basic Christianity, Christ without the theologians. It's interesting, for example, that radical Beatle John Lennon insisted repeatedly that he was "all for Christ." "I'm very big on Christ.

I've always fancied him. He was right." And again, "Christ was all right, really. It was just his friends that thickened things up a bit." And yet again, "I used to go around calling myself a Christian communist."

> (It was during the sixties that Christians and communists discovered that their positions were not mutually exclusive after all, that they could affirm significant parts of each other's theologies.)

But most children of the sixties could not or would not draw Lennon's distinction between Christ and his followers. They found Christianity, even fundamentalist Christianity, too compromised to deserve serious consideration. The result was a great awakening of fuzzed mysticism, often linked with ritual use of soft drugs and sprinkled with paperback Zen philosophy. Tim Leary was religious. Pot was "righteous sacrament"; acid, an avenue to God.

The Western world had been feeling its way tentatively toward the East for many years before the sixties: Thomas Merton (*The Seven Storey Mountain*, 1948; a prolific writer on Eastern subjects until his death in 1968), Hermann Hesse, Gary Snyder, Allen Ginsberg, Alan Watts, Gregory Corso, and even Jack Kerouac (*The Dharma Bums*) functioned as carriers of orientalism. All had large audiences and influenced countless persons.

So you were not a nincompoop if you went around talking the big picture in the sixties. Ordinary folk spoke seriously about God, truth, ultimate reality, vocation, ontology, eschatology. A sense of religious awe and mystery infused even the most mundane activities (and sold J. R. R. Tolkien's religious allegory *Lord of the Rings* by the hundreds of thousands).

Even the intellectual lightweights turned temporarily religious, sliding off the back of the movement with pseudoreligions like astrology and witchcraft and a lot of science fiction theologies invented for fun or profit or both. When the Maharishi Mahesh Yogi and Transcendental Meditation came bouncing into England, and into the consciousnesses of the Beatles, and into the consciousness of the world, older people who had been doing the religious thing for many years found him suspect, simplistic, maybe even slick and commercial. (His association with camp follower Donovan Leitch, with the sticky mush of *A Gift from a Flower to a Garden*, and the contrived love and flowers of Donovan's 1967 tour didn't help much either.) The Maharishi was, however, perfectly attuned to the popular, romantic religiosity of the times and achieved instant assimilation into the artifice of the sixties.

> "It can't be one hundred percent without the inner life, can it?"—George Harrison

George Harrison would transcend it all in *All Things Must Pass.*

My sweet Lord, I really want to know you
I really want to go with you.

The song, the album, the call resonated in the sixties consciousness, and at the close of the age "My Sweet Lord" was everywhere. "Every time I put the radio on, it's 'oh my Lord'!" said Lennon. "I'm beginning to think there must be a God!"

(God had been around AM radio for the duration, however: Ferlin Huskey's "Wings of a Dove" and the Highwaymen's "Michael Row the Boat Ashore" in 1961; later hits like "Oh Happy Day," "Holly Holy"; and three important recordings— by Judy Collins, Joan Baez, and Aretha Franklin— of "Amazing Grace." In 1967 the Electric Prunes did a *Mass in F Minor* complete with Kyrie, Gloria, Credo, Sanctus, Agnus Dei, and Benedictus.)

"I like you too much not to say it. You've got everything except one thing—madness. A man needs a little madness, or else. . . ."
"Or else?"
"He never dares cut the rope and be free."—Zorba, in the movie *Zorba the Greek*

"The painting job, meanwhile, with everybody pitching in in a frenzy of primary colors, yellows, oranges, blues, reds, was sloppy as hell, except for the parts Roy Seburn did, which were nice manic mandalas. Well, it was sloppy, but one thing you had to say for it; it was freaking lurid. The manifest, the destination sign in the front, read: 'Furthur,' with two *u*'s."—Tom Wolfe on the painting of the Merry Prankster bus in *The Electric Kool-Aid Acid Test*

Sixties people would go anywhere, do anything, fill themselves full of (almost) any kind of dope, explore any argument, try any living arrangement, take any class, read (at least part of) any book, look at any movie, listen to any song, talk to any person, tolerate incredible amounts of the most unbelievable pain, aggravation, and plain bullshit just for the sake of doing more. Just to press Furthur. They were the most open-minded people in the world. It is not true that you couldn't tell a sixties person anything: you could tell him everything. He would sit and listen for quite a while and then make up his mind very definitely. He was always ready to go no matter what the hour, no matter what his other commitments might be, no matter what the risks. He was, in fact, quite mad. He had cut the rope; he was free, not uptight. He valued experience for experience's own sake. He was impatient only with sitting on his ass, with habit, with boredom. He was in constant motion. More is better. In fact, he transcended himself and his world in experiences involving himself and his world.

More than anything else, romantics are into themselves. And it was the sanctity of self that underlay the great sixties quest after freedom. It was also the sanctity of self that caused people to pull back from protest, to internalize the revolution, to straighten out their own heads instead of everyone else's, to cut the movement off in mid-march. The sanctity of self was at constant odds with the sixties search for community and meaningful relationships and with the love ethic of the decade. The complexities and paradoxes have yet to be resolved in the heads of most sixties folk: me or her? I or us? How much of myself can I trade yet still retain my integrity? My individuality? My identity?

The importance of self produced a great personalizing of writing, music, and art. The self was all over pop music during the sixties and on into the seventies. Not only rock and schlock rock but songs like "I Gotta Be Me" and "I Did It My Way," which were served to the fifties generation. (Even pop music reviews and criticism are more often about the *I* of the writer than about the song or the album being examined.)

Most prominent among the egos of sixties rock were Paul Simon and Bob Dylan. Simon was an incurable romantic, filled with New York City–inspired angst and lit. crit.–fueled sensitivity, both of which aggravated that disease so common among self-preoccupied artists, self-pity. How Simon suffered! How it showed in his songs! "Bleecker Street" (the best of Simon and Garfunkel's first album) is a poem-song about the inability of people to communicate, more specifically, about the poet's inability to communicate with the audience. "Sounds of Silence" (their first hit) trades in the same currency in slightly clichéd images: the poet walks the cobblestoned streets alone at night, neon lights flashing around him, people deaf to their noncommunication and to him.

"I Am a Rock" continued the isolation and the suffering and the self-pity.

Well, Simon was very young in those days, a Queens College English major doing an occasional gig in the Village or in London or in Paris. In later albums he matured, but he never quite (even in *Bookends*, his best album) outgrew his romanticism. Or his concern for himself. The most intense of *Bookends'* portraits look inside, not out: "A Hazy Shade of Winter," "Fakin' It," "Overs." Songs full of dreams and the death of dreams, full of the nervousness that's bound to develop when self-fulfillment becomes the center of one's life, a kind of unintentional critique of the dangers of self. (In more recent—and less famous—songs like "St. Judy's Comet" and "Run That Body Down" Simon has continued to turn his personal life into song.)

When it came to the self as subject, however, everybody was upstaged by Dylan, whose primary subject in virtually all of his best work is himself.

Look at his albums: invariably a picture of Dylan on the front; more often than not, notes, poetry, story, maybe even a picture by Dylan on the back. And Dylan on the inside, too.

> (*Self-Portrait*, however, consists mainly of songs by other writers—including an abominable version of Simon's "The Boxer." *Self-Portrait* is also Dylan's worst album.)

"I'll tell you another discovery I've made," Dylan once said in an interview. "On a strange level the songs are done for somebody, about somebody, and to somebody. Usually that person is the somebody who is singing that song." Not that sixties heads cared much. Dylan—struggling hero, outlaw, seer, far traveler, lonesome wanderer, confused clown, juggler, thief, artist, and general romantic image of the age—had a self that was the self of the generation, and he spoke for it, about it, and to it.

Two views on the sanctity of self:

> They hate us, don't they? I like it that way, that is the way it's supposed to be. If they didn't hate me I would have to hate myself.
> —George Jackson in a prison letter to Angela Davis (1970)

> Well, the doctor interrupted me just about then,
> Sayin' "Hey, I've been havin' the same old dreams,
> But mine was different you see.
> I dreamt that the only person left after the war was me.
> I didn't see you around."
>
> Well, now time passed and now it seems
> Everybody's having them dreams.
> Everybody sees themselves walkin' around with no one else.
> Half of the people can be part right all of the time,
> Some of the people can be all right part of the time,
> But all of the people can't be right all of the time.
> I think Abraham Lincoln said that.
> "I'll let you be in my dream if I can be in yours."
> I said that.
> —Bob Dylan, "Talkin' World War III Blues" (1963)

Sixties people were disorganized probably because they were so wrapped up in themselves. They could not abide schedules, plans, structures. They tended to leave projects half done, to take on eighty different projects at once and spread the butter too thin. Their work often showed embarrassingly rough edges and imperfections.

This disorganization annoyed their elders, especially parents and professors, and it no doubt has its liabilities. Still, it has a certain art (the randomness of juxtapositions, much like fiddling with a radio dial or listening to the second side of the Beatles' *Abbey Road* album). It gave sixties people a certain breadth. And it produced a healthy disrespect for the real danger: organization in the form of depersonalizing big government, big education, big business, increasing specialization and compartmentalization in all areas.

As eager as sixties people were to explore alternatives, they were—like all other romantics—exceptionally sentimental about their roots. Public history they had little enough respect for, but personal history was something else. Ancestors, heirlooms, photographs, memories—romantics tend their past like a hypochondriac nursing an ulcer. For all their insistence on the now, children of the sixties devoted enormous energy to assimilating the past, pillaging the centuries for whatever they could offer. Professional historians of an older generation accused them of a superficial eclecticism, but in truth the Portobello Road flea market clothing, the refinished washstands and Art Nouveau glass, and the Victorian mansions of Haight-Ashbury, with which children of the sixties fortified themselves against their anxieties, brought them much closer to the touch and feel of history than their more scholarly (and more distanced) critics came.

> "It isn't simply that [the Beatles] have an instinctive nostalgia for period styles, as in 'She's Leaving Home' or 'When I'm Sixty-four,' or that they absorb the past through the media of the popular arts, through music, cinema, theatrical conventions, bands like Sgt. Pepper's, or music hall performers. . . . No, the Beatles have the distinction in their work of *knowing* that this is how they see and feel things and of enjoying the knowledge."
> —Richard Poirier, *Partisan Review*

The romantic seeks a personal tie with the past, not an idea she can understand or a complete sweep of history (certainly not political history, which she dismisses on principle), but a chunk of bygone days—solid, palpable, useful. An Edwardian jacket. An old brownstone to call home. A few Gothic ruins. Here may be bits and fragments, nothing coherent, but here is also intimacy of the past, a *human* past.

This respect for the past has intensified in the seventies as the price of antiques doubles and quadruples and societies spring up everywhere for the preservation of buildings, parks, crafts, even jousting. It is chic to restore an older home. This is remarkable in America. And what makes it more remarkable is that it's the generation of the sixties doing the restoring and preserving and it was their conservative parents, the generation of the fifties, who did the systematic leveling in the name of new housing projects, new expressways, new public office buildings, and all the other manifestations of so-called progress.

Rock has been called the music of the sixties, the music of now, the music of the moment, the music of youth.

As it developed during the sixties, however, rock also came to incorporate much of the musical, social, and cultural past. "How Gentle Is the Rain" stole its tune from Bach; so also did "A Whiter Shade of Pale." Folksingers brought back Guthrie and the Doors brought back Brecht and Weill. The Beatles' white album is an encyclopedia of musical styles. Into the end of "All You Need Is Love" (*Magical Mystery Tour*) they wove fragments of thirties ballroom, the French national anthem, their own "She Loves You," boogie-woogie, "In the Mood," "Greensleeves," and some phrases out of an Indian bazaar.

Rock lyrics also felt the tug of the past. Donovan resurrected Atlantis. The Beatles looked back in "Yesterday" and "In My Life." Dylan looked back with poems like "My Life in a Stolen Moment" and "11 Outlined Epitaphs" and a dozen songs.

> With half-damp eyes I stared to the room
> Where my friends and I spent many an afternoon,
> Where we together weathered many a storm,
> Laughin' and singin' till the early hours of the morn.
>
> By the old wooden stove where our hats was hung,
> Our words were told, our songs were sung,
> Where we longed for nothin' and were quite satisfied
> Talkin' and a-jokin' about the world outside. . . .
>
> I wish, I wish, I wish in vain,
> That we could sit simply in that room again.
> Ten thousand dollars at the drop of a hat,
> I'd give it all gladly if our lives could be like that.
> —"Bob Dylan's Dream"

The Kinks fossilized the past in *Village Green Preservation Society* (1968). Early in the seventies, the Who—epitome of mod and flash and now—looked over their shoulders with *Quadrophenia*. From rock, Dylan turned to country life and country music; he thought the old music would be bedrock upon which to build a new sanity after the confusion of the middle of the decade. And the Band, who most influenced Dylan on his retreat to copper kettle, came reeking of the past, from the Civil War of "The Night They Drove Old Dixie Down" to the American west of "Across the Great Divide" and "Up on Cripple Creek."

The Middle Ages, traditionally a romantic favorite, also infiltrated the music and consciousness of the sixties. The Kinks' *Arthur.* Leonard Cohen's "Joan of Arc." Joan Baez's "Sweet Sir Galahad." David Crosby's "Guinnevere." The title song of Neil Young's *After the Gold Rush.*

> I dreamed I saw the knight in armor coming,
> Saying something about the queen;
> There were peasants singing and drummers drumming,

And the archer split the tree.
There was fanfare blowing to the sun
That was floating on the breeze.

"Time it was, I have a photograph."

"Don't take my Kodachrome away."

In 1967 Marty Balin wrote the most bittersweet memory of all, the Jefferson Airplane's "Comin' Back to Me."

The summer had inhaled and held its breath too long;
The winter looked the same, as if it had never gone;
And through an open window where no curtain hung,
I saw you.
I saw you comin' back to me.

One begins to read between the pages of a book;
The shape of sleepy music, and suddenly you're hooked;
And in the rain upon the trees that kisses on the run,
I saw you.
I saw you comin' back to me.

Strolling the hills overlooking the shore,
I realized I must have been here before;
The shadow on the mist could have been anyone.
I saw you.
I saw you comin' back to me.

Small things like reasons are put in a jar;
What ever happened to wishes wished on a star?
Was it just something that I made up for fun?
I saw you
I saw you comin' back to me.

To the romantic, and to the sixties person, feeling is as valuable a mode of understanding as rational thought. The romantic will rely on intuition rather than on logical argument, or at least in addition to rational thought. He is a mystic and sensualist. The rationalist position—having been commandeered by the liberal establishment that brought America cold war politics, Vietnam, the multiversity, systems and technologies, and all the other demons against which the generation of the sixties rebelled—was suspect from the start. And when gut reaction, the suspicion that something was rotten in Washington (and Mississippi, and Chicago, and Kent State, and elsewhere), was substantiated by establishment actions and reactions to the challenges of youth, and then by the establishment's own investigations— well, reason has never recovered. To this day an opinion is as good as an argument, and all logicians are suspect.

"Diggers are zenlike in that we have totally destroyed words and replaced them with 'doing'—
action becomes the only reality. Like Lao-tzu:
'The way to do is to be.'"—Abbie Hoffman,
Revolution for the Hell of It

"We are only what we feel."—Neil Young

"You think too much. That is your trouble. Clever
people and grocers—they weigh everything."
—Zorba, in the movie *Zorba the Greek*

I remember reading somewhere about an Indian tribe that made a practice of considering all matters of importance twice: once stone sober and
once stoned. Once under the influence of reason, once under the influence
of emotion. Equal weight was given to both conclusions.

One thing sixties people, like all other romantics, really grooved on was
travel. In many respects their antsiness was a legacy from the fifties and the
depression, from Guthrie and a million dust bowl refugees, from Kerouac
and the beat poets. Parents just home from the war might have spent a lot of
time digging in and hunkering down, but their kids were hot to roll, and the
federal highway system was getting put together courtesy of the gasoline
and automobile interests. The sixties migration to nowhere was a national
pastime, a national heritage even, a nationwide consciousness developed
from radio and television and newspaper travelogues; highways lined with
motels, free maps and cheap gas, the 65 MPH speed limit (70, 80, all you
can get out west), a whole generation with summers free, with time and energy and a few dollars scraped together from temporary jobs, squeezed out
of college funds, begged, borrowed, or just gratefully accepted from parents. The economy was opening up, odd jobs were not hard to find, maybe
down at the shore or out on the coast, in Denver or Chicago, overseas. You
might work a couple of weeks or a couple of months, then pack up for another job down the line or spend a few months looking for America.

Even in the course of less footloose lives there was plenty of travel, lots
of driving around town late at night deep in big talk. Fall and spring jour-
neys to and from college were great, heroic adventures, packed five or six to
a '58 Buick, each kicking in $10 and sharing the driving down the old Penn-
sylvania Turnpike with its tunnels and turns, through Wheeling, W. Va., at
2:30 in the morning, across eastern Ohio and a string of small midwestern
towns, on and off the intermittent interstate, fighting through Columbus
traffic in the early hours of the morning, to Springfield, Ohio; or nights on
the Greyhound, perilous with cigarette smoke and ham sandwiches, the
aqua-colored tiles of the Pittsburgh bus station and the dirty restrooms in
Wheeling, and rest stops whiled away at pinball machines, and waitresses
killing the night in conversation with drivers and cops, fits of uncomfort-
able sleep, nearly confessional talk with some chick you never saw before

and would never see again; AND to arrive to a new world full of people from Algoma, Wisconsin, from Kewanee, Illinois, from Chicago and New York and Washington and Cleveland, everybody with tales of summer and of high adventures coming and going; and the year spent chasing around the country after football, basketball, even baseball games, a Peter, Paul, and Mary concert in Dayton or (later in the decade) a demonstration in Columbus or an art flick in Yellow Springs, wheels always somehow available, the going and the coming, the absorption of a continent full of places and a whole country full of people.

And, for the lucky few, the Peace Corps or a summer job in the Bundesrepublik or maybe *Europe on $5 a Day.*

By the close of the decade the underground of travel freaks and itinerant transcendents stretched from California to New York to London to Marrakesh to the Middle East to India and beyond, Tibet, Trinidad, Panama, Turkey, Pakistan, Hong Kong, Mexico, Marseilles, Katmandu—students, beats, dropouts, sons and daughters of the idle rich and the idle poor and the busy middle class, yes, bums and heads and journalists, everybody stoned (some jailed), bulletins floating into clearinghouses in Paris and London and New York from everywhere and by every conceivable carrier: Turkish border officials beating heads; unsigned traveler's checks bringing half face value in Calcutta; blood $50 a pint in Kuwait; bus from Corinth to Athens 40¢; northern Afghanistan cut off because of Moslem-Hindu war; Hotel Thai Son Greet in Bangkok 98¢ for a double.

Travel and the quest after place showed up strongly in the music of the sixties. Where is Washington Square, anyway? Colorado Boulevard? South Street? Saginaw? Muskogee? Galveston? Penny Lane? Abbey Road? Liverpool? Martha and the Vandellas 1964 recitation in "Dancing in the Streets": Baltimore and D.C., Philadelphia, Pa., don't forget the Motor City.

> "I been doin' some hard travelin'."—Woody
> Guthrie

And it has stuck with us, this love of travel, this reverence for the weary traveler, long on the open road, sleepin' in the rain, clothes muddy, thirsty boots kicked into a corner while the wanderer drinks a quick cup of coffee.

The sixties also brought the realization that travel is more than just a groovy way to spend time and to satisfy the yen to see faraway places with strange names. Travel is a protest against habit and convention and a struggle for self-discovery. Travel (sixties style, that is) strips you to the basics and measures you against the need for food, clothing, and shelter. It bumps you into new people, new places, new attitudes. "You who are on the road must have a code," Graham Nash warned in "Teach Your Children." What he did not say, but what everyone knew, was that the road is a means of developing a code—a code based on traditional American values of independence, self-sufficiency, and community developed not by growing up in the same vegetable patch but by struggling together out there on the frontier.

Travel is not escape. It is discovery. As Perceval searched for the Holy Grail, he found himself first, then the Grail. Dorothy's journey along the yellow brick road, though it brought her friends, adventures, and the witch's ruby slippers, was above all else a process of self-realization. In "Tales of the Brave Ulysses" (1967) Eric Clapton suggested that travel is for some the *only* possible self-realization. To Ken Kesey and the Merry Pranksters, travel—like acid—served as a metaphor for living: you were either *on* the bus or *off* the bus.

It is another part of the romantic creed, and a basis for the sixties affirmation, that little people are as important as big people. They are more interesting, they are more deserving, they are the legitimate concern of government and of history and of literature and of decent folk everywhere. Romantics take the side of labor against big business, family grocery store against chain supermarket, individual citizen against government bureaucracy, David against Goliath. The angry farmer rises up and smites the coal company that would devour his land. A few GIs blow the lid on My Lai. John Dean dusts off Richard Nixon.

And so the stories of David, the average farmer or GI, and the kid from Wooster College become important. *Rolling Stone* publishes autobiographies sent in by ordinary readers. Nostalgia books contain interviews with everyday people as well as with big names.

"We are the same, whatever we do," Sly Stone told us.

"Ain't no use a-talking to me," Bob Dylan told us. "It's just the same as talking to you." "Does the Prime Minister realize he's just a bloke?" John Lennon asked.

> "A working class hero is something to be."—John Lennon, "Working Class Hero"

> "Let's drink to the lowly of birth."—the Rolling Stones, "Salt of the Earth"

Little people and outlaws. Because outlaws are little people trying to assert themselves against the big system. Because outlaws have hearts of gold and will protect little people against the big system. Because outlaws are underdogs. Like the mythical figures of the American past resurrected in the folk revival of the late fifties and early sixties: Tom Joad, Pretty Boy Floyd, Joe Hill, other martyred union organizers, and American Robin Hoods.

> There's many a starvin' farmer,
> The same old story told,
> How this outlaw paid their mortgage,
> And saved their little home.

Others tell you of a stranger,
That came to beg a meal,
And underneath his napkin
Left a thousand-dollar bill. . . .

Now as through this world I ramble,
I see lots of funny men,
Some will rob you with a six-gun,
And some with a fountain pen.

But as through this life you travel,
And as through your life you roam,
You won't never see an outlaw
Drive a family from their home.
  —Woody Guthrie, "Pretty Boy Floyd"

Like Paul Simon's fugitive robber of "Wednesday Morning 3 A.M.," like the Kingston Trio's Tom Dooley" (1959), like Bob Dylan's *John Wesley Harding*, a friend to the poor, like Tim Hardin's "Smuggling Man," like the would-be thief in "The Lady Came from Baltimore," like the Shangri-Las' "Leader of the Pack." Like Billy the Kid in a movie Dylan acted in and scored. Like Paul Newman in *Cool Hand Luke*. (Like the driver in *Vanishing Point*: everybody wants him, cops in ten states on his trail, a line of wrecked vehicles long as a turnpike in his wake, and everybody in the whole theater on his side.)

"We're all outlaws in the eyes of America," sang the Jefferson Airplane in "Volunteers." In fact, America is a country of rebels, has a long tradition of outlawry. It's a romantic country; it digs outlaws.

> (The sixties soft-headedness about criminals began with Caryl Chessman. It reached a climax with Ken Kesey's late sixties love-in with the California chapter of Hell's Angels. It reached absurdity with the Black Panther demand that all black prisoners be freed from American jails.)

The sixties were the great age of the common person, the most democratic America has been in a long while. Such was the good effect of this romantic identification with little folk and outlaws. A less desirable effect was the sixties habit of accepting losing as somehow more legitimate, more holy, more worthwhile, and more desirable than winning.

And children of the sixties, suspicious of winners, developed a strong losing habit. Traditionally, romantics are great champions of lost causes. This makes perfect sense because losing builds character. It's more interesting than winning and more psychologically complex. Considerable evidence suggests that part of Gene McCarthy's appeal was the lostness of his cause. Likewise Ho Chi Minh, Bobby Seale, and the New York Mets. The Chairman Mao of the sixties imagination was the Mao of the great march;

the Fidel Castro popular with sixties people was the guerrilla leader of a band of seven men hiding out in the hills. (Castro in power was less interesting than Ché Guevara, who died in action.)

> "Now the rain falls down on last year's man.
> An hour has gone by and he has not moved his hand."—Leonard Cohen

Leonard Cohen lived in a world of losers. People in need of grace, usually a little kinky, strung out, plagued by dope, paranoia, uncertainty. "Suzanne." "Sisters of Mercy." "Bird on the Wire." ("And wasn't it a long way down?") "Joan of Arc." "Winter Lady." He called his 1966 book *Beautiful Losers.* The sixties took the book to their heart because the sixties wanted losers. The sixties liked misfits: honky-tonk women, junkies, hoboes, Mr. Bojangles, gypsies, tramps, thieves. There is no success like failure, sang Dylan in "Love Minus Zero/No limit."

"I'm a Loser," the Beatles sang.

"I am a man of constant sorrow," went the old folk song, quite popular throughout the decade.

It is easier to decide that losing is more holy than winning, and that the worker is more important than the captain of industry, than to transform losers into winners and workers into captains of industry. "My greatest skill has been to want but little," wrote Thoreau.

The same is true of poverty, on which romantics—and most sixties people—usually claim to be keen. The sixties generation saw the poor as rich, the rich as poor. Poverty was most definitely blessed, and wealth could be an embarrassment. College students cultivated the faded, tattered look of madras shirts, cutoff jeans, worn-out tennis shoes, and dingy T-shirts. The idea was to look like a beachcomber or a mechanic. Their parents, who were spending a couple of grand a year to send them to school, wondered what was going on. School administrators wondered, too.

> "Blessed are the meek, for they shall inherit the earth."

Poverty was blessed for two reasons. First, sixties people instinctively distrusted the machines that made the goods and the jobs that made the money. Both were dehumanizing and alienating. Better to do without the riches and make your own tools, clothing, furniture. Poverty meant simple, cheap, handcrafted objects. Folk music. Earth colors. Possessions secondhand, with some history behind them, with some past clinging to them. Second, being children of relatively comfortable, if not affluent, parents, sixties youth had discovered the truth of the axiom that money does not buy happiness. "Fun is the one thing that money can't buy," explained the Beatles in mock melodrama.

(There would have been a lot less bullshit about
blessed poverty had middle-class whites confronted the permanent, genuine, Ray Charles cot-
ton-is-down-to-a-quarter-a-pound-and-I'm-
busted no food and no job poverty that stared at
American blacks.)

Janis Joplin made it sound like fun, singing Kristofferson's "Bobby Mc-
Gee"—"busted flat in Baton Rouge. . . feeling near as faded as my jeans."

Steal This Book is, in a way, a manual of survival in the prison that
is Amerika. It preaches jailbreak. It shows you where and exactly
how to place the dynamite that will destroy the walls. The first section—SURVIVE!— lays out a potential action program for our new
Nation. The chapter headings spell out the demands for a free society. A community where the technology produces goods and services for whoever needs them, come who may. It calls on the Robin
Hoods of Santa Barbara Forest to steal from the robber barons who
own the castles of capitalism. It implies that the reader is already
"ideologically set," in that he understands corporate feudalism as the
only robber worthy of being called "crime," for it is committed
against the people as a whole. Whether the ways it describes to rip-
off shit are legal or illegal is irrelevant. The dictionary of law is written by the bosses of order. Our moral dictionary says no to heisting
from each other. To steal from a brother or sister is evil. To *not* steal
from the institutions that are the pillars of the Pig Empire is equally
immoral.
    —Abbie Hoffman's introduction to *Steal This Book*

(This sort of survival made plenty of outlaws and plenty of losers during the
late sixties. It built a lot of character. Then sixties people got tired of losing.
Their character built, they looked—not very successfully—for the payoff.
Moreover, the causes for which one could lose honorably and proudly were
evaporating at the close of the decade. And the job market tightened up.)

"Consciousness III starts with self. In contrast to
Consciousness II, which accepts society, the public interest, and institutions as the primary reality,
III declares that the individual self is the only true
reality. Thus it returns to the earlier America:
'Myself I sing.' "—Charles Reich in *The Greening
of America*, explaining the generation of the sixties

"God commanded me some time ago to do the
two things that are required of his messengers:
one, not become a martyr and two, to do my
trade union job—to write a Bible and a theology
and a prayer book. So now I have accomplished

that task. *High Priest* is the Bible, the first book
of the Bible, and the *Politics of Ecstasy* is our
theology. *Psychedelic Prayers* is of course our
prayer book."—Tim Leary

"Make love not war."

Romantics love. It's part of their preference for feelings over ideas and
the taproot of their transcendence. It's part of their religiosity. It is the reason they take care of children, dogs, old folks, outlaws, little people, the
poor, themselves.

The sixties loved. Almost indiscriminately.

> Don't you want somebody to love?
> Don't you need somebody to love?
> Wouldn't you love somebody to love?
> You better find somebody to love.
> —Jefferson Airplane, "Somebody to Love"

Love is everywhere in sixties music. There was not a pure hate group to
the decade, not even the Who, self-confessed early in their career as "a
group with built-in aggression." Did they not come ultimately to "love,
reign o'er me"? And the Beatles: "She Loves You." The Stones: "Ruby
Tuesday." Joni Mitchell: "Cactus Tree." "If you can't be with the one you
love, love the one you're with." "Cherish." "You've Got a Friend." Sex.
"Why don't we do it in the road?" "Lola," the transvestite. David Crosby's
ménage a trois, "Triad": "I don't see why we can't go on as three." Jim
Morrison: "Love your neighbor 'til his wife gets home." Johnnie Taylor:
"Who's makin' love to your old lady while you're out makin' love?"
Groupies. "Superstar": "You said you'd be comin' back again baby."
Metaphysics: he ain't heavy, he's my brother. "All You Need Is Love."
"Reach Out in the Darkness," Friend and Lover.

> (I once heard Ralph Bunche speak. Somebody
> asked: "Mr. Bunche, you have spent a lifetime in
> international diplomacy. What has it taught you?"
> Ralph Bunche thought for a moment and an-
> swered, "I have learned that we must be kind to
> each other.")

Despite the disillusionments of growing up, the generation of the sixties
has held to the love ethic: they are still soft touches. "Whenever we have a
case that could go either way," an elderly woman living on social security
told me, "we always try to get assigned to a worker who is around thirty.
They seem to understand better. They will help you more than the older
ones or the kids just out of college." Sixties people remain genuinely kind,
ready to help, always up for one more romance, one more attempt at understanding.

The ability, social consciousness and conscience, political sensitivity, and honest realism of today's students are a prime cause of student disturbances. As one student observed during our investigation, today's students take seriously the ideals taught in schools and churches, and often at home and then they see a system that denies its ideals in actual life. Racial injustice and the war in Vietnam stand out as prime illustrations of our society's deviation from its professed ideals and of the slowness with which the system reforms itself. That they seemingly can do so little to correct the wrongs through conventional political discourse tends to produce in the most idealistic and energetic students a strong sense of frustration.

Many of these idealists have developed with considerable sophistication the thesis that these flaws are endemic in the workings of American democracy.
—Cox Commission reporting on the disturbances at Columbia University in April and May 1968

> In 1948 Allen Ginsberg heard a voice. "My first thought was this was what I was born for, and second thought, never forget—never forget, never renig, never deny. Never deny the voice—no never *forget* it, don't get lost mentally wandering in other spirit worlds or American or job worlds or advertising worlds or war worlds or earth worlds. But the spirit of the universe was what I was born to realize.—interview, Thomas Clark, *The Radical Vision*

We are stardust
We are golden
And we've got to get ourselves
Back to the garden.
—Joni Mitchell, "Woodstock"

> "And in the end the love you take is equal to the love you make."—the Beatles

Ken Kesey, author of *One Flew over the Cuckoo's Nest,* on his Oregon farm, bottom. The destination shown on the front of his bus was "Further"; inside, a cooler filled with acid spiked orange juice; the driver was Neal Cassady, top, real life hero of *On the Road—photo courtesy of Ken Kesey.* Kesey led a band of boisterous nomads called the Merry Pranksters in a search for new joy. *Photo by Paul Fusco, Magnum. Used by permission.*

Astronaut Edwin E. Aldrin, Jr., descending the steps of the lunar module, July 20, 1969. By their moon walk Armstrong and Aldrin physically realized the spiritual intentions of Kesey and his Merry Pranksters and their push against boundaries that don't satisfy. *Photo courtesy of NASA.*

The Grateful Dead. Chaos, bright lights, loud music, and free concerts. *Photo by Chuck Pulin. Used by permission.*

Homemade art in the sixties. Body painting on the eve of an Oregon rock festival. *United Press International Photo. Used by permission.*

Stills (left), Crosby (second from left), Nash and Young. *Photo by Chuck Pulin. Used by permission.*

Bob Dylan and the Band revive rock-n-roll's country roots. *Photo by Chuck Pulin. Used by permission.*

Haight and Ashbury Streets, San Francisco. Flower child's mecca and the center of sixties counterculture. *Wide World Photos. Used by permission.*

People's Park. Street people and students pitched in with rakes, shovels, picks, and other implements to level the ground and beautify the vacant lot appropriated from the University of California, Berkeley, 1969. *Wide World Photos. Used by permission.*

4 | Alternative Life Styles

"Congratulate yourselves if you have done something strange and extravagant and broken the monotony of a decorous age."—Ralph Waldo Emerson

"Our crime was that we were beginning to live a new contagious life style without official authorization. We were tried for being out of control."—Tom Hayden, *Trial*, 1970

Today a friend of mine, Stew Johnson, lives in a $100,000 home in one of those lush Chicago suburbs, half an acre of ex-cornfield well up toward Wisconsin, with a bit of creek and some newly planted shade trees, air conditioning, a garden in which he grows peppers and tomatoes with the help of a garage shelf full of expensive herbicides, pesticides, and fertilizers. He barbecues often on the deck of his house and plays softball in the backyard with his son and mine. He drives an Audi and is a corporate vice-president who defends tax incentives for big business, the profit motive, and Republican politics in general. When he and his blonde wife vacation, they go first-class to the Caribbean or Europe.

He does not appear in even the remotest sense to be a refugee from the sixties.

In fact, during the sixties, you would never have accused Stew of being a child of the times. No beads, no long hair, no marches, and no dope. In 1965 Stew graduated from Cornell University with a degree in chemical engineering and went off to do his duty in Korea; he had been in ROTC at college and had his obligations and was happy enough not to be going to Nam. In 1967 Stew returned home and went looking for a job.

Chemical engineers are different from teachers and philosphers and flower children. They are hardheaded, direct, practical. They think about things like jobs and security and stock options and promotion, which probably explains why they opted for engineering in the first place, which is certainly why they have little time for offing the system. It takes care of them because they make it run. Even in 1967 they made it run.

So Stew interviewed Kodak and General Electric and lots of other giant corporations, looking for a place to fit in and help make it all run.

They would show you this huge room, you know, big as an airplane hangar, all divided up into little cubicles. Each little group of desks

111

was a team, assigned to a special part of the problem, lead by a team leader. He had a special desk for himself, off in the corner. And over each five or eight teams there was a coordinator, and over every five or ten of them was a task force leader, and so on, and so on. An ocean of desks and cubicles and name plates with guys' pictures next to them. And everybody is making $15,000 to start, with insurance and retirement. You work for ten years or so and you get a promotion to team leader and you get a special desk, and in another fifteen years maybe you outlast six other guys and become a coordinator, and maybe after forty years, when you're ready to retire, they make you a task force leader or head overseer or something.

Stew freaked. He took a job with a fledgling corporation of five or six people that offered him a fistful of stock at a penny a share and the chance to travel to Europe and to bust his ass fifteen hours a day seven days a week and maybe to make a decent salary sometime if the company worked out. (It did not, incidentally. It folded, and reconstituted itself, and was bought out by a Swiss conglomerate. Stew moved to another relatively independent position with another relatively small corporation, where he is happy.)

"I just couldn't see myself getting locked into that kind of [big corporate] structure for the rest of my life," he explained. That is the voice of the sixties speaking. Because one thing that everybody agreed on—blacks and whites, lower and middle and upper classes, protesters and flower children, and chemical engineers, and politicians—was that there *had* to be a better way, with all this technology lying around just waiting for people to put it to use. Or at least there had to be a different way that would turn out to be a hell of a lot more *interesting* than the programmed rise of the organization man. And Stew Johnson, sensible engineer-businessman not prone to excess or romanticism, was articulating an attitude not substantially different from the desire for alternative possibilities expressed by Phil Ochs in "The World Began in Eden but It Ended in Los Angeles" (1968).

> Don't you think it's time that we were leaving
> For another chance, another place to start?
> Desperate once they went across the ocean
> And they wondered how it would all turn out.

> "My best education has been living with my children who lived through the nineteen-sixties. They opened up worlds for me that I was reluctant even to understand."—Doris Bernstein, Illinois League of Women Voters, 1977

The sixties felt the typical young, American, Western, post-Renaissance itch to try something different, look at something new, search out another chance, another place to start.

The compulsive need to experiment in alternatives underlay *Easy Rider*, the great sixties quest after an America transformed by pot, sex, hippie communes, and travel ("In the end she will surely know I was not born to follow"). It underlay Stokely Carmichael's black power, with its vision of a new black society with black values and black institutions. It underlay John Kennedy's New Frontier and Lyndon Johnson's Great Society. It explains the middle-class kids who tossed over their parents' affluence for (usually temporary) poverty in San Francisco, the Peace Corps, or rural communes; and it explains the guy who renovates a stone farmhouse rather than buy into a newer or older Levittown. It explains acid and acid rock and perhaps even the protest demonstration. Politically and socially (and musically) we were all looking for an alternative, all vaguely disaffected with established patterns of doing things. The only argument, really, was how far we had to go: some were only bored or impatient; others had more serious objections and more particularized alternatives. Some thought we might get by with minor repairs to the roof and foundation; others were for starting from scratch.

> "One generation abandons the enterprises of another like stranded vessels."—Henry David Thoreau

"The gifted seem to thrive on problem-solving and often select more difficult solutions over easier ones."—AP news story

What we had in mind was something a little more humane, a little more free. Less of "a niche for everyone and everyone in his niche." More flexibility. Fewer rules. We wanted more pluralism, as the professionals say. And we wanted it now. Youth is fleeting. A faculty-student committee on the feasibility of black studies three, four, five years down the road meant nothing at all to the militant junior occupying the dean's office. "How many years until I'm thirty, man? And what good is it all then? We could all be *dead* by then."

> (The mentality of a generation that has known the threat of instant annihilation not as some terrible novelty but as one of life's givens.)

So the sixties exploded across the universe in every conceivable direction at once, gathering momentum and distance as the years unwound, intent on traveling as far and as fast and as many as possible, a shower of stars, a dizzying show of colors and free forms, beauty and a fragile light and something very, very memorable. The campaign of 1968. Flower power. Carnaby Street. Soul. Communes. LSD. Black power. The underground press and underground radio. Free love. Free dope. Free universities. Free speech. The surfer idyl of girls and cars, sea and sand. Meditation. Poster art. The be-in, the teach-in, the love-in. The ugly of beauty and the beauty of ugly. Commitment. Intensity. Transcendence. Self.

Motion.

> For everything there is a season
> and a time for every matter under heaven:
> a time to be born, and a time to die;
> a time to plant, and a time to pluck up what is planted;
> a time to kill, and a time to heal;
> a time to break down, and a time to build up;
> a time to weep, and a time to laugh;
> a time to mourn, and a time to dance;
> a time to cast away stones, and a time to gather stones together;
> a time to embrace, and a time to refrain from embracing;
> a time to seek, and a time to lose;
> a time to keep, and a time to cast away;
> a time to rend, and a time to sew;
> a time to keep silence, and a time to speak;
> a time to love, and a time to hate;
> a time for war, and a time for peace.
> —Ecclesiastes 3:1–8

"Turn, turn, turn"—the Byrds

One of the many alternatives explored by the sixties was dope. The mind expanders dropped, licked, smoked, popped, snorted, ate—marijuana, peyote, LSD, STP, mescaline, morning glory seeds, Benzedrine, Dexedrine, Nembutal, to break through the inhibitions of some twenty-five centuries of rationalist Western thought, to make you *see* things, really *see* things, for the first time, to make you sensitive to touch and feel and sound and smell, to pry loose the lid clamped on the imagination and the senses by reason. "LSD equals love." Ditto pot, coke, uppers and downers, even—in extreme arguments—hard drugs. (Although Paul Kantner called heroin "an ugly drug, a downer. It makes people boring.") When sixties heads talked dope, they were talking liberation of the emotional and sensory self from the prison of intellect. They were talking self-discovery, intensified awareness. They were talking about a door to new perceptions.

> (Which is why so much dope was given away to friends, free. Because you wanted to open for them the worlds that had been opened for you. And it was so beautiful to watch them when the dream came.)

"I am and, for as long as I can remember, I have always been a poor visualizer," wrote Aldous Huxley in his brief statement on mescaline, *The Doors of Perception* (1954). It is a learned book, larded almost to the point of incomprehensibility with big words and psychological jargon. But, like the equally obscure *La Guardia Report on Marijuana* (1944), it enjoyed an immense underground circulation. Dense though its prose may be, *The Doors of Perception* gave sixties heads much of their theory of drug use. (One of the things we have most forgotten about the sixties was the capacity for heavy, learned, mind-fatiguing, and just plain boring research and argument, as long as the effort was to good purpose.)

"Words, even the pregnant words of poets, do not evoke pictures in my mind," Huxley continued. "No hypnagogic visions greet me on the verge of sleep." Which, he concluded, was to be expected for he was too much the thinker and the scholar to be imaginative. His very language betrays where he was coming from: "How can a man at the extreme limits of ectomorphy and cerebrotonia ever put himself in the place of one at the limits of endomorphy and viscerotonia, or . . . share the feelings of one who stands at the limits of mesomorphy and somatotonia?" *But,* one mescaline pill and suddenly three flowers in a small vase become "what Adam had seen on the morning of his creation—the miracle, moment by moment, of naked existence." Colors are indescribably brilliant, a return to "the perceptual innocence of childhood, when the sensum was not immediately and automatically subordinated to the concept." The will suffers a change for the worse, and the causes for which one would ordinarily act and suffer seem irrelevant. The outer world becomes the inner world and vice versa. All things sensory—touch, taste, sound—become sharp and fresh and new.

The cause of this, Huxley argued (borrowing from Bergson), is that the brain functions normally as a screen. Its job is not to create but to shut off. It is a reducing valve that limits our perception to only a minute portion of what might be called the mind at large. Drugs—in Huxley's case mescaline—unlock the doors to perception of total reality, to all those sensory reports that our brain, in making us concentrate, filters out. The drug allows our attention to wander virtually undisciplined over the infinity of things we would normally see but not see, hear but not hear, think but disregard. Under the influence of the drug we cannot think, for thought requires disciplined attention, narrowly reduced sensory input. But while we cannot think logically under its influence, the drug opens the door to intensified feeling and offers an escape from the world of the intellect, from lives "at the worst so painful, at the best so monotonous, poor and limited that the urge to escape . . . is and has always been one of the principal appetites of the soul."

What Huxley said of mescaline, others said of the less esoteric hallucinogens, marijuana and acid. The effects of LSD, British social historian Peter Laurie concluded, are "to break down the processes that limit and channel sense impressions in the deeper interpretive layers of the brain, allowing neuronal excitation to spread indiscriminately sideways." Investigator William Braden reported in his own clinical jargon that acid "stops time. Or in any case, it ceases to be important. . . . The subject is content to exist in the moment—in the here and now. . . . The sense of personal ego is utterly lost. Awareness of individual identity evaporates . . . is expanded to include all that is seen and all that is not seen."

Dr. Jiri Roubichek observed, "LSD inhibits conditioned reflexes."

"Sense of time alters and profound epistemological and ontological disjunctions ensue," wrote English sociologist Jock Young.

"Feed your head," sang the Jefferson Airplane.

"Yippies take acid at breakfast to bring us closer to reality," Jerry Rubin announced.

As with all other sixties explorations, the pharmaceutical revolution proceeded at various paces in various locales. Pot, which had been a staple in places like New Orleans and Greenwich Village since the depression (it was a cheaper high than opium or cocaine), was virtually unknown in white midwestern society until well into the decade. Hollywood, depressed housewives, and the high, fast society had been plenty familiar with downers (Miltown, Equanil, Doriden, Nembutal) even in the fifties. Uppers were popular among college students cramming for exams, musicians on tour, and athletes psyching themselves up for football games. ("Most NFL trainers do more dealing in these drugs than the average junky," wrote former St. Louis linebacker Dave Meggyesy in his book *Out of Their League*.) Mescaline and even lysergic acid diethylamide had been around for over a decade when serious research into their psychotherapeutic capacities began in 1959–1960, bringing them somewhat prematurely to the attention of an eager young and a dour old (and lawmaking) public. In 1962 acid was a rumored secret known firsthand to only a handful of initiates; by 1966 it had become an open secret on both coasts (and the bedrock of hippie society); by the end of the decade, with feds closing in on all sides, probably the only college campus in the country where you *couldn't* buy a tab of acid would have been Bob Jones University. Pot and pills were everywhere, popped and smoked openly.

"An epidemic of drug abuse is sweeping the nation," preached Roland Berg to readers of *Look* magazine, providing conclusive proof that by August 1967 at least the pharmaceutical revolution was a *fait accompli*.

High priest of the movement was Timothy Leary, who inherited the miter and crosier from William S. Burroughs, legendary prophet of an already gone decade and a goner generation. Leary began the sixties decently enough as a Harvard professor, respected, up-and-coming, son of an important Massachusetts family and promising psychologist, future guaranteed by the big H's Center for Research in Personality. Which all goes to show how deceptive appearances can be: Leary ended the decade in a California jail on what could have run into a ten-year sentence for possession of marijuana. Between alpha and omega came heroic proselytizing for the faith, the

International Foundation for Internal Freedom (IF-IF), and IF-IF's house organ, the *Psychedelic Review*.

Mescaline! Experimental Mysticism! Mushrooms! Ecstasy! LSD-25! Expansion of Consciousness! Phantastica! Transcendence! Hashish! Visionary Botany! Ololiuqui! Physiology of Religion! Internal Freedom! Morning Glory! Politics of the Nervous System!

You can see why Harvard canned Leary in 1963. You may also grasp why the east coast immediately deified him, consuming wholesale his *Psychedelic Review* and his books and his message of the mid-sixties: "My advice to myself and to everyone else, particularly young people, is to turn on, tune in, and drop out." A slogan was born.

It was the dropping out that irritated the establishment, which stood to lose prodigiously in such a re-creation of the American soul. Aware that a society turned *on* to pot, acid, mescaline (and, more important, to the spiritual values that Huxley, Leary, and the lower orders of clergy promised would follow) would be a society turned *off* to General Motors and Wall Street, it struggled mightily against any attempt to legalize marijuana and acted quickly to illegalize the new danger, acid. Caffeine, alcohol, nicotine, an occasional adulterous affair—these are officially sanctioned recreational addictions with which the system rewards its faithful (or anesthetizes them). They are token payoffs, necessary, protected by tacit agreement, so that even when booze inhibits an executive's performance the establishment sends him quietly upstairs to dry out rather than toss him publicly in the slammer. But acid, mescaline, and even pot were during the sixties (and are today) seen as subversive to the organized system, vehicles of transcendence, and therefore unacceptable as token rewards or opiates of the people.

(The establishment is right in seeing these drugs as dangerous to it. Drugs underlay virtually every nonpolitical revolution of the sixties. Wasn't it our drug-heightened sensibilities that made color so important and sound and touch? And weren't augmented senses of taste and touch and sound and feel at the root of the revolutions in clothing, music, even sex and life style that constituted the greening of America during the sixties? Without drugs the counterculture of the sixties is unimaginable, and it was the growth of a visible and apparently viable counterculture that so unnerved the establishment during that decade.)

Generally speaking, sixties drug songs saw dope as a means of personal liberation rather than as a mere kick or a reward. The Airplane's "White Rabbit" (1967) is typical in this respect. "One pill makes you larger" (uppers, and a reference to one side of the caterpillar's mushroom) "and the other makes you small" (downers, the other side—of the mushroom, of course); the pothead caterpillar calls; and logic and proportion are warped all out of shape—here is the classic description of a drug experience. Yet the advice is to feed your head, an invitation to wake up to the new realities and personal liberation that drugs could usher in. The song is practically a cop from Huxley.

The Beatles' "Lucy in the Sky" (1967) is another trip song—what with taxi and train and boat, and the tangerine trees and marmalade skies, and the loss of time and the distortion of normal proportions, and the *music*, if nothing else, and of course the LSD of Lucy, sky, and diamonds, a trip song that is an invitation to discover what acid can turn us on to: our senses of touch and taste and sight and smell and wonder. "A Day in the Life," trip song number two on the *Sgt. Pepper* album, is a plea to turn on not so much to dope as spiritual awareness, transcendence, love. The Yellow Submarine led to Pepperland and to the heroic victory of yes over the Blue Meanies. And "Dr. Robert" "helps you to understand, to see yourself." ("There's this fellow in New York," Paul explained, "and in the States we'd hear people say, 'You can get everything off him; any pills you want. . . .' That's what Dr. Robert is all about, just a pill doctor who sees you all right.")

Dylan's "Rainy Day Women #12 & 35" isn't so much a dope song as it is a pun—and a useful pun at that—and a protest song in the mold of "Subterranean Homesick Blues": they stone you when you're trying to be good, and ultimately everybody must get stoned.

> (You have to be careful about dope songs. There was a lot of pressure to recant, and a lot of FCC paranoia, which meant a lot of bullshit all ways. Roger McGuinn equivocated on "Eight Miles High," Paul McCartney explained away "Lucy in the Sky," and Peter Yarrow excused "Puff, the Magic Dragon," but very few children of the sixties bought any of their excuses because we all knew about the heat from the FCC, so naturally somebody was going to have to say something *public* for the straights who couldn't grasp the metaphoric significance of dope.)

Drug songs that *were* drug songs came in several varieties.

Roger McGuinn's "5-D," which titles a 1966 Byrds album, sounds like a straight cop from Timothy Leary's prose as it hypes a drug-induced insight into the fifth dimension.

All my two-dimensional boundaries were gone. . . .
But I found my senses still working
And as I continued to drop through the hole

I found all surroundings to show me
That joy innocently is
Just be quiet and feel it all around you
And I opened my heart to the whole universe
And I found it was loving
And I saw the great blunder my teachers had made
Scientific delirium madness.

The sixties abounded in frank celebrations: the Association's "Along Comes Mary" (1966), the Strawberry Alarm Clock's "Incense and Peppermints" (1967), Steppenwolf's "Faster Than the Speed of Life" (1968), less popular songs like the Rainy Daze's "Acapulco Gold," Country Joe McDonald's 1967 "Acid Commercial" and his 1967 pot commercial "Bass Strings," and the early classic "I Couldn't Get High" (Ken Weaver, 1965): "So I threw down my pipe as mad as could be, and I gobbled up a cube of LSD."

Donovan Leitch was a master salesman: "Sunshine Superman," "Sunny Goodge Street," "Mellow Yellow" (a myth—the mighty Chiquita will not take you higher—but who cared?). And the Stones: "Jumpin' Jack Flash [Methedrine] is a gas, gas, gas." And Creedence Clearwater Revival, rollin' on the river in "Proud Mary," riding the flyin' spoon in "Out My Back Door."

There were also protests. Protests about price, as in the Jefferson Airplane's "3/5 of a Mile in 10 Seconds": "Sometimes the price is $65." Protests about addiction, as in the Stones' "Sister Morphine" or Joni Mitchell's great "Cold Blue Steel and Sweet Fire" (both bittersweet). Protests about drug laws, as in Graham Nash's "Prison Song" or Phil Ochs's "Miranda." Protests about dealers, as in Steppenwolf's "Pusher Man," which came packaged in sixties consciousness with *Easy Rider*.

Occasionally there were warnings: "You're gonna trip, stumble, and fall," sang the Mamas and Papas in 1966.

> (Be it noted here that the sixties were scrupulous about bad drugs. PA announcements warned Woodstock celebrants against bad acid. Dr. Hippocrates warned *Berkeley Barb* readers against cyclopropane and other dangerous highs. "Speed kills" was as common a slogan as "Turn on, tune in, and drop out.")

A fistful of lyrics turned drugs into women, until the two fused as had cars and girls in the fifties: the Airplane's "Plastic Fantastic Lover," the Stones' "Lady Jane," the Association's "Along Comes Mary," Lucy, Mother Mary, the Rainy Day Women.

Another fistful of sixties songs explored the obvious parallels between the world of drugs and the world of children's and fantasy literature. Thus you got a dopey version of Pooh and Alice (and Puff).

The best of the drug songs was undoubtedly Dylan's "Mr. Tambourine Man." Mr. Tambourine Man is the pusher and the drug and the musician and the music all at once. And the magic, swirling, sensual ship on which the weary Dylan trips is at once the drug and the music and the act of making the music. Ultimately it is Bob Dylan himself, the same Bob Dylan who stands blind and enervated, leaden footed in the empty streets of the first stanza, who provides escape. The spell is cast, as much the magic of music as of pot, of art as of drugs, and we and Dylan and the sixties are off, escaping, swinging madly across the sun, free and alive in a reefer, in a song, in the interior of our minds, in the person of Dylan.

> Then take me disappearin' through the smoke rings of my mind,
> Down the foggy ruins of time, far past the frozen leaves,
> The haunted, frightened trees, out to the windy beach,
> Far from the twisted reach of crazy sorrow.
> Yes, to dance beneath the diamond sky with one hand waving free,
> Silhouetted by the sea, circled by the circus sands,
> With all memory and fate driven deep beneath the waves,
> Let me forget about today until tomorrow.

Another major area of sixties liberation was sex.

> "The key energy for our revolution is erotic. A free person is one whose erotic energy has been liberated and can be expressed in increasingly more beautiful, complex ways. Sexual revolution is not just part of the atmosphere of freedom that is generating within kids. I think it is the center of it."—Timothy Leary

Granted, the sexual revolution is by now a commonplace—recorded, quantified, tabulated, sloganized, popularized, established. Nor did the sixties invent sex, or even free love, or even "recreational sex." The twenties were full of free love; beat subcultures of the fifties were full of free love; and despite Debbie Reynolds' everlasting virginity the fifties mainstream must have known how to enjoy itself.

In addition, it is in the media interest to hype sex. Not just *Playboy* and its assorted imitations, all media. Sex sells books and magazines, and sex—properly distorted—can be used to sell cars, clothes, perfume, aftershave. But to use sex this way you have to convince the audience that everybody else is getting lots more than he/she. Otherwise, he/she won't have any reason to buy your aphrodisiac magazine or movie or sports car or aftershave or cereal. Another thing about sex: people invent a lot because that's what they're most uptight about, even today. And, most important, the sixties were not all of a piece sexually. The decade began in innocence and ended in experience; 1962 sex was plenty different from 1969 sex.

(And from 1979 sex, which raises another point: unlike most other experiments, the sexual revolution continued into the seventies. Not as a media event, but as a significant transmutation of male-female relationships. It's had tough going, the sexual revolution, and I suspect there's less raw sex abroad now than then, but from a seventies perspective even 1969 sex seems slightly crude and quite chauvinistic.)

The decade began in full retreat from the musical and sexual revolution of rock-n-roll. Elvis, as somebody once remarked, told us in the mid-fifties that there was a way of making it without formalities, which is essentially what rock-n-roll was all about and why it generated such hostility among grown-ups. But by 1960 the establishment commanded the field: when Elvis returned from the army and retreated into shlock rock and bad movies, every one of us realized that he'd had his balls cut off along with his hair. Rock-n-roll had been prettified into Dick Clark–promoted cuteness. By and large we were not far from soppy fifties hits. "Goin' to the chapel, and we're gonna get married," warbled the Dixie Cups in 1964. Bad girls did, but *nice* girls still did not, and the distinction between the two was still drawn. Most women in most colleges still had curfews (sign out with your date's name, your destination, your intention, so that the dean of women can check up on you), students were expelled for shacking up, and girls were expelled from straight society for getting pregnant. Virginity and the Puritan code of abstinence were still big in the hearts of women and men and most of all parents.

Couples did not live with each other. Young people expected as a matter of course to get married and raise kids. Except, maybe, in the Village and other centers of beatdom, where free love was neither more nor less popular than it had been for most of the twentieth century.

The seeds of the sexual revolution, however, were already sown. First was the memory of that sexual awareness that burst into middle-class consciousness in fifties rock-n-roll music, a memory not quite forgotten in the 1960 sellout of rock-n-roll or in the high seriousness of civil rights or nuclear disarmament protest. Second, there was a general exporting of Bohemian attitudes in the folk music flowering of the early sixties, which brought Village mores along with Village folk music into the field of vision of Americans from Kankakee to Miami. Third, there was *Playboy* magazine, which, though it certainly was *not* sixties sex (being too glossy, too commercial, and generally too plastic), was a spur to sixties sex. It was an accepted, widely circulated publication devoted to preaching sexual liberation (of men) and is not to be underestimated as a root of the sixties sexual revolution.

Several other factors were important, perhaps crucial: developments in contraception ("The pill, the pill, they're gonna bless the pill") and in the treatment of VD, which made sex safer and infinitely more fun, and a new assertiveness among the young, an emerging sense of me and now. This attitude was most prominent in areas like civil rights and nuclear disarmament, but it was bound to spill over into matters such as sex. Gratification of personal desires began to take precedence over what mommy, daddy, church, university, or society set down. Tomorrow being irrelevant, there was no point in preserving one's virginity. If desegregation could not wait, why should getting laid?

Initially the sexual revolution was plenty male, plenty macho. "I am just a poor boy, trying to connect," sang Dylan, telling his girl that she could go or she could stay, but if she decided to stay it was for the night. Take it or leave it. "You just happened to be there, that's all," he sang in "One of Us Must Know (Sooner or Later)." Clinging vines—which included all women who looked for something beyond the quick, convenient lay—were shunned with a callous "it ain't me, babe." The assumption was still that good girls did not and bad girls did; you had to *work*, coax, trick, cajole, and otherwise con a girl into bed. And it was masculine to be strong, aloof, invulnerable: don't offer anything that might be considered an entangling promise.

> (Women, for their part, were advised by the Excitors in 1963 to swallow their pride and "tell him that you're never gonna leave him, tell him that you're always gonna love him." Men screwed and forgot; women loved and were true.)

This aggressive male principle remained fairly prominent in rock, and in sixties thought, well into the decade. "Show me the way to the next little girl," the Doors sang in 1967 in a resurrected Brecht-Weill tune. "This could be the last time," the Stones bullied in 1965. "Bang, Bang," you shot me down, Cher sang suggestively in 1966. At the end of the decade, the aggressive, male, brutal Stones wrote a couple of the most aggressive, male, and brutal sixties songs: "Parachute Woman" ("Won't you blow me out?") and "Honky Tonk Women" ("She blew my nose and then she blew my mind"). Sex was out in the open, all right, but relations between the sexes had not changed appreciably.

The other tradition, that of good girls wooed and won with promises of eternal affection (and eternal fidelity), also survived the decade surprisingly well: the Temptations' "My Girl" and Herman's "Mrs. Brown You've Got a Lovely Daughter" (1965), the Righteous Brothers' "Soul and Inspiration" and the Association's "Cherish" (1966), the Association's "Never My Love" and Stevie Wonder's "I Was Made to Love Her" (1967), O. C. Smith's shlocky "Little Green Apples" and Herb Alpert's shlockier "This Guy's in

Love with You" (1968). The fact of the matter is that at the end of the decade, many sixties people found themselves married and raising kids.

A counter tradition, however, had developed over the course of the decade, a tradition of experimentation in all kinds of sexual arrangements, a tradition of open sexuality that obliterated or reversed the old bad girl–good girl distinction, a tradition that makes sixties people still think that there ought to be no rules in the bedroom no matter how they act elsewhere.

The Beatles' "Norwegian Wood," for example, is noteworthy in that in 1965 it presented an aggressive woman who was not aggressive: "I once had a girl, or should I say she once had me." More noteworthy, Nancy Sinatra's 1966 hit "These Boots Are Made for Walkin'"—a shlock pop song that made the rock charts and was revolutionary—presented woman as assertive, independent, even liberated. Maybe even equal. Certainly she was not about to put up with a lot of macho bullshit. "We Can Work It Out," from the Beatles in 1966, also implied equality between the sexes, a direct contrast to something like Dylan's "It Ain't Me, Babe." The Airplane's "Somebody to Love" and Otis Redding's "Respect" (popularized by Aretha Franklin in 1967) said that both men *and* women need somebody to love. Both men *and* women deserve respect.

We were approaching the day when either sex could honestly say, "I love you." Or, "Let's fuck."

"How sweet it is to be loved by you," sang Jr. Walker and the All Stars in 1966.

"Set the night on fire," suggested the Doors in 1967.

"Witness the quickness with which we get it on," sang Stephen Stills in "Carry On" (1969). It sure beat holding hands.

What we like to think of as sixties sex (*late* sixties sex) was a lot different from the lovemaking of our fathers. For one thing, it was a lot more out front. Nowhere is this difference more obvious than in sixties invitations to make it. This kind of song has been around a long time. But sixties invitations show just how very much out front love and sex were. In the twenties you got indirect and very witty invites like Cole Porter's "birds do it, bees do it, even educated fleas do it, let's fall in love." Clever, sophisticated, so slick that you almost forgot what you were about. Metaphoric, because in the twenties you couldn't come right out and say, "Let's fuck"; you had to be subtle. Ditto the thirties and the forties and even the rock-n-roll fifties. The metaphors changed, but metaphoric indirection remained: "Do You Want to Dance?" "Let's Dance." "Rock me all night long." "Good golly, Miss Molly, sure like to ball!" (Little Richard was careful to explain that "ball" in this song referred to dancing—but what he didn't say was that dancing was fifties slang for getting it on.)

And the metaphoric covers continued into the early sixties, with the Beatles' "I'm Happy Just to Dance with You" (1964) and "Drive My Car"

(1966). Gradually, however, sex came out of the closet. "Let's Spend the Night Together," sang the Stones (but not on Ed Sullivan's television show, where Mick Jagger changed it to "Let's spend some time together") in 1967. "I Want You," sang the Beatles in 1969, and Bob Dylan in 1966. "Why Don't We Do It in the Road?" (followed on the Beatles' white album, with typical Beatles humor, by "I Will") represented something of an ultimate in naked invitations to sex.

> Why don't we do it in the road?
> No one will be watching us,
> Why don't we do it in the road?

"Let's Get It On," invited Marvin Gaye, carrying the revolution in frankness into 1973.

This kind of directness was a far cry from the games people played throughout the fifties. The pleasure, sixties people decided, came not in the yes-no-maybe, coax-me-a-little-more struggle, but in the simple and spectacular act of getting it on (preferably while high, which doubled your pleasure by doubling the fun). And it got things out in the open: you could either yes get it on, or no not get it on.

Another thing about sixties sex was that it was innovative. "No holds barred experimentation," one veteran called it. "If you can't be with the one you love," Stephen Stills suggested, "love the one you're with." "You better find somebody to love," the Airplane warned.

(Certainly not your wife or husband. Marriage didn't fare very well in sixties sexual theory: it was too straight, too restrictive, too traditional. Most sex was premarital or extramarital. "There's so many times I've played around," admitted Peter, Paul, and Mary in—would you believe?—John Denver's "Leavin' on a Jet Plane," but playing around seemed no reason in the world not to go ahead and get married.)

In "Triad," David Crosby sang about a sexual threesome. In "Stray Cat," the Stones suggested the same arrangement: your wild friend—bring her upstairs and she can join in, too. "Love your neighbor 'til his wife gets home," suggested the Doors in "Soft Parade" (1969). And earlier (1966), "Break on through to the other side." In fact, most Doors songs were loaded with Freudian sex and sexual symbolism—"The End" (1967) features a ritual killing of father and balling of mother and sister. As the decade reached its conclusion, Mick Jagger moved increasingly in the direction of androgyny, a mode that carried into the seventies. Even seediness had its moment in songs like the Jaggers' "Rapper" and "Vehicle," by the Ides of March (1970): "I'm the friendly stranger in the black sedan"; and in Laugh-In's dirty old man Tyrone.

Through all this, the grown-ups assumed that the world was going to hell, sex was losing its mystery, love was losing its sanctity, and male-female relationships were becoming cheap. But to the sixties, the new sex was a supermystical experience that got richer and richer the more you explored it; or an avenue to understanding (what the Bible would call *knowing*); or a terrific time. Even the last was groovy: the sixties, in the matter of sex as elsewhere, saw nothing wrong with having a good time. Today. Now. Before the Bomb explodes or you turn thirty.

The sixties also enthusiastically explored flower power. Beautiful people, tribes, flower children, the love generation—hippies came literally from the shadows in 1967 to take the world by surprise. Suddenly they were everywhere (or seemed to be): New York, San Francisco, Philadelphia, Detroit, London, but most of all on television and in magazines. Overnight hippie culture became synonymous with drugs and sex and music, and anyone who smoked pot, grooved to the Airplane, and smelled suspiciously of sex was a hippie freak.

A whole generation
With a new explanation
People in motion
People in motion

Some of the popular conception of hippiedom was of course myth. Flower culture did involve large doses of drugs, sex, and music, but it's a mistake to assume that hedonism in any or all of these forms was the core of hippie philosophy. Also, there's nothing particularly hippie about sex, as the midnight hustlers along Haight Street quickly discovered. To the extent that sexuality was marketed or substituted for deeper, more personal communication, sex of some kinds was outside hippie philosophy. "Promiscuity? That's such a cute word. Oh wow!" answered a San Francisco freak when asked the obvious question by a straight reporter. "What is promiscuous, man? Sex without feeling, without tuning in?"

The girls of the great San Francisco acid rock songs were different, really, from the girls of straighter rock. The "California Girls" extolled by the Beach Boys were broads, bodies ripe and ready and willing and able. Ditto, to grab another random example, the girls of Ricky Nelson's 1962 "Travelin' Man." Hippie chicks were barefoot, ethereal creatures, beautiful *heads*, jeweled hair and visionary eyes, whistling, laughing, dancing, and living on the street—as in the Grateful Dead's "Golden Road"—or "children of Orpheus" called to a trip of love—as in John Phillips's "Strange Young Girls" (1966).

Strange young girls
Colored with sadness
Eyes of innocence
Hiding their madness
Walking the Strip
Sweet, soft, and placid
Offering their youth
On an altar of acid. . . .

Gentle young girls
Holding hands walking
Wisdom flows childlike
While softly talking.

Emphasis was on the mind, the spirit (and the clothes). The body? Well, everyone comes with the same basic body, don't they?

As for drugs, they were everywhere in the sixties. As the Who's Jimmy observed in *Quadrophenia*, each has his own poison. Your average hippie was pretty choosy about her dope: pot was a black-bread staple, acid she used regularly, heroin was a bad trip. Speed killed. She almost never touched hard liquor. And although there might have been a lot of dope floating around the hippie community (and didn't some of the best sixties dope songs come from hippieland, along with a few antiwar numbers?), in a pinch it could have been done without. "I don't need Timothy Leary or LSD," Jerry Garcia once told an interviewer. "Nobody in the Haight-Ashbury follows Leary. [They all followed Ken Kesey, who was also an acid freak. But let it pass.] The people here would have done this thing without acid, without Leary. I would have been a member of some weird society wherever I went. Don't ask why. Don't try to analyze it, man. It just is, that's all. This is where we're at. This is our trip." So acid was not essential.

Likewise, hippie life was neither consumption without production nor do your own thing and screw the other guy. Most hippies worked occasionally (for pay or other rewards), and most lived relatively structured lives, with group work, group play, group meditation, group dancing and music, group meals. Thoughtless self-indulgence was a drag. A Digger, part of that selfless community that undertook to feed hippie tribes in San Francisco and elsewhere during the golden years of flower power, reflected on the end of free food in 1967.

> Well, man, it took a lot of organization to get that done. We had to scuffle to get the food. Then the chicks or somebody had to prepare it. Then we got to serve it. A lot of people got to do a lot of things at the right time or it doesn't come off. Well, it got so that people weren't doing it. I mean a cat wouldn't let us have his truck when we needed it or some chick is grooving somewhere else and can't help out. Now you hate to get into a power bag and start telling people what to do, but without that, man, well."—John Howard, *The Cutting Edge*

The real essence of the hippie life style was community, the social expression of a wider metaphysical truth, love.

> "San Francisco's secret was not the dancing, the lightshows, the posters, the long sets, or the complete lack of a stage act, but the idea that all of them together were the creation and recreation of

a community. Everybody did their thing and all
things were equal."—Michael Lydon

Community was what made hippie life so very positive, so alluring to
middle-class and upper middle-class orphans who had never known real
community in their secure, establishment, suburban dwellings. And why
hippie philosophy so vehemently rejected social structures that tend to isolate individuals, while *at the same time* it developed intricate and often rigid
(but *unifying*) rituals within the community. And why the hippie rejected
all the freight of goods that require specialization (and thus isolation) to pile
up. And why he rejected competition, which pits neighbor against neighbor, separates man from wife from children in the mad rush to get ahead.
And why the hippie felt and loved and danced and sang and shared—her
dope, her pad, her music, her mate. The values of hippie philosophy were
those that tend toward community; the values rejected by hippie thought,
those that create competition and isolation. In this respect the long-haired,
delicately clothed, dispossessed, possessionless flower children of the late
sixties were the culmination of a dream that had been building through the
late fifties and all the sixties. They embodied more perfectly than any other
sixties experiment the search for an alternative to establishment thought and
establishment life. *All* children of the sixties saw in the hippie an ideal of
love, peace, and joy, which they sought, consciously or unconsciously, to
approximate.

> "The Revolution has ceased to be an ideological
> concern. Instead, people are trying it out right
> now—communism in small communities, new
> family organization. A million people in America
> and another million in England and Europe. . . .
> How do they recognize each other? Not always by
> beards, long hair, bare feet or beads. The signal is
> a bright and tender look; calmness and gentleness,
> freshness and ease of manner."—Gary Snyder

So the communities sprang up, mostly in large urban areas with decadent and decaying cores—Los Angeles, Boston, New York, London, especially San Francisco—but also occasionally in rural areas—the hills of Big
Sur, upstate New York, northern California. A return to the romanticized
tribalism of the American Indian. A return to the values of the American
frontier, lost somewhere between the dawn of the twentieth century and
1967, which require you to open your home and your heart to that wagon
struggling up the trail and when you see your neighbor carryin' somethin' to
help him with his load.

> (Like all other revolutions, the hippie revolution
> was in many respects a return to the past, a con-
> servative revolution. Gridley Wright, a west coast

high priest and founder of the Strawberry Fields
community, began as a William F. Buckley–Yale
University conservative.)

Hippiedom represented a threat to the establishment far more dangerous
than free sex, loud music, even drugs. People who argued that the state can
tolerate hippies because they drop out and are thus no threat to the power
structure were misinformed, Paul Goodman argued.

> Proportionate to its numbers, this group is by far the most harassed,
> beat up, and jailed by the police. Negroes go scot free in comparison.
> The social response to the demonstrating Negroes is, primarily,
> "Why don't they go away?" It is at the point of riot that the deep
> anxiety begins to be aroused. But with the hippies there is a gut reac-
> tion from the beginning—they are dirty, indecent, shiftless; they
> threaten the self-justification of the system.

Well, what else could you expect from the mainstream? Hippies were
not compelled by money, fame, or power. They did not consume. They did
not abide by rules, listen to orders. They insisted on choices other than
those offered by General Motors, General Foods, and political parties.
There were the Diggers and the Provos handing out free food, free clothing,
free dope, a free place to sleep. Hippie bands played loud. "We spent two
years with loud, and we've spent six months with deafening" (Garcia
again). Pads full of no furniture, no food, no television sets, just people and
animals and cheap posters and dope. No consumption and thus no commitment to making the system run. Public nudity and open sex and thus an end
to the sublimated sexuality with which the system powers itself. Lots of play
and thus an end to the Puritan work ethic. Politics? The only way to end the
war is for everybody to turn his back and say, "Fuck it."

"What you represent to them is Freedom," lawyer Jack Nicholson explained to Captain America and Billy in *Easy Rider*, taking a toke and
spreading America before them. "But talkin' about freedom and bein' free
are two different things." Whop on the head in the middle of the night.

Acid rock—the sound of San Francisco—the sound of the Quicksilver
Messenger Service, the Jefferson Airplane, Big Brother and the Holding
Company, the (Ken Kesey–Owsley Stanley–supported) Grateful Dead,
Moby Grape, Sopwith Camel, the Mind Benders, Weeds, Loading Zone.
Acid rock embodied the whole San Francisco hippie scene, packaged it in a
typically noncommercial package, and carried the alternative across the nation's airwaves and into hearts and minds thousands of miles away. Lyrically there could be no mistaking the philosophy: it got preached again and
again, and again and again. "You better find somebody to love." "We
should be together." "Try to love one another right now." "You're gonna
find some gentle people there" (John Phillips' "San Francisco" served in 1967
as a musical photograph of what had come in the summer of 1966 and what

everybody hoped would return in summers ever after). The celebration of dope and hippie chicks, of San Francisco people (Country Joe's "Janis" and "Grace," for example), of Vietnam protest, of doing it in the road.

Acid rock was at first simple music, in keeping with the sixties' romantic penchant for the uncomplicated, easy, accessible sounds of the people: a few basic chords, some narrow drums, hypnotic repetition. Through the simplicity, however, acid rock wove a Victorian improvisation on exotic instruments—recorder, sitar, mandolin, maybe electric violin or electric oboe —which gave the music its head appeal. The simple became incredibly complex, the raga turned baroque. You listen again and again to the long, rambling jams of the Doors or to the Dead's guitarist Jerry Garcia, snaking his way through time in an almost visual or tactile trip, each phrase a whole new world and no two times do you hear exactly the same thing. Bits and pieces of a dozen different musical styles form an exquisite filigree, sounds as exotic as the instruments themselves, a rifling of the musical past analogous to the hippies' rifling of Salvation Army clothes racks for buckskin vests and feather boas. Color. Variety. A mosaic monument to the fecundity of life in the sixties.

> "Nobody has to fool around with musty old scores, weird notation, and scholarship bullshit; you can just go into a record store and pick a century, pick a country, pick *anything*, and dig it, make it a part of you, add it to the stuff you carry around, and see that it's all music."—Jerry Garcia

Volume was important, too, and length. Acid rock blasted apart the neat world of record company rules and AM radio three-minute singles, warped equipment out of shape, got you right there *inside* the music, where you could chew on each note, really taste and assimilate it. Communication proceeded on several levels at once: you could hear the words (maybe), you could hear the music, and you could actually feel the sound washing over you, pressing against your ribs, throwing you back against the wall.

The personal relationships and organizational structures of acid rock groups, though largely irrelevant to the music they produced, also tended to reflect attitudes of the hippie community. The Airplane, for example, could restructure itself as occasion demanded, splitting into Hot Tuna, Slick and Kantner, reconstituting itself as the Jefferson Starship, picking up at various moments David Crosby, Graham Nash, John Barbata, Papa John Creach. The great, big, brawling, sprawling family that was the Grateful Dead, backstage, onstage, in the big pad at 710 Ashbury. The Family Dog. Country Joe McDonald and the Fish, packed together in New York's Chelsea Hotel for a summer and a fall cutting their second album and living and fighting and being a (troubled) musical community. A random coming and going, everyone free to do his own thing with the group or with other groups (record company lawyers went berserk). Commitment to the moment and the community—but never to record company rules, censorship, and packaging, or to radio programming format, or to money.

Most significantly, a lot of this goodness was free. Acid rock groups confounded, astounded, and otherwise perplexed their recording companies first by laying down tracks far too long and too formless for AM air play, then by filling their songs with four-letter words that would never pass censorship, then by behaving outrageously onstage and off, and then by giving their music away in free concert after free concert. (And, finally, by making a *success* out of this kind of totally noncommercial life style.) All the San Francisco groups did freebies, and in emulation of them all big-name groups and individual performers started giving free concerts just for the art or the fans. The Grateful Dead especially were known for slopping on a few extra hours, even when the concert had been played for a veritable pittance, or for nothing, in the first place. Music became what music always should have been: just a stoned groove, a joy, a great cry of affirmation and love and beauty. I recall one absolutely free Dead concert (much opposed by authorities at Ohio University, incidentally) that began at 7:30 and pumped on until the electricity was cut off at 1:00—when the Dead reassembled themselves elsewhere and played three hours more.

> (Eventually, of course, the predators came, and the rip-offs, and the lawyers, and the heat, and all the harpies of the establishment crushing in from every side, exploiting, abusing, applying the screws and the rack, and there were drug busts and legal hassles about lyrics and who could play with whom, and before you could say "1968" acid rock had gone the way of all flesh, with its light shows and Kesey–Dead–Bill Graham Trips Festivals, and Graham was calling the new breed of rock group a rip-off and closing up shop, and the Dead had gone country, and Joe had left the Fish, and the Haight was full of hustlers and perverts, and that was the end of a brave experiment and a very lovely dream.)

Another sixties experiment that had largely evaporated by the seventies was the movement toward black power. Early on, black power meant higher salaries, more jobs, lots of voters at the polls, lots of clerks working at the courthouse. But as the sixties developed, black power became a concerted effort on the part of the American black community to dissociate itself from any and all elements of the white, racist, American establishment and to develop alternative structures based largely on non-Western (non-white) cultural values. It stressed black control of all institutions that governed black lives: government, businesses, schools. But control was merely a means of insuring substantially different *kinds* of government, business, and education. Local (i.e., black) control of local (i.e., black) schools, a starting point fought every inch of the way not only by city hall politicos and school board members but by teachers' unions as well, was intended to create schools substantially different from white schools. Black power was not a change of color but a change of value. And the qualities most admired by late sixties black power theoreticians were the same qualities valued by the white counterculture: simplicity and even primitivism, spontaneity, ethnic identity, respect for individuality, cooperation rather than competition, joy, love. Black power could have been, should have been, often was as valuable a source of humanization as was the hippie community.

> (In demanding *different* institutions, black power spokesmen recognized immediately that there could be no cooperation with, let alone assimilation into, the white community. Thus, black power represented a major change of direction from earlier civil rights activity, which aimed at black entrance into existing systems. "Thus we reject the goal of assimilation into middle-class America because the values of that class are in themselves anti-humanist and because that class as a social force perpetuates racism."—Stokely Carmichael and Charles Hamilton in *Black Power*, 1967.)

Like flower power, black power drew a lot of heat: wanting *into* the system might mean cramped quarters until a little more room could be carved out of somebody else's backyard; wanting *out* not only deprived the barons of a servant class but also called into question the appropriateness of the whole structure. It questioned the ability of the system to deliver the goods, along with the very desirability of the goods. So the more separatist the movement became, the more black heads got smashed. Compared with hippies, black power people did *not* get off scot-free.

> It's more than just Evolution,
> Well, you know, you got to clean your brain
> —Nina Simone, "Revolution (Part 1)," 1969

The black regeneration (or just plain generation) of black consciousness relied heavily on music. Music, as Malcolm X observed in the late fifties, was the only part of the American scene in which black people traditionally had been free to create. As a consequence, blacks became adept at musical creation and, as LeRoi Jones pointed out, "the most expressive Negro music of any given period will be an exact reflection of what the Negro himself is. It will be a portrait of the Negro in America at that particular time." The goal of black power was to develop the kind of independent spinning of gold from straw in all social and political spheres that Malcolm X had seen taking place in music.

> And in that atmosphere, brothers and sisters, you'd be surprised what will come out of the bosom of this black man. I've seen it happen. I've seen black musicians when they'd be jamming at a jam session with white musicians—a whole lot of difference. The white musician can jam if he's got some sheet music in front of him. He can jam on something that he's heard before. But that black musician, he picks up his horn and starts blowing some sounds that he never thought before. He improvises, he creates, it comes from within. It's his soul; it's that soul music.

The black thinker did not really "come up with a philosophy that nobody has heard of yet," as Malcolm had hoped—"a society, a social system, an economic system, a political system, that is different from anything that exists or has ever existed anywhere on this earth." In retrospect, one senses that the greatest glory of black power was the myths it regenerated and its soul music.

> "Thus close followers of events in the jazz milieu were less than wholly surprised when Stokely Carmichael first raised the cry of 'Black Power!' After all, the disputes, debates, and deluge of literature which Stokely's cry unleashed had for some time been a permanent fixture in the narrower jazz world."—Frank Kofsky, *Black Nationalism and the Revolution in Music*

The musical assertion of black independence had begun in the forties, with the retrieval of jazz from cool white musicians of the proto-beat generation and the infusion of open resentment into black bebop. Kofsky read bebop in its social aspect as "a manifesto of rebellious black musicians unwilling to submit to further exploitation," and he was right. But the proclamation was in musical terms only; social corollaries remained implicit. In fact, even the musical manifesto was aborted by economic dislocations in the postwar period. Then came the ascendance of the cool, disengaged style of Chet Baker, Dave Brubeck, the west coast jazz crowd, which meant that the wild, ranging, engaged, *hot* style of hard bop was as out as the literary extravagancies of Jack Kerouac.

With the sixties, however, out came in, and everyone realized, in the words of the poet Don L. Lee ("But He Was Cool, or: he even stopped for green lights"), "to be black is to be very-hot." And with the release in 1960 of Ben E. King's "Spanish Harlem" came sweet soul music.

Soul music was the black state of mind throughout the sixties. Rhythm and blues, the black sound of the fifties, was dated or had been co-opted by white rock-n-roll. Blues seemed vaguely rural, southern, and antiquated. But soul was the contemporary expression of urban black consciousness. It offered a lot of love, a lot of passion, and a protest that became more and more explicit as the decade developed.

If blues had become synonymous with Chess Records, and rockabilly with Sun, soul music belonged to Atlantic Records, which in the mid-sixties became the Atlantic/Stax/Volt conglomerate. Booker T. and the MGs ("Green Onions"). Wilson Pickett ("In the Midnight Hour," "Soul Dance Number Three," "Funky Broadway"). Sam and Dave ("Hold On I'm Coming," "Soul Man," "Brown Sugar"). Otis Redding ("Respect," "Dock of the Bay"). The Drifters ("Up on the Roof," "On Broadway"). Aretha Franklin. Ray Charles. Second liners like Arthur "Sweet Soul Music" Conley, the Bar-Keys ("Soul Finger"), Archie "Tighten Up" Bell and the Drells, the Crazy World of Arthur "Fire" Brown, and Clarence "Slip Away" Carter. Even the white soul music of the Young Rascals. Names infinitely more prominent in the black community than in the white: Eddie Floyd, Solomon Burke, Percy Sledge.

Atlantic, however, had no absolute monopoly on soul music, especially as black consciousness developed (and, perhaps more important, proved itself commercially profitable) in the middle and late sixties. Soul brother number one, James Brown, recorded for King Records and Polydor; Motown gave Atlantic a run with Smokey Robinson and the Miracles ("Shop Around" was the company's first million seller), Jr. Walker and the All Stars, Marvin Gaye, and other recognizably soul sounds early in the sixties. But as the decade wore on, Motown became increasingly slick, produced, and then overproduced. The Supremes and the Marvellettes and other formula groups became so overplayed, so mechanical, so impersonal, so interchangeable, so smooth in a world that was becoming increasingly rough, innovative, personal, and passionate that Motown lost its rep for soul.

Because what soul was, was an attempt to create something different from the status quo, a musical alternative that did not leave social ramifications implicit.

> "We will no longer call ourselves lazy, apathetic, dumb, good-timers, shiftless, etc. Those are words used by white America to define us. . . . From now on we shall view ourselves as African-Americans and as black people who are in fact energetic, determined, intelligent, beautiful and peace-loving."—Stokely Carmichael and Charles Hamilton, *Black Power*

Energy. More than a dance beat (perhaps Motown seemed cheap precisely because it was *only* dance music), more than a sex drive, soul music was a definite commitment to keep on pushin', to move up a little higher, reach that higher goal (the phrases are from Curtis Mayfield's "Keep On Pushin'"). The total energy of a James Brown concert, a superhuman expenditure of blood, sweat, and tears and of cuff links hurled into the crowd and of faints and gasps and collapses that went on 365 days a year, maybe twice a day, as many years as people would have it. The total energy necessary to pay the bills and to be the boss.

Determination. Soul was the determination to drive so hard that "no matter how hard you try you can't stop me now" (the Temptations). To lay on Mr. Charlie a bit of the old backlash blues (Nina Simone). To demand proper re, re, re, respect (just a little bit). Not to quit until we get what we deserve. To ride that train all the way to Jordan.

Pride. As in "Say It Loud—I'm Black and I'm Proud," the soul anthem of James Brown. As in Curtis Mayfield's "Mighty Mighty Spade and Whitey" or "This Is My Country." As in "Black Pearl, precious little girl." As in "Black Is Beautiful," words and music by Charles Wood and Jon Cacavas, record by Nancy Wilson.

> Black is the velvet of the midnight sky,
> Black is so beautiful it makes you cry.
> Black is oil, Black is coal,
> Black is soil, Black is soul.
> Black is you and me,
> Black is beautiful, don't you see.

"Young, Gifted and Black." "We're a Winner."

Anger. A willingness to burn and to let burn. "Fire."

Black assertiveness filled the air in the late sixties. It most certainly represented a change of direction in both music and attitude from what the fifties and earlier decades had known, presenting at almost every point the exact opposite of what the Colored People were always thought to have been thinking. Smiling faces, they don't tell the truth. But black soul music presented an alternative not substantially different from that of white counterculture. There was less bullshit about blessed poverty but in the Impressions' "Woman's Got Soul" you heard the same disdain for the world's goods that the hippies voiced: "I don't need a Cadillac car or diamonds and such." And the Shirelles could forget Paris and Rome and diamonds and pearls because in the long run, baby, "it's love alone that counts." And (Mayfield again), "I'm richer than the richest gold if the woman's got soul."

Like white counterculture–turned–mainstream pop, black power soul music was filled with the assertiveness of individuals, cries against the immorality of Vietnam and outrage at social stagnation at home, hatred of Nixon, and general distrust of classic liberalism. It was heavy on sex, and, against the wishes of most theoreticians of the black power movement, soul singers included in their new society a lot of the dope that flavored hippie culture: the Temptations' "Cloud Nine" and "Psychedelic Shack," Sly and the Family Stone's "I Want to Take You Higher."

(There existed in black society the same split between heads and political revolutionaries that divided the white counterculture. While the SDS
and the New Left apologists attacked hippies for
dropping out and giving up, black radical A. X.
Nicholas attacked the Temptations and Sly:
"These songs, as opposed to the blues, are
counter-revolutionary, and should be boycotted
by the Black community.")

The affinities between white counterculture and its aims and the goals of
black nationalism were recognized early by Malcolm X. "The young whites,
and blacks, too, are the only hope that America has," he once told Alex
Haley. White youth had come by themselves to black rhythm and blues
back there in the fifties, seeing in it the only living music in America. That
they were forced to settle for white imitations and covers of black originals
is more a testimonial to the absorptive capacity of the establishment (soon
to be considered) than a reflection of their own preference for bleached
products.

An old friend of mine and a veteran of the times thinks back:

You had to believe that if it was ever going to come, it was going to
come from the blacks. When things got down to the nitty-gritty,
flower children could always run home to daddy, women could opt
for marriage and motherhood, radicals could organize banks and
congressional campaigns instead of protest marches. But blacks, you
half hoped, half feared, had no security to retreat to, no alternative
but to level the whole system. In a way, it's too bad that they burned
their houses, that the Panthers were exterminated, and that the rest
fell for Nixon's black capitalism bullshit.

In 1971 Bob Dylan took time off from his country retreat to write a song
about George Jackson. And in 1975 he did the same for Rubin "Hurricane"
Carter. Great Black Hopes never really die.

The mention of Bob Dylan raises yet another major area of sixties exploration, the country. Musically—and spiritually—Dylan cleared out in 1968
with *John Wesley Harding*. Musically—and spiritually—he was followed in
his retreat to the hills by a lot of other refugees from the urban, twentieth-
century Mobiles that had given us all a bad case of the Memphis blues. Socially the retreat to the country began with hippies and heads looking to escape the heat of the metropolis; initially the Leary commune in Millbrook,
New York, and Ken Kesey's farm near Eugene, Oregon, although not the
first communes of the sixties, popularized the idea. The notion became immediately attractive to hippies tired of watching the city scene turn sour;
tired of the American Express–style tourist buses packed with middle-class
paunches, their cameras cocked, hot for the first sight of a frazzle-haired
freak in beads and sandals; tired of the straights looking for a quick hit or a

quick feel; tired of hustlers looking for a fix or for someone to rip off; tired of plastic flowers and pulse-taking journalists; tired most of all of being hassled. By the end of 1967, hippies were ready to update the centuries-old dream of a rural utopian community where all God's children could live in love and get back to the good earth without persecution or prosecution. (Substitute Parliament and the Church of England for San Francisco cops to see just how old and how traditionally American this vision is.)

> "I went to the woods because I wished to live de-
> liberately, to front only the essential facts of life,
> and see if I could not learn what it had to teach,
> and not, when I came to die, discover that I had
> not lived. I did not wish to live what was not life,
> living is so dear; nor did I wish to practice resigna-
> tion, unless it was quite necessary."
> —Henry David Thoreau

"People started to spread out to the country," recalled Ron Thelin, owner of the Haight's Psychedelic Shop, who departed San Francisco in October 1967. "It started to get a feeling like, 'Well, it's *gotta* be real.' The feeling was, grow your own food, get to know your own community, the system's gonna die. My friends started to come out here and we had a collective commune, a real experiment." Stephen Gaskin, onetime English professor at San Francisco State and lecturer at the Straight Theater and the Family Dog, cleared out in 1969 for a 1,700-acre farm in Tennessee, which remains to this day a self-sufficient community of several hundred. Stewart Brand, who with Ken Kesey fathered the San Francisco Trips Festival in 1966, created *The Whole Earth Catalog*. Its "purpose" explains as can nothing else the late sixties return to the country.

> We are as gods and might as well get good at it. So far remotely done
> power and glory—as via government, big business, formal educa-
> tion, church—has succeeded to point where gross defects obscure ac-
> tual gains. In response to this dilemma and to these gains a realm of
> intimate, personal power is developing—power of the individual to
> conduct his own education, find his own inspiration, shape his own
> environment, and share his adventure with whoever is interested.
> Tools that aid this process are sought and promoted by the WHOLE
> EARTH CATALOG.

Inside, everything: *The Way of Chinese Paintings*; Lee electric flour mills; how to make hard cheese; Terramycin soluble powder; pig tooth nipper; balling gun; tipis; Honda electric generators; surveying made simple; geodesic domes; *British Columbia Land Bulletins*, free for areas 1–10; *The Book of Tea*; how to make and fly paper airplanes; *New Schools Exchange Newsletter*; the dialectic of sex; wooden toys; yoga; wild edible plants; fishing techniques; auto factory service manuals; mountain climbing; LeClerk

looms; *Jewelry Making and Design*; Solidox welding torches; music synthe-
sizers; *The Tibetan Book of the Great Liberation*. Everything you might
need or care to know in order to set up your own commune in rural California, the Pacific Northwest, Nevada, upstate New York, Minnesota, Iowa,
Tennessee, Pennsylvania.

The transition from urban park to country commune, however, worked
a profound effect on the counterculture. There may have been fewer hassles
from interlopers, journalists, and police, but there was more work. With no
stores to rip off, no Diggers to provide free food, no university to offer a
free library, lectures, lecturers, no quick food joints, well, the work got
done by the members of the commune or it did not get done at all. Buildings
had to be built, not liberated. Children had to be taught, medical care organized, heat provided, food grown and prepared.

This is not to say that country experiments fell apart for lack of willing
workers. (They fell apart for the same reason that Utopian societies have always collapsed: the assertive individual ego, material and sexual possessive-
ness, the original sin of the human species.) Hippie life was very different
from country life. The move to the country meant changes. It meant a more
structured life, with appointed times for community work, meals, play, and
meditation. It meant a little less dope: you simply cannot get the work done
when you're stoned all the time. Pot, of course, continued as a staple, but
the heavy pharmaceuticals, the ten- and twelve-hour trips, tended to disappear in the successful country communes. Natural foods, natural highs. A
cleaning out. A simplification and a purification of body, mind, and spirit.
Less Dionysius. A new moral orthodoxy. A new seriousness. (Stewart
Brand observed in discontinuing *Whole Earth* in 1971, "Traditionally the
most failures have been among the serious ones, the ones with great Utopian ideas who think they are going to do something spectacular and change
the whole world. The stronger communities are kind of frivolous.")

A new conservativism was developing, from scratch almost, through
the necessity of survival. Those communes that operated under the premise
that "God is the sole owner of the land and we, as his children, are not
meant to fight, quarrel, and kill over the land, but rather to share this
natural resource—to each according to his needs" (the quote comes from the
Morning Star Ranch, a commune founded by Limelighters' Lou Gottlieb, no
rules, no structures, open to anyone, and no one asked to leave)—such
communes failed. Those that developed structures and rituals succeeded,
maybe. "The more people, the more structure; the less thoroughly members
know and understand each other, the more structure. And finally, the less
time members spend together, the more structure"—this was the rule of
thumb generated in 1972 by Those Who Study Communes.

For better or worse (in some ways, I think, for better), the movement retreated to the country. Following this vanguard, America moved to the
country. And with it, the music of the counterculture and of America
moved to the country.

"Now I won't be back 'till later on (if I do come
back at all)."—Neil Young

Beginning somewhere around 1968, pop music developed an affection
for the simple, honest life of the farm. Rock has always had country blood
under its mulatto skin, even black rock-n-rollers like Little Richard, but the
country side of rock was pretty much an embarrassment, the well-guarded
secret in the family closet. Never mind that the Buffalo Springfield, Dylan,
even the Stones sounded very country in odd moments, that Country Joe
McDonald was, after all, *Country* Joe—nobody but *nobody* was doing
honest to Opry country in the mid-sixties. Not *Sweetheart of the Rodeo*
stuff (Byrds, November 1968), not Flying Burrito Brothers or Johnny Cash,
Los Angeles or Nashville country music. Country rock emerged at the close
of the decade, right along with the return to America's rural roots.

And the metaphysics of the music were—initially at least—almost exactly the same as those of hippie refugees and radical reformers tired of smashing their heads into billy clubs: a desire to return to fundamentals, to purge
the head of accumulated shit, to simplify, to get down to bedrock upon
which to build.

> (To the original sixties heads who joined com-
> munes, experience taught the necessity of organi-
> zation, and hard work imposed from within the
> group through participatory democracy. The ad-
> vantage of commune over straight society was not
> that there were no rules, but that rules were self-
> imposed. But children of the seventies proved
> unable to distinguish self-imposed structure from
> externally imposed structure and settled comfort-
> ably into the Nixon era. Likewise, the metaphysics
> of country rock were all too quickly lost on a
> generation for which country music became not a
> metaphor for the genuine and the homemade but
> an easy, formulaic, shlock simplicity.)

It was with *Harding*, you will recall, that Dylan broke through his own
nightmare visions to the quintessentially Nashville sound of "I'll Be Your
Baby Tonight"). Both the philosophy and the country music continued on
his next album, *Nashville Skyline*, which caught him dueting with Johnny
Cash (who also wrote the jacket notes), which freaked out everyone because this was 1969, the year of *Abbey Road, Crown of Creation*, Woodstock, Altamont, the beginning of the end. What *was* this shit? "He's lost
touch with the distressing reality of our psychotic times," said New Left
spokesman Carl Oglesby, expressing the consensus.

The innuendos of "Lay, Lady, Lay" and "Country Pie"—really not characteristic of country music—could not save the unbelievably bad, clichéd,

stupid language of "one thing is certain, you'll surely be a-hurtin'," and "love to spend the night with Peggy Day," and "turn my head up high to that dark and rolling sky."

Then came more of the same in *New Morning*, this time without the puns: "I'd be sad and blue, if not for you." "Winterlude, this dude thinks you're grand." Many people turned Bob Dylan off, and many more wrote him off.

In the trajectory of *New Morning*, however, was an explanation for those who cared to listen, and it was precisely that offered by the heads on the country communes. This album opens with Bob receiving his honorary doctorate at Princeton University. The song "Day of the Locusts" is reminiscent of pre–*John Wesley Harding* lyrics. Here in the album's beginning is a nightmare reminiscent of *Blonde on Blonde*, and in the old manner Bob Dylan clears out: "Sure was glad to get out of there alive." Next song finds Dylan where he's cleared out to: up in the mountains, where time passes slowly and people try hard to stay right. Country living is an antidote to the city's poisons. In "Went to See the Gypsy," it's a little Minnesota town (Dylan going back to his roots). In "New Morning" it's a place down the road a country mile or two. In "Sign on the Window," it's a cabin in Utah, a wife, a bunch of kids, rainbow trout. "That must be what it's all about," concludes Bob Dylan the temperate man, someone who has thought long and hard and tortuously about it.

Similar long and hard and tortuous thinking had been done by the best of the turn-of-the-decade followers of Dylan into country music. It certainly underlay the conversion of some of my friends: "Look, it's cliché and shit and all, but at least it's honest cliché. There's no pretension, no promo, no phony hype." That may not be the case today, but it's certainly what Bernie Leadon of the Eagles was driving at when he told *Rolling Stone* in 1975, "There's so much bullshit in the pop world. So much of it is just lower-chakra music. No finesse. It's just sexually oriented. That's a form of escape. I like to think our band is more than that. That there's some thought, some living behind it." The kind of thought and living behind John Sebastian's "Nashville Cats" or Buffy Sainte-Marie's *I'm a Country Girl Again* (1969). Or the Eagles' "take it easy, take it easy, don't let the sound of your own wheels make you crazy." What country meant to Joan Baez, who, having spent a life in the movement, married a draft resister, walked the protest lines, refused to pay her federal taxes, visited Hanoi under Nixon's bombs, could see in the country life qualities of honesty and decency that would make her fill *David's Album* (1969) with "Green, Green Grass of Home" and "Hickory Wind" and "My Home's across the Blue Ridge Mountains" and *One Day at a Time* (1970) with country stylistics and the in-1964-heretical "Take Me Back to the Sweet Sunny South." Or to Stephen Stills in "Colorado" and "Fallen Eagle" and "Colorado Rocky Mountains saved my senses."

What the country meant to the Who in a song like "Gettin' in Tune to the Straight and Narrow" or "Baba O'Riley."

> Out here in the fields
> I fight for my meals,
> I get my back into my living;
> I don't need to fight
> To prove that I'm right,
> I don't need to be forgiven.

What country meant to the Band. And to those who made it their business in the fifties and sixties and even the seventies to support folk festivals from Big Sur to Monterey to Newport and a hundred fiddlers' conventions and a thousand bluegrass jamborees the establishment was too busy and too jaded to notice.

> "The feeling of the music, as well as the sounds and the words, and the voices, reflected a smokey fire and stonewall atmosphere. When the Band went on stage it was instantly obvious that this was no Hollywood studio group in buckskin and beads playing what they had learned off Carter Family records. Whatever this band played was real. It was honest and true and it was them."
> —Ralph Gleason on the Band

While some sixties heads went stampeding for the farm, others were stepping out into the future. I mean the far-out future—science fiction, space exploration, technology, fantasy. *Superman* comic books. *Star Trek* (much more popular as a rerun than as a bright, new hopeful). J. R. R. Tolkien. *2001.* Kurt Vonnegut. Philip José Farmer. Even C. S. Lewis.

The Jefferson Airplane's manager, Bill Thompson, explained the transformation of Airplane into Starship, and Grunt Records, and *Blows against the Empire* (1970): "For one thing, you learn that you can't change people by beating them over the head, or bombing, or whatever. That's the old style of revolution. You try it, it fails, you move on to something else." The notice on *Empire* said it better.

> Starship   Starship   Starship
>   People (people!)   Needed Now
>   Earth Getting Too Thick
>   Move on Out
>   to the
>   Cool & the Dark

We intend to hijack the first sound interstellar or interplanetary starship built by the people of this planet. A time of 3–7 months will be needed for tantronic conversion of the machinery to make it usable for practical travel—involving light years. We need people on earth now to begin preparing the necessary tools. There will be room for 7000 or more people. If it seems that your head is into this please write & talk about something for a bit. You will not be contacted immediately. Please just prepare your minds & your bodies. . . . Search out Atlantis.

The album features egg-snatching Mau Maus come to bestow upon Dick and his grade b movie star governor and their entire silent majority race a baby tree on "an island way out in the sea" that would presumably repopulate the world; another Pooh song ("Wave goodbye to Amerika, say hello to the garden"); and "Hi Jack," in which the great caper actually comes off: seven thousand people zipping past the sun, "free minds free bodies free dope free music," past Uranus and Pluto and a thousand other suns that glow beyond. With "Starship" we discover ourselves light-years from earth, heads locked onto Andromeda, a million pounds lighter and all the clinging years melted off our bodies, forgotten like the snows of long ago.

"If I do come back at all"—Neil Young

"The silence of their leaving is all that they reply"—Phil Ochs

Here was, as Paul Kantner explained, one solution to the population problem: "It's the only way it's all going to get together and work. Unless we have a war or a big disease or a famine, there's just too many people, and they're going to have to get off the planet. This is my way of starting off earlier. You don't have to stay anywhere, we'll land wherever we want and then take off again."

You can see why Starship albums, mostly Slick-Kantner projects, soon started popping up on clearance racks, any record for $1.79. Earlier in the sixties the Airplane had spoken for the San Francisco scene, for a whole tribe of 1966, 1967, 1968 heads; the Starship was a (fragmented) band of loonies and wild visionaries way out in front of—of not very many freaks. And this was just *not* a well thought out plan such as might attract followers of the science fiction writers acknowledged in *Empire's* printed lyrics: Sturgeon, Vonnegut, Heinlein. In fact, *Empire* is pretty stupid, and it's maddeningly, alienatingly, self-assuredly mindless at that. About the only thing good on the album is the music—weird approximations of the sounds of outer space, or what Slick Kantner and Jerry Garcia imagined space sounds to be.

> (Footnote on the Starship: with *Sunfighter* it landed back on earth, returning to revolution, communes, and radical, tough-talk profanity. Thereafter it took off only intermittently, the most notable voyage being Gracie Slick's "Hyperdrive" on *Dragon Fly*, 1974.)

There was other space rock around. The genre, in fact, can be traced to the days of "Telstar" and Walter Brennan's sticky "Epic Ride of John M. Glenn" (1962). Those were the days when space was a great adventure, a new frontier, and a sigh of relief after the scare of sputnik. As the sixties wore on, however, space lost a lot of its glamour, both in fiction and in song. Science fiction writers especially used space more to examine moral dilemmas than to spin Buck Rogers adventure tales. Rock headed in that direction as well. And as it did, space rock lost much of its tinsel.

By 1968, for example, the Grateful Dead had found space slightly ambiguous, a "Dead Star." The frontier is open, but it's dead, and the song alludes to T. S. Eliot's "Prufrock": "Shall we go, you and I, while we can, through the transitive nightfall of diamonds?" The Byrds' "Space Odyssey" (on *The Notorious Byrd Brothers*, also 1968) is a cool, dark, unenthusiastic piece of music. The year 1969 brought the shlock rock "In the Year 2525," promoted as "a terrifying glimpse into the future from two bright young poets." (Well, the first claim was right, anyway: in 2525 the world looked plenty bleak, plenty inhuman and inhumane, plenty frightening, although for no identifiable reason.) In 1970 Pearls before Swine contributed *The Use of Ashes* to the symposium on space. By 1972 Elton John's "Rocket Man" was finding his interplanetary voyaging just another job, lonely, isolated, a drag. (Mention might also be made of the British group Hawkwind's *In Search of Space*—a veritable catalogue of alternative realities, none of them having much to do with space as a glamour business—and Tom Rapp's "For the Dead in Space," which deglamourized space travel with dead astronauts the way the Grateful Dead had deglamourized it with dead stars.)

Whereas the ride of John Glenn was greeted with musical applause, the lunar landing of Neil Armstrong in 1969 aroused a chorus of yawns, sowhats, boos, and hisses. John Stewart, in "Armstrong," pointed out what heads all over America were saying: kids are dying in Calcutta, black children in Chicago grow up in a world of patent double standards, the globe is suffocating in its own pollution, and the United States puts a man on the moon. So what? Why? In "Moonshot," Buffy Sainte-Marie taunted NASA with her Indian boyfriend who could call her up anytime "without a telephone."

The best space rock was probably David Bowie's, although it lies somewhat beyond the pale of the sixties in both date and concept (no selfrespecting child of the sixties would have been caught too deeply inside Bowieland, you better believe). Most important were the albums *Space Oddity*, *Diamond Dogs*, and *The Rise and Fall of Ziggy Stardust and the Spiders from Mars*. (This last with Ron Davies's "It Ain't Easy" and "Starman" circling above us in a light-filled starship.) As did science fiction writers, Bowie saw in space the opportunity for moral statement. Ziggie's is the familiar story of a rocker who can't endure stardom; his is also the tale of a modern Everyman confronting his own past, terrifying present, and the bleak, intergalactic amplitudes of the future. *Diamond Dogs* borrowed from George Orwell's *1984* to paint a world in which man cannot accept what is, cannot change from anything except what is. It is an album of frustration with the sixties and almost zero hope for the future although its despair is infinitely more intelligent than Kantner's naive hijacking. (In the early seventies Bowie decked himself in what *Melody Maker* called "*Vogue's* idea of what the well dressed astronaut should be wearing" and— word had it—was preparing to play Heinlein's hero in *Stranger in a Strange Land.*)

My own attitude toward science fiction and the exploration of space, the future, and fantasy lands is ambivalent. Insofar as they examine moral dilemmas and philosophical possibilities, I—and other children of the sixties—found them attractive. But as escape, which space and the future tended too easily to become, they seem more characteristic of the seventies, more reflective of the impractical whims of the heirs of the revolution. Sixties types viewed the space program on the one hand as an element of their own romantic quest, and it caught their fancy; on the other hand, they saw in it conclusive proof that the establishment had determined to ignore pressing social issues at home and to dazzle the poor and the disinherited with technological sideshows. Born in the fifties, they were, after all, practical about their own impracticality: if they were to escape, it would have to be to something they could actually reach, something *they* could actually *do.* They were not about to be conned by grandiose interstellar visions.

But I do not really think children of the sixties ever fully intended to escape. It's true that in drugs, black power, sex, country communes, the multimedia acid test head shows, and a hundred other lesser devices they sought alternatives to the establishment they considered hopeless, on the verge of collapse, or already dead. Still, sixties people could not bring themselves finally to leave, to cut the rope and walk off. Their younger brothers and sisters, who as adolescents had written off both the establishment *and* countercultural causes, were more than happy to grab whatever kicks could be had, speculate about whatever worlds were exploitable, and then split. Children of the sixties kept threatening, "We're leaving, we're leaving," but departure was a trump card that could never be played. Beyond leaving could lie only doing nothing, and they could not resign themselves to that fate.

It was the generation of the seventies that actually dropped out: politically, socially, educationally (and musically).

> "The biggest deterrent to the progress, expansion, and success of contemporary music is Top-40 radio."—Tom Donahue, then program director of KMPX-FM San Francisco, in November 1967

The sixties were not, generally speaking, an era of important novels or of significant glossy magazines. Memorable examples of both (and of theater) come to mind, of course, but *Ramparts* and *Rolling Stone* aside, the printed medium belonged to the older generation. Sixties people invented their own vehicles: the cheap poster (political, or dayglow mind-bender, or a combination thereof); the underground press (in which emerged the new journalism that accounted for the best books of the decade, Mailer's *Armies of the Night* and *Why Are We in Vietnam?* and Wolfe's *Electric Kool-Aid Acid Test*); the light show–plus rock concert–plus dope-in–plus be-in, born as the San Francisco Trips Festival and cloned throughout the universe in a medium of strobe lights, loud music, projected oil emulsions, and good vibrations; and rock music. (To these might be added the music festival, the protest march, and guerrilla theater.) Through these vehicles, all forms of pop art, the sixties expressed themselves.

In each case the medium, as well as the message, was revolutionary because each medium was exploratory. In each case the sixties constructed in relatively virgin land something new and strange, and in each case they ended up getting ripped off by the establishment. (This was the most discouraging thing of all, for when medium is message, and you have gone to great lengths to develop new media for new messages, and they get slurped up so quickly, well, then you're bought off before you even know you've been bought off.)

Alternatives also developed during the sixties to standard methods of creation, production, and dissemination of pop music because in the struggle for control of the medium of music lies one of the brightest and the darkest stories of the decade.

> "American radio is the product of American business! It is just as much that kind of product as the vacuum cleaner, the washing machine, the automobile, and the airplane."—George Storer, of Storer Broadcasting Network

What the major record company wanted was not alternatives to establishment-think but product that would sell—defined as music that appealed to public taste, which the record company thought it could manipulate; radio broadcasters, whom it sought both to please and to purchase as tools for manipulating public taste; and media moguls, some internal (corporate execs, the artist and repertoire men) and some external (the FCC). This father-knows-best approach saw the artist as somebody who would show up Tuesday at 11:00; sing twelve songs that company wise men had selected, set to arrangements cranked out by company arrangers and played by company-hired studio musicians; walk out the door at 4:00; and leave editing, promotion, album design, jacket notes, and public appearance scheduling to daddy. These robots could pick up a (modest) royalty check every now and then, but they had better keep quiet and do as they're told. "And she fines you every time you slam the door," Dylan added. (Record companies did, too.)

It's a fact of life that all artists who try to work for a living are in the same boat. The musician may in some respects be better off than many other artists: songs are more marketable than paintings, easier to take directly to the public than a movie or a television show or a book. Still, there is a lot of built-in structure and a lot of pressure to conform. The odd, the new, the kinky, the politically or socially (or musically) subversive is filtered out before the record is cut. So rock artists sought alternatives to big record companies owned by bigger conglomerates, to big music publishers, and to big radio.

The simplest, and in some ways the most important, step in circumventing the majors is to set up a music publishing company. You need almost no equipment, few employees, virtually no capital beyond the incorporation fee. You farm out the dirty work to someone who has an offset machine— or maybe you mimeograph your own lyrics. Copyright law does not much care *how* a song is published, only that it has been published and is somehow commercially available to the public. You won't sell many songs this way, though. Unless you happen to be a big star, whose every song is going to be recorded (by yourself) and rerecorded (by your imitators and interpreters and the Muzak shlockmeisters) and sold in the hundreds of thousands and even millions of copies to loyal fans. *Then* the two- or three-cent royalty per song per album will start to mount up: royalties on a $6.95 album may be only 24¢, but a million records means $240,000, which is nice change even for a rock star. They all own their own publishing companies (with terrific names like Dwarf Music, Siquomb, Faithful Virtue, Canaan, Barricade Music), along with a lawyer or two to keep track of all those pennies flowing in.

> (Do not underestimate the importance of simple control in this scheme. Anyone wanting to use a Bob Dylan song must ask not only Bob Dylan but also Warner–Seven Arts. And just because Dylan says okay is no guarantee that the lawyers who handle his songs at Warner–Seven Arts will also approve.)

Of course, artist-owned music publishing companies could happen only because rock developed big stars who wrote their own material. Most of them did, as a matter of artistic integrity. But *none* of the fifties big names wrote their own stuff, not Dean Martin or Frank Sinatra or Patti Page. Record companies found and arranged their songs for them, so that A&R men relied heavily on Tin Pan Alley and ASCAP for their tunes, which meant that rock-n-roll challenged not only the Legion of Decency and the KKK, and major record companies, and Republican ascendancy, but ASCAP and Tin Pan Alley as well, which meant bloody battles indeed, including the payola scandals in which Alan Freed, Dale Young, and Tom Clay—but not

Dick Clark—went down. Ultimately what broke Tin Pan Alley was the emergence—or reemergence—of an alternative recording structure and the development of AM and later FM radio programming that would carry these alternative sounds to the consciousness of America.

Between 1946 and 1952, one hundred sixty-three records were million-sellers in the United States. Of this number one hundred fifty-eight had been released by the six major record companies: Columbia, Capitol, Decca, Mercury, MGM, and Victor. The smaller, independent companies (of which, Nat Shapiro estimated, there were probably four hundred in the forties, maybe one hundred in 1952) settled for those tiny markets the majors deemed too insubstantial to merit their attention (you guessed it, the r&b and country audiences in which white teenagers of the fifties discovered everything that was vital and meaningful in American music). Most of the majors had been around a long time (Columbia and Victor had survived both the depression and the war), and they were set up to outlive any given generation of stars, perpetuating easy listening and profits in a gently rising curve from here to eternity. (They did, incidentally, survive the fifties, and the sixties, and they should survive, as programmed, forever.)

> "Since I have been with Mercury, things haven't been going too well . . . I have kept in constant contact with Chess Records. I like little companies because there's a warmer relationship between the artist and the executive. I shall be going back soon, to Chess Records [and so he did]."—Chuck Berry

Meanwhile, independent record companies came and went. During the twenties they came; with the depression they went or got bought out by the majors. With the war they came again, as the majors yielded up marginal markets under the duress of wartime shortages of materials. After the war they went again, as the majors moved in to swallow up the industry. Country singer Hank Williams rang up eleven million-sellers for MGM, and the market settled into fifties orthodoxy.

Until the rock-n-roll revolution, that is. Here independents exerted an influence out of proportion to their size, eventually forcing the majors to buy into rock-n-roll by the standard expedient of purchasing contracts (Decca bought Bill Haley from Essex; RCA, with considerable fanfare, bought Elvis from Sun; and so on. It's worth noting that none of Presley's many million-sellers came on the Sun label). Still the independents maintained their suddenly enlarged share of the market: by 1958 the biggest of the big—Columbia, RCA, Decca, and Capitol—had seen their share of the *Billboard* top sellers dwindle from 75% in 1948 to 36%—despite Haley and Presley. The companies having the impact were Chess, Atlantic, Imperial, Vee Jay, Aladdin, Specialty, King, Savoy, Peacock, and over a hundred other small operations concentrated in Los Angeles, Nashville, and New York.

The independents had the impact they did because they were different and vital and because the demand (created, in part, by pioneer DJs like Al Benson, Jack L. Cooper, Dr. Jive Gordon, Ed McKenzie, and Alan Freed) was for something fresh and vital. They offered, in short, an alternative. And after they had been gobbled up by the majors (often offering themselves not unwillingly) the sixties generated new independents to provide new alternatives following the 1958–1963 drought.

The independents had several advantages over the big companies. They were willing to listen to and offer something different. They could give personal attention and freedom to their artists. And they had a better sense of local taste, which allowed them to tap an audience the majors could not even identify. These were virtues much prized by the sixties, and by the beginning of the decade record *producers* as well as artists were going independent. By the end of the sixties maybe 75% of all rock records were being produced by independents.

> "I'm fed up with arrangers and people. We've done all the music ourselves."—Mick Jagger, 1967

> "Some of the new groups are good, but a little crazy. They are absolutely noncommercial and have to be taught to conform a little to make money."—Max Weiss, Fantasy Records, 1968

> "The best artists in the business—the aristocracy —are moving into positions of power. They're making fewer compromises with commercialism. There's hardly anything interesting happening outside of this exclusive circle—but what's happening inside may be the most remarkable story of our time."—Derek Taylor, press agent for the Beatles (later the Byrds and the Beach Boys), 1963

Traditionally, good rock artists began with the independents, where they could develop style and personality; made it big; and then opted for the promotion departments and studio equipment and cash offered by the major record companies. But majors can't promote hundreds or even dozens of artists at once (Capitol had trouble promoting two—the Beatles and the Beach Boys; the Beach Boys always felt like the slighted child of the house), and for whatever is gained something's lost. The late sixties witnessed the remarkable spectacle of big-name artists leaving the majors for their own or independent record companies. Chuck Berry returned to Chess in 1969. The Beatles formed Apple in 1968. The Stones left Decca to form Rolling Stones Records in 1970. The Mothers of Invention formed Bizarre. The Airplane alias Starship formed Grunt. The Beach Boys formed Brother

Records. "We'd just get that much more control over everything," Paul Kantner told Ben Fong-Torres of *Rolling Stone* in contemplating Grunt Records. Grace Slick added, "So the band makes the music and the tapes go away, and they come out as records. But RCA is too big to even refer to. It's like saying, 'Well, how are you dealing with the government?' I mean, what dealing? You don't deal with the government at all."

> (One of the things the Airplane wanted control over was censorship of things like *"motherfuck-ers"* in "We Should Be Together." Censorship fights, when they arise in a major company, are *always* won by the company. The Airplane, by the by, once contemplated pirate radio as a means to bypass the FCC, something "to circumvent whatever repressions we feel from corporations or the government.")

The move toward complete independence and self-control led the Beatles, the Grateful Dead, and the Airplane/Starship to dump their managers and handle their own affairs on a cooperative basis. This worked for a short while. "There were thirty of us making a creative effort. After all, it was *our* thing" (Rock Scully of the Airplane congratulating himself and others on their northwest tour of 1968).

The generation of the sixties also experimented in rock music programming. This effort was important since radio plays a crucial role in rock music as a vehicle of communication. The disc jockey and the program director exercised enormous power over artist and record company alike. In order to sell, a song must be heard; to be heard, it must be played. And here the odds are against most singles and the vast majority of albums.

A four-hour top-forty radio show, for example, will air the same list today, tomorrow, and the day after, and maybe for several weeks, as long as the records remain in the top forty. In one week the record industry will generate upward of two hundred singles, all trying to break into that top forty and thus into public consciousness. Odds, then, are five to one against —only they are considerably poorer because hit records hang around for plenty longer than one week. The only way to beat the odds, and get through to the audiences, was (or so record companies thought until they discovered late in the sixties the alternatives of rock festivals, free concerts, and hype in the underground rock press) either to get your song "broken" by a key disc jockey on an important station or to plug into *American Bandstand.* "If WABC [New York] or KHJ [Los Angeles] goes on a song," Steve Chapple and Reebee Garofalo reported, "it has been proven again and again that that means a minimum of 50,000 units of additional sales, almost automatically. If a major chain makes a commitment to a song nationally, sales will be boosted several hundred thousand units."

During the early and middle fifties, AM radio programming was fairly decentralized, which had advantages and disadvantages. On the good side was pluralism: somewhere somebody was bound to play your record once, maybe twice, and you could get maybe a local hit without paying off too many people. On the bad side was provincialism: to get a really big national hit, you had to contact plenty of disc jockeys on plenty of stations and maybe slip them an extra twenty or fifty. It took lots of time and lots of money and gave rise to the system of payola sanctimoniously unearthed by Congressman Owen Harris (who was, it developed, himself on the take) in 1960.

In 1955, however, Todd Storz pioneered the concept of top-forty programming, an idea he'd gotten at lunch one day after hearing the same tune played again and again and yet again on the jukebox: if people wanted to hear their favorites, he reasoned, why not play their favorites for them? Again and again and then one more time. So Storz picked out the top forty tunes each week and played them endlessly—first on radio WTIX in New Orleans, then all across the South, then all across the country. As *Billboard* charts became more sophisticated, Storz had a ready-made top forty and an easy answer to the problem of how to break new records into that magic XXXX. In fact, the Storz formula worked so well, was so rigidly adhered to, that Storz's stations came through payola scandals virtually unscathed: since the play lists were out of their hands, since they had so little to do but shout and push buttons, there was no point laying a sawbuck on Storz disc jockeys or program directors.

Then Bill Drake, ABC radio and Metromedia, got hold of the Storz formula and developed the standard we all grew up with: boss radio. Top forty was cut to thirty-three records picked from *Billboard*'s Hot 100 and standard top-forty lists. Three of these were "hit bound," which marked them for heavy play. Mixed with the thirty and three transients were four hundred golden gassers, knocked out nifties, moldy oldies, which were sprinkled across the airwaves at preset intervals. Music was programmed at one, three, seven, eleven, sixteen, and 20 minutes in the half hour, sandwiched between fewer commercials, less talk, shorter jingles, self-promotion for a station "where the hits just keep happening." Drake's formula also took into consideration "momentum" (comers receive more air play than goers) and "pacing" (two similar-sounding records—for example, two female vocalists, two acid rock songs, two Bob Dylan–style ballads— should not follow each other). The list of thirty-three magic singles was carefully balanced to cover all musical possibilities, no matter who had or had not produced a good single in the past month. The trick that artists and record companies had to master was timing: if everyone else was releasing heavy blues, you could slip a mediocre country rock song into that slot in the boss radio formula.

You don't have to have these formulas in front of you ro recall that mid-sixties radio, even the top-forty radio of the fifties, played a lot of junk. It was good as long as the singles were good. But it tended to filter out the new and the vital and anything over two minutes and thirty seconds (although AM radio could request—and receive—shortened versions of longer songs from record companies eager to please and to sell). It tended to discourage experimentation and—the worst crime of all—it tended to ignore the embarrassingly obvious fact that what was left was bad. Bad as the singles might have become, top forty and boss radio just kept pumping them at you, telling you how dynamite they were.

AM radio became a leveler.

> "Top-40 radio, as we know it today and have known it for the last ten years, is dead, and its rotting corpse is stinking up the airwaves."—Tom Donahue, 1967

This bankruptcy of AM radio gave rise in the late sixties to FM or underground radio. Progressive rock programming was the experiment of Russ the Moose Syracuse on his midnight-to-dawn shift at KYA. In the long hours of the night time, Moose played what daytime AM radio ignored: albums, music that hadn't made or wouldn't make the charts, songs that were too politically or socially charged to pass the AM censors—Dylan, Baez, the Dead, the Airplane. He reviewed new material, took time off from the fast talk to become a radio personality. And he clicked instantly with college kids, the generation of the sixties.

Then into the Bay area came Larry Miller from Detroit, with an all-night program on KMPX-FM, a play list of two or three hundred records, and telephone requests, and ultimately Tom Donahue as the program director of what has come to be recognized as the country's first free-form, twenty-four-hour-a-day, progressive FM station. By the end of the decade, Donahue's evening show on KMPX topped everything else in the San Francisco area—including AM radio.

By the early seventies there were about four hundred free-form FM stations in America. And there were many, many more FM stations on college campuses, some of them part of public broadcasting, underwritten, ironically, by the federal government. Free-form commercial radio also spread quickly to college radio.

Initially, then, FM programming was an alternative. Like all other sixties alternatives it opened up new possibilities: the chance to hear "Satisfaction" or the uncut version of "Light My Fire" or the Chambers Brothers' "The Time Has Come" or Phil Ochs or Joan Baez or long Bob Dylan songs or maybe a whole side of *Sgt. Pepper* without interruption. The chance also to hear bluegrass or jazz or the Kinks or the Mothers of Invention. Time for a disc jockey to talk seriously about music in other than eight-second slogans. The chance for a broadcaster and even a listener to stamp upon the program her own personality. To circumvent the FCC (not until FM radio began attracting big advertisers and audiences did FCC censors really tune in, although when they arrived, they arrived with their pistols loaded). An opportunity to experiment.

Naturally some great things were done, tough, creative, unpolished, kinky scenes, but great. FM radio was a world full of surprises, like the world of early television or the world that Jean Shepherd found in the late fifties when he spun his radio dial away from New York and tuned in America.

Ultimately FM went the way of every other sixties innovation, but not before it helped independent producers, independent companies, and independent artists turn popular music on its ear. In the mid-fifties classical music was the bread and butter of record companies; popular music was only a sideline. Today, for better or worse, the situation is reversed. Record sales in 1955 totaled not quite $300 million; record and tape sales in 1973 totaled over $2 billion. That $2 billion topped the movie industry ($1.6 billion) and all sports events combined ($600 million). If you combine record and tape sales, radio advertisements and concerts, and tape recorder and stereo and radio sales, the music biz grosses more than $7 billion annually.

> "Progressive radio as a whole didn't turn out the way I had hoped. I'm disappointed. There's too much FM rock, too much competition, too much bad music. We've turned into what we wanted to be an alternative to."—Larry Miller, 1970

"And, in the end, FM rock stands naked. It is, after all, just another commercial radio station."
—Ben Fong-Torres, 1970

Big, big dollars draw establishment types. They made rock a big business. And rock music, like every other alternative developed by the sixties, like the very generation of the sixties, found itself a victim of its own success. *Because* it succeeded, it drew the packagers and the handlers, the formulizers and the merchandisers, who had built the grey machine against which the music and the generation rebelled. In the end the music and the generation found themselves absorbed by the system against which they had revolted.

Bullet holes in the door of
Black Panther headquarters
in Chicago after July 31,
1969 raid. Police returned
in December, fired eighty-
two rounds into the room,
and killed Panthers Mark
Clark and Fred Hampton,
who slept inside. *United
Press International Photo.
Used by permission.*

"Hippie chick," *Playboy*
style. The shadow of the
peace sign forms the
Playboy bunny symbol.
*Photo courtesy of Playboy.
Used by permission.*

Woodstock Music Festival, 1969.

If there's one thing Anvil does understand, it's what you wear.

We don't pretend to understand every-thing that's going on in your world today. But there is one thing we do know. We make slacks and jeans that a lot of guys go for. For a lot of good reasons. Like the way they fit. The way they'll stand up through any occasion. The fabrics they come in, made with Celanese

Fortrel®. And how little they sell for, start-ing at $7.00.
   Granted, we're not hip to everything that's happening today, but what we are hip to, you might like.
   Our company may be 72 years old, but our slacks and jeans are definitely for the under 30.

Anvil
BRAND

Anvil Brand. For the under 30.

Anvil Brand Inc., a Glen Alden Company. Empire State Building, 67th Floor, New York City 10001.

CELANESE FORTREL
Fortrel® is a registered trademark of Fiber Industries.

Madison Avenue Woodstock. *Photo courtesy of Anvil Brand. Used by permission.*

| 5 | The Tug of Gravity: Co-option, Absorption, and Shlock Rock

"The old magic of the woman and the piano and the night and the rhythm being one is gone. But everything goes, one way or another. The '20's are gone and lots of fine things in Harlem night life have disappeared like snow in the sun—since it became utterly commercial, planned for the downtown tourist trade, and therefore dull."—Langston Hughes, *The Big Sea*, 1940

"But when Almighty God shall have brought you to our most reverend brother the Bishop Augustine, tell him that I have long been considering with myself about the case of the Anglii; to wit, that the temples of idols in that nation should not be destroyed, . . . since, if these same temples are well built, it is needful that they should be transferred from the worship of idols to the service of the true God."—Pope Gregory, Bishop of Rome, to Mellitus, Abbot, Rome, June 22, 601

The capacity to absorb: Western society's most salient characteristic, the key to its longevity, the source of its ubiquity. Almost never does Western society reject alternatives outright; very infrequently these days does it engage in one-on-one, head-on Athens versus Sparta struggles to exterminate. Not with serious contenders. Albigensians, American Indians, Vietnamese may be rubbed out with impunity, for they are weak, pose no genuine threat, involve no serious risk. But when big powers collide, there is always less explosion than noise, and always there is reconciliation in the end.

This is especially true of ideologies that pose the real alternatives and offer the real conflicts. Protestantism and Roman Catholicism, monarchy and democracy, capitalism and communism: after all the fierce talk, when the boys are finally in the ring they waltz around like overweight prize fighters and suddenly what you thought was a clear-cut choice between mutually exclusive opposites is resolved into a muddled both/and. A middle ground appears, and the sharp distinctions blur ultimately to invisibility; before you know it, Outside is Inside and the powers that be have grown a little fatter.

Pagan temples are rebuilt and dedicated to Christian saints. Harlem jazz is absorbed into New York City social life.

It should be comforting to realize that Armageddon is probably never going to arrive, that the world will not end tomorrow. Since the final whistle today *would* be the final whistle, we surely ought to be doing everything we can to avoid blowing it. Reconciliation beats confrontation. Still, this wholesale absorption is discouraging. It undermines our sense of winning and losing. I sometimes think that the American (Western) fascination with inconsequential sports, elections, ratings, and beauty pageants stems directly from this muddling of distinctions everywhere else in life. At least in the World Series somebody wins and somebody loses; the runs, hits, and errors —and winners' and losers' shares of the take—are there in the paper, undeniable, unambiguous, palpable, distinct. And for all the if-onlys and what-ifs and shoulda-beens, when the election is over, one candidate goes to Washington and the other returns to law practice.

Reconciliation confounds our sense of definition. Alternatives (political, social, educational, ideological) never turn out to be what we thought they were because ultimately they are all assimilated piecemeal into the establishment and thus made compatible with what is, from which they're supposed to be distinct.

The game that's played, as the Stones observed in "Street Fighting Man," is compromise solution. It is not a very satisfying game.

> "Be sure to come again the next time we Republicans have a love-in."—Reaganite to reporter Sandy Darlington after a fund-raiser at the Oakland Coliseum, 1968

When religion dominated our lives, the game was called scholasticism. When politics dominated our lives, it was called balance of power diplomacy. Today, when commerce calls the shots, the game is known as commercialism, or the big buy-off. Black power theoreticians called the game co-option, this incessant sucking of life out of revolutions, this absorption of energies. And they spoke out unequivocally, if futilely, against it. "We reject the goal of assimilation into middle-class America," wrote Carmichael and Hamilton in *Black Power*. Even temporary coalitions were suspect: "In fact, one might well argue that such coalitions on subordinate issues are, in the long run, harmful. They could lead whites [the establishment] and blacks [the alternative] into thinking either that their long-term interests do *not* conflict when in fact they do, or that such lesser issues are the *only* issues which can be solved." Both would be equally fatal to the goals of black power, which were nothing less than the total reconstruction of society by the creation of alternative, more humane, less racist institutions.

Black power failed, not heroically, in a shoot-out show of integrity, not in a mushroom cloud that leveled New York City, black and white together, but in Richard Nixon's black capitalism and in "academically sound" black studies programs. In a federal grant. In the resolution of little issues. In blurred distinctions. In the big buy-off. In the way the system resolves everything: by absorption.

> "They are discovering new ways to divide us faster than we are discovering new ways to unite."
> —Eldridge Cleaver, 1969

Absorption depends on three basic tactics used by the establishment in dealing with threats to its ascendancy. Each would be persuasive in itself, but together they have proven virtually overpowering.

Tactic A, exercised only when an alternative is exceptionally threatening *and* exceptionally impotent is the naked rub out. You shoot the bastards, or you lock them in a dungeon eighty miles underground, or perhaps you lobotomize them, or maybe you send them scurrying into self-imposed exile. Like what happened in *One Flew over the Cuckoo's Nest*, or *Easy Rider*, or *Cool Hand Luke*, or *Chinatown*. Like what happened in real life to the Black Panthers, the Weathermen, Martin Luther King, Jr. Or to John Kennedy, the first and the most traumatic and the most naked rub out of the sixties, from which many children of the decade never fully recovered.

> "He knew more than anybody but he didn't know there was doors to go through and ladders to climb. He thought it was just 1, 2, 3."
> —Phil Spector on Lenny Bruce

This doesn't happen often, because there are so many other, more genial means of co-option. Tactic B is the buy-off, usually an unsubtle combination of punishments on the one hand, rewards on the other, with an offer that no sensible person could refuse. "Why, we could really use you, son, and here, have some money, and besides, you wouldn't want your arm broken, would you now?" The kind of trip they laid on Ken Kesey: fame and dough while he behaved; then one bust and then another when he started dabbling too publicly in acid; then the power trip that sent him packing to Mexico; then a pinch by some FBI sharpie when Ken absentmindedly returned to the land of the free; and then jail. And then the big sting: if Ken will do some public-spirited, noble, good, establishment thing like calling all his followers together and telling them to lay off dope and be good Americans, then he can have his freedom.

In music the buy-off amounted to plenty of air play, television exposure, dough, women, and contracts for good little boys and girls. As long as you cooperated in public, you could do damned near anything in private. "Just think of *Satyricon* with four musicians going through it," John Lennon recalled of the early (clean) Beatle days. For the not so clean Stones, right from early on (and for Lennon later), and for everyone else who refused to cooperate, air play was restricted, television access was limited, engagements got canceled, hassles were constant, busts were frequent for dope, for obscenity, for whatever (the Stones were busted for pissing against a wall when the men's room was locked).

Tactic B is remarkably persuasive, the kind of deal you cannot really refuse. Either they buy you off (Elvis Presley) or you disappear (the MC5). Take your choice. "We want people to hear us," said Rock Scully of the Grateful Dead, "but we won't do what the system says—make single hits, take big gigs, do the success number. . . . So we've never had enough bread to get beyond week-to-week survival, and now we're $50,000 in debt." If you avoided compromise completely, you ended up like Captain Beefheart (Don van Vliet), and who ever heard of him ten years after? (He, at least, had the candor to see the situation for what it was, and the honesty to remain true to himself and pass on Judas Priest's pile of tens, and the good fortune to write his own apologia in an A&M single: "Out of the frying pan into the fire/Anything you say they's gonna call you a liar.")

> "I found I was continually having to please the sort of people I'd always hated when I was a child."—John Lennon

Tactic C is no option at all. It is pure co-option, and it goes on every day, every year, so constantly as to be a standardized process. George Melly described it in *Revolt into Style.*

> A local enthusiasm for some form of music gradually crystallizes around a particular group or artist. At this point an entrepreneur, sometimes a local enthusiast with an eye to the main chance, sometimes an outsider led towards the scene by apparently fortuitous accident, recognizes the commercial potential of the group or artist and signs them up. . . . If he is successful, his "property" becomes first nationally and then internationally famous. In the wake, other groups or artists, many from the same local or musical background, some simply recognizing that a particular sound or image has become commercial, swim along feeding on the vast plankton of popular favour. Then, inevitably, the interest and hysteria die away, and there is a variable time-lag before the same thing happens again.
>
> It is this process which led me to paraphrase the line from Thom Gunn's poem about Presley as the title of the book. "He turns revolt into a style" wrote Gunn. And this is what happens in pop; what starts as revolt finishes as style—as mannerism.

This tactic is the most effective and the most commonly exercised of all: you flood the market with cheap, harmless, and *manageable* imitations;

soon enough the original can be neither heard nor recognized. The only trick, and it is one that is easily mastered, is that the style must maintain the appearance of revolt as long as possible. "The trick is to shift the emphasis so that the pop idol, originally representing a masculine rebel, is transformed into a masturbation fantasy-object for adolescent girls" (Melly again). This goal is most effectively achieved by liberal use of Brill Building assembly line rock-n-roll lyrics (ground out mostly for major record companies by the employees of Don Kirshner and Al Nevins at Aldon Music) and similarly liberal use of cover songs.

> (The use of white covers for black originals was the first form of co-option of rock-n-roll and one of the most vicious. In a chapter of *Rock 'n' Roll is Here to Pay* entitled "Black Roots, White Fruits," Chapple and Garofalo listed forty-three "cover records and questionable revivals" by artists ranging from Perry Como, the McGuire Sisters, Steve Lawrence, and Andy Williams to Elvis Presley, the Beatles, the Stones, and Grand Funk Railroad.)

In advanced stages, the whole stylized, undifferentiated mess can be resurrected. At the distance of a decade or two, there is no distinction between "All Shook Up" and "Love Letters in the Sand," between "Rock around the Clock" and "Hello, Mary Lou," between "I Ain't Marchin' Any More" and "Eve of Destruction," between "Get Off My Cloud" and "Mrs. Brown, You've Got a Lovely Daughter." They're all golden oldies, tuneful memories, and few remember that there once was a difference.

> "Rock is progressive, pop reactionary."—Gary Herman, writing on the Who in 1971

The difference between rock and pop is measured by our response. Does it take us further along or not? Does it press back the frontiers of our collective experience, does it challenge, does it open new worlds? Or does it reinforce old habits, reaffirm old prejudices, settle in comfortably. Does it lead *out* or back *in*? That's the real rating system by which you measure a record or any other work of art. It's the only way you can tell whether you've got a genuine article or a piece of co-opted pop shlock.

The history of the sixties, of rock music, of all human experience is one continual tug between forces pressing out and away and gravity which pulls back. I suppose we need both, but rock and the sixties line up unhesitatingly behind the quest for alternatives. It pains us to sit still. It hurts to admit we need an occasional good night's sleep. It hurts more to see ourselves and others conned by the comfortable, to see exits become entrances, to see how successful the establishment can be in the process of absorption.

Maybe this business is not as overtly sinister as I've made it sound. Your average record company may be crass; it may be reactionary by managerial instinct; it may turn music into a commodity like cars or refrigerators; but it is not dedicated to God, apple pie, and motherhood any more than it is dedicated to revolution, dope, and free love. The music biz is an ideological whore. It is dedicated to maximum profit, and it won't wring the neck of a goose that lays golden discs out of pure philosophical differences. But it happens that a smoothly functioning system generates more golden discs than a haphazard nonsystem, because it turns out the most product for the least effort. *And* a smoothly functioning system is by nature exploitive, not innovative. It prefers formulas and mass production to experimentation and innovation.

Escape necessitates the expenditure of energy and generates motion. Co-option reduces the expenditure of energy, slows change, freezes motion. Escape is the product of rock. Co-option is a natural product of systems. Co-option means certain death to any generation that predicates its being on motion—specifically, the generation of the sixties. Rule number one: representatives of the system, no matter how genial, are not on our side.

> I played "Ohio" for [Albert Grossman, Dylan's "dear landlord"] last night and he got angry. He said, "What are you trying to do?" And I said, "Well, actually, if you really want to know, I'm not really trying to do anything. But I think we're gonna help tear it apart a little bit." And he said, "Well, man, you're just children, and you don't understand what's going on." Went into that kind of rap, and I said, "Albert, you're comin' on hip all the time, but in truth you're just another old man who's really got all his marbles in this system. And the real truth of it is, man, I just scared you. You don't want that system to go."—David Crosby, 1970

Rule number two: there is no such thing as half a loaf. There is no such thing as working within the system. All the alternatives developed by children of the sixties were gobbled up.

Music, despite the independent record companies and producers, and the FM stations, and the underground concert circuit, proved particularly vulnerable to absorption. There was a tremendous amount of money to be made selling records, especially after the newly developed teenage market was sold rock-n-roll as "a thing of our very own," especially during a decade of economic expansion. Thus, not long after the Beatles made their own peculiar alternative popular and profitable, every record company around was dragging the Mersey for four stiffs with guitars and thick Liverpool accents, rushing to cash in on the new sound. Musical innovation turned quickly into musical formula. The wealth of imitation overburdened program directors and DJs. Overworked and maybe underpaid, they were susceptible to pressures other than public demand and to considerations other than good taste and any obligation they might have felt to innovation or art. As a consequence of the big bucks, artists themselves confronted daily a smorgasbord of smothering goodies offered to nobody but nobody else in the world. Politicians, writers, robber barons, even jocks and movie stars— who had money, groupies, dope tossed at them like the Beatles? Even the Order of the British Empire! *Satyricon* with four musicians.

> Paul's response: "I know what he was talking about, but at the same time I was sitting there thinking, 'no, it wasn't.' It was as much a dream as anything else is, as much crap as anything else is."

The really surprising thing about the sixties is that so many artists managed to resist for so long, to keep their heads above the rising pile of garbage, to keep pushing up and out when there was such strong gravity pulling back, to maintain their vision and not turn cynical.

> "Everybody screwed everybody in those days."— Phil Spector

In the late fifties and throughout the sixties and the seventies, the biggest single pollutant of rock music was *American Bandstand*, hosted by Dick Clark. *Bandstand* has been glorified in retrospect—as has most other fifties shlock ("the golden age of hype," Nik Cohn called the decade). In fact, it was an almost incredible parade of one South Philadelphia mediocrity after another, many of them reprocessed especially for the occasion: voice lessons, makeup, new clothes, new accents, new teeth, maybe even a good song (although this was incidental—witness Fabiano Forte, Fabian, who went the whole hundred yards on pure image, and nobody ever guessed). Sprinkled among the natives were auslanders, also mediocrities. Annette Funicello had eight big hits on the Disney label! All were polished smoother than cue balls and hyped to instant stardom by a smooth pitchman who sold to an average of ten million record buyers weekly.

Usually what interested Clark was what could make him (or, occasionally, a good friend) money. Example: the Silhouettes' "Get a Job," produced on the Junior label, Philadelphia, Pennsylvania, went nowhere. It was bought by Ember Records and the copyright transferred to a company controlled by *Bandstand*'s producer. *Bandstand* catapulted "Get a Job" onto the hit parade. Example: Bill Parsons's "All American Boy" was processed by a Clark-owned company; bingo, *Bandstand* pushed the song, an overnight hit. "Dick Clark got right behind 'Venus'," enthused Philadelphia's own Frankie Avalon, who had recorded the song on Chancellor Records, in which Clark owned stock. "It sold 1.5 million copies. He's the greatest." (Avalon was *Bandstand* promoted and Beatle buried—along with Paul Anka, Dion, Fabian, Chubby Checker, Deedee Sharp, Bobby Rydell, Freddie Cannon, Bobby Darin, the list goes on). Example: "Sixteen Candles" (Clark owned the copyright) was promoted on *Bandstand* into a national hit and made Clark a cool $12,000. It's a dumb song (but no worse than Paul Anka's "Diana," which sold nine million records). Example: between 1958 and 1960, Dick Clark played the eleven records of Duane Eddy well over two hundred times on *Bandstand* (Clark owned all Eddy's publishing rights and stock in his record company as well).

Over half the records released by companies in which Clark had an interest—and he dealt himself into thirty-three companies—received air play on *Bandstand*, and two-thirds of these were heard on *Bandstand* before they appeared on a *Billboard* chart. Clark came to control the copyrights to one hundred sixty songs, almost all of them "gifts." He made a lot of money off these inane lyrics, whose composers hoped, correctly, would be promoted by Clark into big money-makers. It was all very legal.

> (While we're admitting things, let's also note that Alan Freed plugged Chuck Berry's "Maybellene" pretty heavily after he acquired one-third interest in the song. They all did it, although some did it more than others, and some got away with it.)

What's worse is that Dick Clark dumped upon the American musical consciousness an unrivaled amount of mediocre songs. In the beginning *Bandstand* was tied into some big artists (although Freed, who went down in the payola scandals that left Clark Mr. Clean, had better taste and better artists); things slid progressively downhill into the dog days of the late fifties: the Royal Teens, Ricky Nelson, Connie Francis. The real kicker is that young Dick Clark, freshman Philadelphia disc jockey in 1957, pulled in "at least $50,000." By 1973, Clark, still young and now ensconced in Malibu decadence, was grossing in excess of $5 million a year. Dishing out the same stuff.

But how can you fault him? He was a promoter. "You're a fucking idealist," he reportedly told *Rolling Stone*'s Ben Fong-Torres. "And I'm a whore."

> "They don't listen to music, man, they listen to money."—David Walley, interviewing the MC5

"I don't make culture. I sell it."—Dick Clark

"I saw her face, now I'm a believer." Remember the song? Think about it for a minute: love at first sight, innocent love without a whisper of sex, nothing earthy or compelling. Hum the tune a few times—light, bouncy, a hint of hard rock, but rock reduced to a musical formula, rock toned down almost but not quite to Muzak level. Look at the words: a bit of wit, the cute rhyme of "believer" and "leave 'er." But no bite, nothing new, no challenge of comfortable assumptions, no alternative—especially in 1967, when everybody knew better than this cutsiness.

It topped Aretha Franklin's recording of "Respect," the Stones' "Ruby Tuesday," the Beatles' "All You Need Is Love," the Procol Harum's "Whiter Shade of Pale," Scott McKenzie's "San Francisco," the Buffalo Springfield's "For What It's Worth," the Airplane's "Somebody to Love" and "White Rabbit," and the Esquires' "Get On Up," each of them better songs with more to say, important thrusts *out* of the establishment mode of thought. I suppose the conclusion is inescapable: shlock outsells real rock three to one any day; the American record-buying public really grooved to Dick Clark's kind of sound. (Also ahead of most of those important songs were Lulu's soppy "To Sir with Love," the Association's "Windy" and "Never My Love," the Monkees' "Daydream Believer," Frank and Nancy Sinatra's "Somethin' Stupid," and Frankie Valli's "Can't Take My Eyes Off of You.")

The success of "I'm a Believer" was a tribute to the financial effectiveness of flooding the pop market. For the Monkees, who recorded "I'm a Believer" (and "Last Train to Clarksville," 1966; "Daydream Believer," 1967; "Valleri," 1968; and a total of seven drippy LPs), were from the beginning a deliberate commercial imitation of the Beatles, so crass as to congeal the blood of every struggling sixties rock group and of all their fans. *A Hard Day's Night* and *Help!* had worked so very well, and made so very much money, that ABC decided the Beatles should have their very own weekly television spot. Not the real Beatles, of course, since they would want an impossible amount of money and be unmanageable; and not any existing rock band because they also might create problems of control or want to inject some of their own musical ideas into the program. Something as close to the real Beatles as possible. The Lovin' Spoonful tried, but they could not fill the bill for a sunshine moptop group. One was created from scratch. From, an oft denied story runs, an ad in *Variety*.

Talk about crass. And talent, naturally, was never a consideration.

Thus emerged the Monkees. Peter Tork (Ringo), a veteran of the Greenwich Village coffeehouse scene with musical experience but no background in acting. Mike Nesmith (George), also a musician, with roots in country music. Micky Dolenz (John), a child actor who had served time in the *Circus Boy* television shows, strummed a guitar and banged a drum occasionally, and had been lead singer with a short-lived group called the Missing Links. And Davey Jones (Paul, the cute one), who had played the Artful Dodger in Broadway's *Oliver* and knew virtually nothing about music.

Once a week American television fans got *A Hard Day's Night*.

Television pseudo-Beatles, however, required pseudo-Beatles lyrics— mostly, since by 1967 the real Beatles had turned philosophers, *early* Beatles lyrics. These were provided by Bobby Hart of Hart and Boyce, a professional songwriting team. The word was that, often as not, the Monkees were not even playing the songs they had not even written; it was all done by the best studio musicians money could buy. The only people crying were the legitimate rock artists who knew that they'd just had a large part of their younger audience ripped off.

(The story is not, however, entirely unhappy. When the Monkees realized they had become men who, in Thoreau's words, had been made "tools of their tools," they revolted. Learned their instruments and attempted to grow up with a 1968 film *Heads*. But the movie lost them their youthful audience without really squaring them with the counterculture, and within a couple of years the Monkees were no more. Nesmith returned to country music in a series of relatively heavy second generation country revival albums with the First and Second National Bands. He was a classic bit of counterabsorption, of pop shlock that came in out of the cold.)

The Monkees were not the only imitation Beatles, of course. In the first frantic years of Beatlemania we'd gotten the Searchers, Gerry and the Pacemakers, Billy J. Kramer, the Mojos, the Swinging Blue Jeans, the Undertakers, Tommy Quickly, the Merseybeats, the Big Three, all vacuumed up in Liverpool by record company reps. In 1967, the Bee Gees, London by way of Manchester and Australia, sounded more like the early Beatles than the early Beatles (and certainly more than the 1967 Beatles, who were miles away from "I Want to Hold Your Hand," leaving rock's softer heads yearning for the good old uncomplicated days). The Bee Gees were not without experience, although they lacked imagination and shied consistently away from the musical frontiers. They had performed in England as kids, and they had performed in Australia before returning to England, where they were processed into the Beatles' mold by none other than Brian Epstein.

The result was another surge of slush, mostly derivative, all very clever and polished fluff, all without redemptive social value: "I Started a Joke," "Lemons Never Forget," "I've Gotta Get a Message to You," "Lonely Days." A decade later the Bee Gees were still neck deep in pop shlock, making millions off disco.

Herman and his Hermits present a more difficult case, in part because they were earlier than either the Bee Gees or the Monkees and thus not quite as retrogressive. Still, although I find their songs tuneful, I'm forced to admit that nothing compelling goes on in "Mrs. Brown, You've Got a Lovely Daughter" (1965), "Must to Avoid" (1965), "There's a Kind of Hush' (1967), or "Leaning on the Lamp Post." Mostly it's teenage love with a British accent, and very very clean. A lot of Herman's material covered British hits done in their own country by other groups. It is significant that Herman and his Hermits were virtually unknown in their native land (where they came packaged as the Heartbeats), whereas they cleaned up in America. Lillian Roxon's *Rock Encyclopedia* description is too accurate not to repeat: "Goopy, squishy, adorable bundles from Britain; dear little marshmallow-soft English boys that a girl of thirteen could listen to without effort, bear-hug to death in her Barbie-doll dreams, and scream over without upsetting her mother and, particularly, her father."

Herman was, in short, the masturbation fantasy with which the establishment sought constantly to replace more potent symbols of rebellion. These fantasies proliferated, depreciated the coinage of rebellion, effectively stopped the British invasion, and killed a number of solid British rock groups like the Zombies, the Animals, and the Kinks.

Then there was bubble-gum.

It is difficult for true children of the sixties to deal calmly with bubble-gum music. It's like mentioning Richard Nixon—they start foaming at the mouth, flinging out irrational and often wildly outrageous accusations that are often only half-truths but that together present a very accurate picture.

> "That's shit, the Archies; that's pure, unadulter-ated shit. When I see and hear stuff like that I want to throw up."—Phil Spector

"Total lack of nutrition"—Albert Goldman

Don Kirshner unloaded upon America the Archies and the archetypal bubble-gum hit "Sugar, Sugar." Kirshner and Al Nevins were, at the beginning of the sixties, known primarily as the propietors of the Brill Building, music publishers who had grown fat off the talents of Gerry Goffin and Carole King, Barry Mann and Cynthia Weil, Neil Sedaka, and Howard Greenfield, whom they housed in honeycomb cubicles vaguely reminiscent of jail cells, while Kirshner and Nevins made millions peddling tunes. A classic Maggie's Farm and very profitable: four hundred of five hundred Kirshner-published tunes had by 1970 made the charts. Then there were the Monkees, and the Archies, and *In Concert*. No concern for art or for content. A restrictive form through which really talented artists might break (Carole King) but one designed more to co-opt emerging musical alternatives, to ride and exploit, than to generate genuinely new and exciting and different sounds.

Tony Orlando ("Candida," "Tie a Yellow Ribbon," "Knock Three Times") is no meteor who burst upon the music scene at the dawn of the seventies with sunny vacuity and bouncy tunes. He'd been hanging around for years, looking for his opportunity, lurking in the shadows and in what company you might expect. Childhood hero: Bobby Darin, shlockmeister of the fifties. First employer: Don Kirshner, Darin's best friend. So Tony

Orlando worked out "Half Way to Paradise" with Carole King and Gerry Goffin, sang the demo (in 1961, at age sixteen) because Kirshner liked his sound because he sounded black and black was in (pure Presley-style fifties co-option), and Kirshner sold the demo to Epic, and Tony Orlando had contributed one small bacterium to that blight which back there at the beginning of the sixties checked the first flowering of rock-n-roll. Kirshner followed "Half Way to Paradise" with "Bless You," and Tony Orlando was running all over the country with none other than—you guessed it—Dick Clark.

Then came the Beatles, and the second and greatest flowering of rock, a low point for the shlocksters, although ultimately the Beatles gave them a fresh alternative to suck on—as we have seen in the saga of Don Kirshner, Hollywood, the Monkees, and the Archies. Tony drifted into CBS's music division, worked his way up to vice-president by signing sweet, suffering James Taylor (and also, I want to be fair, Laura Nyro and Blood, Sweat, and Tears). Next thing you knew, Tony picked up the phone; it's Hank Medress and Dave Appell (producers who in their day and his had handled Bobby Rydell); they wondered whether maybe Tony wouldn't be into doing a master for them, "Candida." And lo, the same flotsam that washed ashore at the outset of the sixties came washing back at the outset of the seventies, with all the same faces and all the same sounds.

In 1973 Tony's manager summed it up: "I think I know why they're into Tony's music. In the sixties musicianship was what counted—the progressive rock artists were musicians first, entertainers second. . . . I think audiences just want to be entertained again." Not that early Dylan, Beatles, or Stones could be accounted high musicianship. But certainly audiences of the seventies were very much into being just entertained again. (It was about this time that sixties people quit listening to pop music.)

The Muzak Corporation was founded in 1934 and has plenty of detailed psychological study behind it. *Effects of Muzak on Industrial Efficiency. Application of Functional Music to Worker Efficiency. Research Findings on the Physiological and Psychological Effects of Music and Muzak.* With appropriate tunes, Muzak can speed up your breathing, typing, or buying; delay fatigue; improve attention and production and—presumably—worker satisfaction with tedious jobs. Carry you over the early afternoon slump, help teachers with discipline, help students with homework, help Neil Armstrong wile away the long hours to the moon, help employers compensate for those periods when "employees' residual energy is lowest." It's all computerized now, and musical programs can be tailored to any and all parameters.

Music, as the Greeks understood, has direct, measurable, predictable effects on the psyche; Muzak is in the business of measuring these effects and enlisting them in the service of whatever system cares to pay for such services. It is the ultimate musical whore. And it absorbs everything that is usable, because for everything there is a season, and a time for every music under heaven. Thirty thousand compositions in the computer, with three hundred additions each year. No hard rock, however, because somehow it doesn't lend itself, it's "a little too obvious," and fees would be astronomical. No, the rock is rearranged and rerecorded by the best studio musicians—toned down, dry-cleaned "professional rock."

What's missing from Muzak is the music that most resists co-option, the best rock. The Beatles and the Stones, who, a Muzak spokesman claims, "do not lend themselves to the Muzak process." The Carpenters, who took off in 1970 with a cover of the Beatles' "Ticket to Ride," were, however, highly popular with Muzak. But the direct, frontal attacks on the system by Frank Zappa, angry Airplane, protesting Phil Ochs—the sort of music that might make a student pitch his homework out the school window or a worker walk off the assembly line; the sort of stuff that makes the blood pressure rise *too* high, that turns on the head, that keys the emotions to the point at which a listener does something other than type faster, purchase more, whistle merrily along—for this the computer has no use; it stands outside the Muzak system.

> (Which is why the almost ubiquitous Muzak, far from increasing their productivity, drives sixties people nuts. A man knows when his foot is asleep, dammit, and he knows when Maggie's father is sticking a needle in his vein.)

The marshmallow absorption goes on constantly, on every front. Two years after the Beatles slipped "I'd love to turn you on" into *Sgt. Pepper*, we had turned-on colors of lipstick and turned-on flavors of ice cream, and youth turned on to politics and Christ, and you just wanted to forget it. Dick Nixon was doing "sock it to me" lines. Cosmetics and cars were revolutionary, and an Opel would light your fire. The flowers and beads of San Francisco filled glittery Fifth Avenue boutiques, and display windows along Chestnut Street, Michigan Avenue, Regent Street, and shopping malls in Dallas, Los Angeles, St. Louis.

It is, however, one thing to see cheap rock drive out dear. It's another thing entirely to see the young, lean, angry good guys turn into fat, well-serviced, middle-aged bad guys. Elvis Presley's life is the best example of the big buy-off.

Right now a proper perspective on Presley is difficult to achieve, what with the apotheosis following his desperate death. Colonel Parker has seen to it that we've been Elvis-the-King'd to distraction, which is not surprising because raking in the bills was what Elvis was about during the sixties, and maybe he would have dug the hoopla and the long green sloshing around his grave. In fact, the deification of Elvis, at the expense of historical fact and common sense, began well before his departure from life (but well after his departure from serious rock-n-roll).

Elvis Presley was, right from the start, a compromise: the white kid with the black sound. If you were unkind, you could accuse him of being a cover artist: the first song he ever recorded at Sun Records was the Ink Spots' "My Happiness"; his first hit—regional—was Arthur "Big Boy" Crudup's "That's All Right." "Hound Dog," "Mystery Train," "Lawdy Miss Clawdy," and many other early Elvis songs were also versions of black originals. The famous Presley hip action, Bo Diddley once claimed, was learned in Harlem's Apollo Theater. Elvis openly admitted his debts: "I dug the real low-down Mississippi singers, mostly Big Bill Broonzy and Big Boy Crudup." And again, looking back: "When ["That's All Right"] came out a lot of people liked it, and you could hear folk around town saying 'Is he, is he?' and I'm going 'Am I, am I?'"

And that is precisely what Sam Phillips and Sun Records manager Marian Keisker recognized in the infant King: "The reason I taped Elvis was this: over and over I remember Sam saying, 'If I could find a white man who had the Negro sound and the Negro feel, I could make a billion dollars.' This is what I heard in Elvis, this . . . what I guess they now call 'soul,' this Negro sound. So I taped it. I wanted Sam to know." Elvis was the man of the hour in July 1954.

Now the reason Sam Phillips was looking for a white man with the "Negro feel" is obvious: a black singer with a black sound was just not going to break into the big dough because the big dough was white and racist. With Presley, Phillips thought he had a chance. The time was, as they say, ripe: already in Cleveland adventurous, white, middle-class kids had taken the initiative in Leo Mintz's record store. Elvis became the King thanks mainly to American racism and his ability to sing blue-eyed soul.

But to his credit, Elvis, like all other covers, did introduce the black sound to an audience it would probably not otherwise have reached. Most Americans who *would* watch the *Ed Sullivan Show* would not have sought out the "race" records of Leo Mintz's back shelves and would not have caught the late night–early morning radio programs of Jack L. Cooper, "Professor Bop," "Jocky Jack" Gibson, or "Sugar Daddy" from Birmingham, Alabama. Maybe a small percentage of those who heard Elvis on Sullivan fought their way upstream to black originality.

Elvis did have a certain talent, a certain musical sound. Early Elvis is pretty good stuff: not exclusively a cover of r&b but a fusion of country, blues, and his own style, the very fusion that made rock-n-roll something distinct from r&b and country. It has a certain pop style as well, which is basically what interested RCA Records when the bidding began that would take the King away from Sam Phillips and Sun. "Heartbreak Hotel" was an unusual record for 1956 in that its style appealed to r&b, country, and pop audiences. Elvis's early recordings were not the "production rock" under which Charlie Gillett classified Presley in *The Sound of the City.*

But musically Presley went straight downhill from his first Sun hits, "Mystery Train" and "I Forgot to Remember to Forget." More and more ballads, less and less rhythm and blues—and what r&b there was came toned down. Less personality, less dynamics, less roughness. More formula, more polish, more sentimentality. More money. For a few moments the Sun magic held on RCA: "Jailhouse Rock" (1957) is not a bad song although the movie is an abomination. "All Shook Up" is also a pretty fair number although the beat and vocal mannerisms approach habit. In 1958, with "Wear My Ring around Your Neck" (backed with "Doncha Think It's Time"), Elvis was promoting the same true-blue purity, the same adult-sanctioned teenage mindlessness that his swivel-hipped, black-voiced "There's Good Rockin' Tonight" had assaulted in 1954. By the end of that year Presley was well on his way to RCA production pop: a Christmas album, *Viva Las Vegas; A Date with Elvis.* Movie after movie after grade B movie.

> "By the time [Elvis] came back to civilian life again, he was almost as respectable as an Andy Williams or Perry Como."—Nik Cohn

The difference between Presley and Dylan was that whereas both developed early a relatively individualistic style based on patent imitation of a variety of originals, and whereas the style, still derivative, burst in both cases upon the national scene hyped as something fresh and innovative and very, very genuine, Dylan took his sudden fame as a point of departure for development up and out; Elvis took the long, easy, lucrative road downhill. Where Dylan fought like hell to remain an avenue *out*, Elvis became in three or four short years an avenue back *in.* And this he became, to all outward appearances, quite willingly. Not that he deliberately opted for the great American road show in preference to playing the prophet. Not that he made public statements to the effect that look, fellas, it's all a show anyway, you guys are performing and we're all performing, and I'm gonna be the biggest performer of them all. It was not a public shuck because Elvis never really stood *above* the performance. Nobody believed in Elvis more than Elvis. And the myth of Elvis became a static myth; it became the myth of American consumer society, a myth Presley didn't invent, a myth that invented him. (And invented others long before him and manufactures others after him and loves and rewards nothing so much as the idols it manufactures because it has them locked in its pocket.)

As he turned thirty and then forty, even when he came back for some cash and flash personal appearances, even when, with the fifties revival, Elvis rejuvenated himself as a museum piece on tour, it was increasingly apparent to everyone that he cast no shadow. Elvis was Elvis when he was onstage; offstage, he was nobody—he was invisible. The motion had ceased somewhere back in the fifties, when Elvis Presley had his hair cut off by the U.S. Army.

"All the time he wasn't onstage for that hour, I guess the man was just bored and trying to find different things to do," Sonny West, one of his exbodyguards, declared in an interview following the publication (four days before the King's death) of *Elvis: What Happened?* His days were poisoned by an obsession with death and an active hatred of singers he considered competition, which led him on one occasion to shoot out a television screen showing Robert Goulet. (That the King of rock-n-roll considered Robert Goulet competition tells you everything about his descent.) His money went to buy gifts for strangers who might become friends. His life was very much wrapped up in drugs taken not to get high but to sleep, to act, to perform.

The key questions were posed in a postmortem conference held by his bodyguards, his former friends.

Q: Couldn't you have stopped him from doing all those things?
Dave Hebler: How can you?
Q: He hired you to protect him.
Hebler: Of course, protect him. How do you protect a man from himself?
Q: Was Elvis happy when you left him? Was he a happy man?
Hebler: I don't think so. I think in many ways Elvis was a tormented man. I think he was a victim of himself, the image and the legend.

"The sad part was that he became a product," wrote Chris Hodenfield of Elvis's movies. "Because an Elvis picture guaranteed easy profits, he was eventually given nothing but the flimsiest of scripts, ground out sometimes at the rate of three a year." But the real tragedy is that Elvis never demanded better. Did he storm off movie sets? Did he challenge the formula of twelve songs a picture? He did not, no matter what he thought to himself. "It was just that Hollywood's image of me was wrong," he once told Pierre Aldridge, "and I knew it, and couldn't say anything about it."

Well, you can always say *no*. Except that you can't, once they've got you, once they've turned you into production rock, movie product. The legend of Elvis Presley is told in music by the Band: it is the morality play of "Daniel and the Sacred Harp."

Now Daniel looked quite satisfied,
And the harp it seemed to go;
But the price that Daniel had really paid
He did not even know.

Back to his brother he took his troubled mind,
And he said, "Dear brother, I'm in a bind."
But the brother would not hear his tale,
He said, "Oh, Daniel's gonna land in jail."

So to his father Daniel did run,
And he said, "Oh father, what have I done?"
His father said, "Son, you've given in—
You know you won your harp, but you're lost in sin."

Then Daniel took his harp and went up high on the hill,
And he blew across the meadow like a whippoorwill.
He played out his heart just the time to pass,
But as he looked at the ground he noticed no shadow did he cast.

This is a stern moral judgment indeed, this business of lost souls. But rock—
in fact, the entire culture of the sixties—would offer the Band one justification after another.

> "One has to completely humiliate oneself to be
> what the Beatles were, and that's what I resent."
>
> —John Lennon

"We do not ride on the railroad, it rides on us."
    —Henry David Thoreau

Nobody was more aware of the price of being a rock star than rock stars
themselves. They spoke of it constantly, openly, sometimes in music, sometimes in candid interviews. *Tommy* is a rock star, off on a power trip, raped
and forsaken by his fans, in his end more pitiful than in his beginning. "So
you want to be a rock 'n' roll star?" asked Roger McGuinn and Chris Hill-
man. You sell your soul to the company, you make the charts, the girls rip
you to shreds, you end up "a little insane" with all the money and the hype,
and you're a rock-n-roll star. Maybe you end up dead, like Brian Jones:
"What the Stones Sang, He Was," headlined the *Rolling Stone* obituary.
Maybe you clean yourself up or get yourself cleaned up—like Buddy Holly
or the Everly Brothers or Elvis—or like Ray Charles, washed not quite clean
of the blues in the waters of ABC-Paramount for his 1962 hits "You Are My
Sunshine," "You Don't Know Me," and "I Can't Stop Loving You." Or like
the fab moptops from Liverpool, cleaned and pressed, dressed, shampooed,
sanitized in 1962 by Brian Epstein.

Maybe you end up broken apart. "It got harder and harder to talk to
Artie because we were spending so much time working together that when
we weren't working we'd just as soon not be around each other," explained
Paul Simon. The Mamas and the Papas, two and a half years together,

burned out in 1968: "The last album was torture to make, just torture." The Buffalo Springfield, *Last Time Around*, their core disintegrating, isolation slowly engulfing one member after another, one song after another.

Maybe you end up compromised. "You can't always tell a recording company not to do this and not to do that," Chuck Berry explained, looking over his shoulder at the late fifties, "because they have a little authority over the product they put out, and if they feel that it's commercial, they can take your name and turn it inside out."

Maybe you just feel pressured by the company or by the public. Pete Townshend admitted, "I've often gone on the stage with a guitar and said, 'Tonight I'm not going to smash a guitar and I don't give a shit'—you know what the pressure is on me—whether I feel like doing it musically or whatever, I'm just not going to do it. And I've gone on and *every* time I've done it." Maybe you feel pressured by society: "The song—'Acid Queen'—is not about just acid; it's the whole drug thing, the drink thing, the sex thing wrapped into one big ball," Townshend continued. "It's about how you get it laid on you that you haven't lived if you haven't fucked forty birds, taken sixty trips, drunk fourteen pints of beer—or whatever. Society—people— force you. She represents this force."

It hurts to read that Joan Baez played a Las Vegas casino the other night in a sexy dress.

It bugs you when soul music, the best and purest expression of the black community and its new values, turns increasingly formulaic, increasingly neutral, increasingly bland, and ends up finally in Tamla-Motown, whose highest value is success and whose notion of success is, according to Jon Landau, "to be able to put each of its groups into the big nightclub scene."

It bugs you to think that there on the Columbia campus in 1969, right where the heat was busy busting heads a year before, you had the Sha Na Na doing 1950s nostalgia, museum pieces purged of social and political content a decade after their moment: "Get a Job," "Rock and Roll Is Here to Stay," "Come Go with Me." One year it's the revolution against slumlord Columbia fucking over the poor blacks of Morningside Heights, a kind of holy war against institutional racism and insensitivity; the next year it's "Grease under the Stars."

Then to watch the rock-n-roll revival run its inevitable course, from the Garden Party of November 1969, with the Coasters, the Shirelles, Chuck Berry, the Platters, and Bill Haley, to the return of Little Richard, to Ricky Nelson and Dion and a Dick Clark *Bandstand* retrospective, gathering steam and bucks as it tumbled down the ladder of quality, a grotesque parody, a loop through time-space.

Or Grace Slick and Paul Kantner, following the lead of the Quicksilver Messenger Service, clearing out of San Francisco to live as idle rich in a Marin County special by the ocean, with a redwood deck–enclosed swimming pool, a studio in the basement, a geodesic dome for meditation, a beamed living room ceiling, and a fireplace—Paul busy fixing the place up.

Or Sam Brown, onetime leader of antiwar youth and Eugene McCarthy organizer, in 1978 director of Jimmy Carter's Action, writing off the Peace Corps, the great sixties Peace Corps, with the flip comment, "This is our country. When we mess up and make mistakes, we ought not to make them in other countries."

> "Don't try to get yourself elected: If you do, you had better cut your hair."—David Crosby, "Long Time Gone"

Or *Rolling Stone's* obituary for Detroit's MC5: "They wanted to be bigger than the Beatles; he wanted them to be bigger than Mao." And the Five and John Sinclair at each other's throats over who paid whose bills, and who was using whom, and the group living on a farm out in Hamburg, Michigan, returning to early adolescent dreams of gold-plated sports cars and screwing around a lot.

(The litany continues.)

Jimi Hendrix, pressured by his manager to go commercial, avoid experimentation, pressured by black militants to turn political, caught in the bind of having to please everybody with no time to please himself and getting himself torn into a hundred pieces while so doing.

The Stones, tangled in censorship hassles over "half-assed games," which was finally cut out in air play in the United States. The Stones, slurring "Let's spend the night together" for the *Ed Sullivan Show*. (Mick Jagger: "They would have cut it off if I had said *night*.")

Eric Clapton on music charts: "Personally, I don't think they're amoral, you know, musically. I think they're anti-music and anti-progress. They're obsolete. . . . They bring the whole thing down to a very immature level."

Ravi Shankar on the absorption of Indian philosophy and Indian music into the American experience:

All this big wave of Hare Krishna and beads, bells and joss sticks in their ears or between their teeth like Carmen carries a rose, always sort of hurt me very much. . . . The whole mix-up of sex and spiritual exercise all became one, you know. All of a sudden I saw it was more like a pagan ritual like you find in those peculiar books or those peculiar films, you know, orgies and religious things together. And it makes me sad because I happen to be a Hindu, a Brahmin, and belong to a very religious family and I know what has happened in India and what is happening. And it is absolutely gross, I mean, a distortion of facts.

Paul Simon, the only living boy in New York, rides thorugh the city in a big black Cadillac he rents from a limo service.

The Beatles sue manager Allen Klein for "excessive commissions." Klein sues George, Ringo, John, Yoko, and Apple for $63 million in damages and future earnings and Paul McCartney for $34 million plus interest. The court battles last almost as long as Lennon's battle against American immigration authorities.

The gumdropping of counterculture in Hollywood shlock movies: *The Activist* (1969), *The Strawberry Statement* (1970), *RPM* (1970), and a lot of skin flicks full of phony hippie chicks.

"Since [the Monterey Pop Festival in 1967] what San Francisco started has become so diffuse, copied, exploited, rebelled against, and simply accepted, that it has become nearly invisible"—*Rampart's/Rolling Stone's* Michael Lydon, August 23, 1969. And again, "There was no doubt that the bourgeoisie loved love and flower power since they were very easily turned into a product. . . . The Plastic hippie was created—from $38.00 sandals to the $15.00 leather handbag"—Joe Ferrandino, 1972

Woodstock was something *we* produced out of our own national genius and energy, it was a beautiful experience for hundreds of thousands of our people which we produced ourselves, but the mother-country record companies and movie companies and vampires of all kinds swooped down on it and grabbed it and took it into their factories and cooked the reality of Woodstock down into records and movies and shit which they now sell back to us at $3.50 and $12.00 a shot. We control no part of it, yet it's entirely produced by us.—John Sinclair, "We Are a People"

Then there was Richard Nixon's proclamation making October 1970 "Country Music Month," along with his invitation to Johnny Cash and Merle Haggard to the White House. Everybody cringed to think of Nixon's grey jowls crinkling at the corners to "Okie from Muskogee" and "The Fightin' Side of Me" and "Welfare Cadillac."

"Right now I'm pretty busy with the lousy Repression, it's so real, so operative," explained a "company freak" to interviewer Danny Fields in 1970.

It's a full-time thing, countering the repression. Kokaine Kharma was dropped from WFMU, and that's supposed to be the hippest radio station in the New York area, and that show was probably the best, liveliest, freshest, hippest show in American radio, with Bob Rudnick and Dennis Frawley. The MC5 is fired by Elektra, which is the hippest record company, and the Smothers Brothers are fired off the hippest network, and Columbia records is dropping its ads in the underground press. The hard rain is falling, it's falling right now.

Interviewer: Did Alan Freed actually co-author the tune with you?
Chuck Berry: No, that was a very strange thing. He got that money solely for doing us some favors in those days.   .

April 30, 1970: the FCC ruled that Jerry Garcia was "obscene" on radio and slapped a fine on the educational FM station for broadcasting an interview with him; Peter Yarrow was busted for taking "indecent liberties" with a fourteen-year-old chick.

(And the jocks. Remember the athletes with their fists in the air at the 1968 Olympics. And Jack Scott's Institute for the Study of Sport and Society. And Dave Meggyesy's radical *Out of Their League,* in which he ripped football apart. There is no such idealism today. Only bucks.)

Phil Spector on the record industry:

They're a bunch of cigar-smoking sharpies in record distribution. They've all been in the business for years, and they resent you if you're young. That's one reason so many kids go broke in this business. They're always starting new record companies—or they used to, the business is very soft right now. They start a company and pour all their money into a record, and it can be successful and they're still broke because these characters don't even pay you until you've had three or four hit records in a row. They order the records and sell them and don't pay you. You start yelling for the money and they tell you, "What-ya mean, I have all these records coming back from the retailers, and what about my right to return records and blah-blah." They look at everything as a product. They don't care about the work and sweat you put into a record.

Jesse Kornbluth on racism and the majors: "This year someone seems to have decided that the scene is blues, and Columbia Records has signed a Texas albino named Johnny Winter for $300,000, a sum that would buy a dozen black guitarists of equal heaviness."

Do you recall the persecution of the Panthers? The arrest of Huey Newton on October 28, 1967, in Oakland; the raid on Eldridge Cleaver's home on January 16, 1968; Judge Julius Hoffman's sentence of forty-eight months for Bobby Seale; the raid of Chicago police on the apartment of Fred Hampton and Mark Clark on December 6, 1969, a murder in the middle of the night. And the policeman who commented, "These guys were denouncing the President, and the courts are supine, never convict; something had to be done."

(Cleaver has taken to campaigning against Soviet bloc countries and calls himself a social democrat these days.)

Abbie Hoffman recalled an incident during the Chicago Eight trial: "A stocky built man about 48 in a chauffeur's suit stopped us and smiled, 'Abbie, I'm Mick's [Mick Jagger's] private chauffeur. My name's Al.' We chatted trial-gossip for a while waiting for the performance to begin and then Al dropped the clunker. 'It's really a small world. You know who I chauffeur during the day???' He paused to suck me in real good and lowered the boom. 'Judge Julius Hoffman!' "

"Neil [Young], married for a year now, plans to stay at his redwood hillside Topanga Canyon house, their home since August 1968. He's even building a 16-track recording studio under the house. [David] Crosby has settled into a ranch in Novato, in north Marin County, and Steve [Stills] is looking for a house in Marin County." (*Rolling Stone* in a piece by Ben Fong-Torres on Crosby, Stills, Nash, Young, Dallas Taylor, and Greg Reeves)

Stanley Cohen (*Folk Devils and Moral Panics*) on the dilution of mod by commercialism:

> Carnaby Street, Cathy McGowan, Twiggy, transistor radios always on to Radio Caroline (opened on Easter Sunday, 1964), boutiques, the extravagant velvets, satins and colours of the more flamboyant of the early Mods. By the middle of 1964 there were at least six magazines appealing mainly to Mods, the weeklies with a circulation of about 500,000, the monthlies about 250,000. There was also "Ready, Steady, Go," a TV programme aimed very much at the Mods, with its own magazine related to the programme and which organized the famous Mod ball in Wembley.

Derek Taylor, former press officer for the Beatles, turned publicity agent for a bunch of top-forty singers:

> The myth is that the industry has grown up. All the marvelous elements have come together, all the groovy people are now in command. Okay. But when the awards come out at the end of 1966, you open *Record World* and what do you find? The top vocalist of the year is Staff Sergeant Barry Sadler. I'm sure Barry Sadler is a very good soldier, but what has that got to do with music? All right. The most promising male vocal group is Tommy James and the Shondells. Here's a group that made one record that hung around for two years because nobody would touch it. Then, by some freak, it sells more than a million copies—"Hanky Panky," the all-time definitive piece of crap, a very poor recreation of "Be Bop a Lula," a famous Gene Vincent song—and on the basis of *that*, they're voted the most promising male vocal group in the single market.
>
> In *Cash Box*, somewhere on their list is Bob Dylan, who has just beaten out John Gary, but above Dylan is *Al Martino*. All of which goes to prove that it's quite untrue that the record industry has grown up. And the reason is that there's no growing up of the public taste. The same crap is being bought that was bought ten years ago.

> (The most promising group of 1966 was the Monkees.)

"The accounting we receive from MGM is so bullshit it's not to be believed. Sales are estimated from 300,000 to 800,000. A suit has been filed and we are auditing their books. . . . I think I would

rather not record than go back with MGM"—
Frank Zappa.

And the underground press, another alternative become what it was
supposed to have been an alternative to.

And John Lennon's Toronto Peace Festival ("Free. For $1.") that never
was, killed by egos and finances and the bonds required by Ontario police:
$875,000 for security, $425,000 for water, $377,000 for sewage, $50,000 for
garbage, $1,500,000 for medical care.

> So you've a right to sing your own song;
> No one else can tell you if you're right or wrong;
> Livin' your own life, that's what America means. . . .
>   —This commercial about believing in yourself was brought to you
>   by the makers of Budweiser Beer. . . .

And John and Yoko, busted in their own apartment, taken to the police
station by cops with dogs, and booked for grass. October 1968.

> That's what it was, man, the fuckin' paranoia. The hassles, the unbe-
> lievable hassles. You try and keep your head straight, and you can't.
> There are rules about everything, and you can't keep from filling
> your head with them, because it's like you do something and you
> think "crunch, now it's gonna come," and it always does come, and
> you have to keep fighting to keep from saying "well, this time maybe
> I'd better cool it," and life becomes one big fight with yourself and
> with them. You try to keep your head straight, man, but you just get
> burnt out trying to make yourself ignore the shit.

And CBS squashing Pete Seeger's "Big Muddy" over Tom and Dick
Smothers' protest: "It may be your show, but it's our network."

And CBS squashing the Smothers Brothers with the argument that
"someone has to be the judge of the difference between entertainment and
propaganda."

And the Chuck Berry–Pete Townshend jam that never was, killed by a
show biz squabble over who should get top billing.

And Mick Jagger busted. And Ray Charles busted. And Joe Cocker
busted.

And the Airplane fined $1,000 in Kansas City for saying "that's a bunch
of bullshit" onstage and forced each appearance thereafter to post a cash
bond to be forfeited if there were any "illegal, indecent, obscene, lewd, or
immoral exhibition" while they were performing.

And Mick Jagger unable to make the Bangladesh concert because he
could not get a U.S. visa.

And Phil Ochs, so paranoid that he came to suspect shortly before his
death that the CIA and the Mafia had a contract out on him. So he carried a
lead pipe, a hammer, a pitchfork around wherever he went. And he made

the bartenders in his SoHo bar carry meat hooks, and he kept insisting there were snipers on the roof across the street.

We've seen it over and over, in the sellouts and the compromises of our heroes, in the rubouts of our heroes, in the proliferation of shlock, in the reports of bust after bust, in the establishment's use of political trial as a tool of repression, as a means of punishment. Nobody was immune as long as she posed a genuine alternative to the system. And everyone was forgiven as soon as she repented. And all those who took the one step forward were rewarded a hundred fold, even the cardboard cutouts the system created itself.

> (An interesting analogy presents itself. A worker intent on fleeing East Germany faces no real danger these days: either he escapes or he is caught, jailed for two years, and then expatriated. Either way he's out of the East. The communist position is that the system created him and it can create a million others like him. This fellow is only a troublemaker anyway, uncooperative. Flush him away and make others. American record companies operate on much the same principle.)

There is only one way to deal with this process of absorption: you must keep moving. This is the single most important lesson we can learn about ourselves, about the sixties, about rock-n-roll, about life. You have to put your head down, look neither to the left nor to the right, ignore the threats and the sweetmeats, just assume that you're going to have to fight a lot of inertia, and keep moving straight ahead. "He who's not busy bein' born is busy dyin'."

Leave your stepping stones behind, something calls for you.
Forget the dead you've left, they will not follow you.

How often has Dylan, at the very height of one phase of his musical career, walked out the door, trucked on down the road, struck another match, and started all over again? At the very top of the heap, when he was number-one folksinger, number-one rocker? *At the height of his popularity,* when he had audiences and tours and groupies and money and adulation, risked the whole heap of trophies to maintain his artistic integrity, to move closer to the philosophical and musical edge, to go back out in the rain and battle the elements, to put himself on the line again and again, to hear the critics carp and moan about how he's sold out on protest, or abandoned rock, or obviously misunderstood the dislocations of our crazy times?

> "It must have been a big, big step for him, 'cause it's hard when your people around you are all tuned to one way of life, and then you just come

and change it for them. He took a *big* risk, as an artist, by doing that. A big, big risk. He really deserves a lot more credit. He can't get anymore, I guess, but that was a big, big step for him to do that. 'Cause the people really wanted somethin' else from him."—Phil Spector on *John Wesley Harding*

Dylan was the brightest and the best of the sixties rockers and by far the most perceptive. He realized what Presley and Joplin and Hendrix and Ochs did not, what Lennon and McCartney suggested when they admitted the Beatles knew from the beginning that they could not go on forever being thirty-year old Beatles. Dylan understood that the greatest threat is the threat of image: the enervating sweetness of success, the annihilation of person by role.

Rock was tough enough on the big fish; it was murder on the small fry. It made it all too easy for essentially weak people, loners, not too bright kids with a little talent and a lot of the American dream, kids whose very vulnerability could turn them into symbols with whom a generation could identify; made these loners into stars and sometimes superstars. The danger was in taking the goodies you'd always dreamt about and then believing in them and the role you'd created for yourself or had created for you or fell easily, almost unconsciously into. Only the strongest survived that temptation, and among them Dylan alone rejected it consciously.

The Stones fought absorption with self-parody. The Beatles fought it with dissolution, but only after the myth itself became hollow, only after the dream had turned into a nightmare. Janis Joplin, Jim Morrison, and Jimi Hendrix fought it by living themselves to death. But Bob Dylan was willing to walk away at the moment of triumph to remain his own man.

Mick Jagger and Keith Richards of the Rolling Stones. "The only performance that really makes it is one that achieves madness"—Mick Jagger. *United Press International Photo. Used by permission.*

Mick Jagger. *Photo by Mike Putland, Retna. Used by permission.*

Pete Townshend of the Who in motion. *Photo by Chuck Pulin. Used by permission.*

Art Garfunkel and Paul Simon. *Photo by Chuck Pulin. Used by permission.*

Janis Joplin; died October 4, 1970. *Photo courtesy of Retna. Used by permission.*

Jim Morrison; died July 9, 1971. *Photo by Alice Ochs. Used by permission.*

Jimi Hendrix; died September 19, 1970. *Photo courtesy of Retna. Used by permission.*

Black Panthers walk out of Omaha's central police station after questioning, 1969. *Wide World Photos. Used by permission.*

Watts during the "long, hot summer" of 1965. *United Press International Photo. Used by permission.*

State troopers and tear gas move in on freedom marchers in Canton, Mississippi, 1966. *United Press International Photo. Used by permission.*

Toward the end of the decade, the focus and energy of individual movements were lost in the proliferation of related causes.

"Burn, baby, burn." Arson and looting in Washington, D.C., following the assassination of Dr. Martin Luther King, Jr. *United Press International Photo. Used by permission.*

Police and antiwar demonstrators clash during 1968 Democratic national convention in Chicago. *United Press International Photo. Used by permission.*

Conspiracy defendant Abbie Hoffman makes a somersaulting entrance at the trial of the Chicago Eight, September 1969. *United Press International Photo. Used by permission.*

Defendant Bobby Seale, bound and gagged at the trial of the Chicago Eight. *United Press International Photo. Used by permission.*

Jerry Rubin as Santa Claus, "the red peril," at the House Un-American Activities Committee hearings, December, 1968. *United Press International Photo. Used by permission.*

My Lai massacre, Songmy, Vietnam, March 1968. *Photo by Ron Haeberle, Life,© Time Inc. Used by permission.*

Kent State University, 1970. " What if you knew her and found her dead on the ground/How can you run when you know"—Neil Young, "Ohio." *Photo* © *1970 Howard E. Ruffner. Used by permission.*

|6| Artiness, Absurdity, and Excess

> "It was good for a time; then we went so far that we lost it."—Timothy Leary

Overwhelming as the establishment loomed, it was not pop shlock alone that ultimately undid rock—and the counterculture—at the close of the sixties, but three inside enemies: artiness, absurdity, and excess. The drive toward artistic expression took children of the sixties out of the arena of real social and political struggle, and into the fairy-tale world of hypothetical people, problems, and solutions. The late sixties sense of the absurd—however justified by the madness of the world—leveled indiscriminately, until any commitment seemed futile. And the excesses of artists, revolutionaries, and drug freaks led not to more freedom now but to a conservative reassertion of the safe, sane, Republican center.

> "You've got yourself to blame."—the Who, *Quadrophenia*, 1973

The least expected, least guarded against internal flaw was the tendency of the counterculture to turn itself into (self-conscious) pop art and of rock music to turn itself into fine art. What fine art has become in the twentieth century is too often obscure art about art, or pure style. In reviewing "The Lollipopping of the West" for the *New York Times* in 1977, England's George Steiner talked about modern art.

> The claim that the modern arts have completely rejected common human needs and understanding is silly. But there *is* something to the widespread sentiment that ordinary men and women, in their daily existence, can no longer draw from the great springs of the imagination the strengths, the delights, the bracing hopes they once did.
>
> Paintings are opaque scrawls; sculptures seem to be lumps of ugly matter; music banishes melody. Modern writing is so often autistic, technically demanding, defensive (the schism between poet and public, which dates back to Baudelaire and Mallarme, has not been healed).

Such is indeed the case. And was certainly the case during the sixties, when the counterculture, which initially had been gloriously indifferent to fine

179

art, began moving in all of its aspects in the direction of artiness. Political rappings turned into the Theater of Ideas. Rock guitarists became musicians. Rock concerts became theatrical or operatic performances. Rock lyrics became, or attempted to become, poetry.

> "I sincerely believe in the generalization that there is not very much of what I would call valid artistic expression, you know, anything to do with a higher plane of expression, in any present-day progressive or rock music. In most cases it hasn't even reached the point of being a true craft, which is a stage through which it must go before it can become art."—Jethro Tull, 1970

"In the long run, the Beatles were not good for rock-n-roll."—Nik Cohn, *Rock from the Beginning*, 1969

As the sixties unfolded, rock—real rock—grew increasingly obsessed with becoming an art. This trend had several effects on rock, some of them good, many of them detrimental. For one thing, rock became much more sophisticated musically, lyrically, structurally, in every way imaginable. To a point this development was healthy because you can go only so far on three chords, "let's dance, do-wop." And by incorporating new sounds, new styles, and new instruments rock opened new worlds to the generation of the sixties. For another thing, art is sometimes the only form of subversion tolerated by the uncomprehending toughs hired by the establishment to defend itself. So artiness might not have been such a bad tendency but for some other effects it had on rock.

Like squaring it with the critics and teachers, who often legitimize what has been revolutionary. When the Beatles are taught in schools, cooed over by serious music critics, and published in poetry anthologies, you know that something's been lost for something gained.

Or like consuming in the creation of art energies that might better have been expended in creating real social or political alternatives. Sixties life was being *intellectualized*. Art rock tended to produce discontented thinkers. Simple, proletarian rock-n-roll produced discontented *doers*. Substitute one for the other, and there goes your motion.

The great moment of awakening, when the sixties suddenly realized that rock could have form and shape, could be an artifice, could fill itself up with imagery and metaphor and tensions and ambiguities, was the release of the Beatles' *Sgt. Pepper's Lonely Hearts Club Band*. But it was the folk music flowering of the early sixties, and folksinger Bob Dylan in particular, that underlay *St. Pepper* and rock's impulse to become art.

This is not to say that folk music, protest songs, or even the young Dylan were inherently artsy. In fact, all three were anti-artsy, preferring homemade, unpolished simplicity to the sophistication of professional art. Folk music is nothing if not un-self-conscious; protest songs obviously place social considerations ahead of aesthetic concerns; and folksingers, Bob Dylan included, always try their best to be untutored hayseeds from the north country. Dave van Ronk recalled Dylan blown in from the Midwest.

> Being a hayseed, that was part of his image, or what he considered his image at the time. Like, once I asked him, "Do you know the French symbolists?" and he said, "Huh?"—the stupidist "Huh?" you can imagine—and later, when he had a place of his own, I went up there and on the bookshelf was a volume of French poets from Nerval to the present. I think it ended at Apollinaire, and it included Rimbaud, and it was all well-thumbed with passages underlined and notes in the margins. The man wanted to be a primitive, a natural kind of genius. He never talked about somebody like Rimbaud. But he *knew* Rimbaud all right. You see that in his later songs.

As long as the folk songs themselves remained old border ballads, union songs, and Woody Guthrie dust bowl laments, the *quality* of the music was largely untouched by its environment. But when the popular verdict came down, around 1962, in favor of allowing folksingers to perform their own material—written in the middle of the Village in the middle of the twentieth century—then the door was opened to a new kind of folk music. Then the climate of the Village and the college campus—intellectually charged, artistically sophisticated—would almost inevitably infiltrate not only folk music but the mind of the nation as well.

Folk music's inherent emphasis on words as meaning turned popular music in the direction of art and poetry. Fifties rock-n-roll was rarely big on words. With the conspicuous exception of Chuck Berry, most rockers viewed them as something to hang, well, not a tune but some noise on. That was groovy, but it would never be poetry or art. Folk songs come closer to art just because their lyrics are more central to their message, so folksingers spend more time on their words. In fact, ballads and blues lyrics and other folk songs have been considered poetry ("art") for some time now by curators who relegate pop music, including rock-n-roll, to the kitsch heap. Rock lyrics approached art only after the Byrds fused folk and rock in 1965.

> (The folk music they chose to electrify leaned heavily on Bob Dylan, who by 1965 was well into his French symbolist period. Musically the Byrds had a hard, crisp edge that sounded very artistic.)

The proto-poetic qualities of folk music can be seen in "Michael Row the Boat Ashore," which the Highwaymen sang into the top ten in 1961.

> River Jordan is chilly and cold,
> Hallelujah;

Chills the body but not the soul,
Hallelujah.

The song is allusive, symbolic, understated, loaded with hidden meaning. Like traditional folk music it's slightly biblical, slightly rural, and slightly dated. The same thing could be said of "Poor Wayfaring Stranger" and "House of the Rising Sun" and most of the other folk songs that filled the song bags of Village folkniks in the early sixties.

The intensification of poetic qualities in folk music by the climate of the sixties is obvious. You can't help connecting Bob Dylan's story about playing an East Orange coffeehouse, where he was constantly interrupted by chess players and he dreamed of being paid in chess pieces (the story, with a muffed punch line, is recorded on a bootleg tape), with his song on the death of Medgar Evers: "Only a Pawn in Their Game." It becomes obvious where Dylan got his metaphor, and it becomes obvious just how much the Village environment influenced folk music.

Other Dylan folk songs are nearly English class exercises in such standard poetic techniques as symbol, simile, metaphor, irony, and alliteration. In "Blowin' in the Wind" the symbols are so conventional as to hurt: white dove (peace) and cannon balls (war), roads and seas (hardship). In "A Hard Rain's A-Gonna Fall," the imagery is more original and more prominent. Word pictures hang like clusters of ripe grapes, a whole handful in each stanza, a potential song in each line. Fresh or clichéd, however, the images and metaphors are everywhere, along with ironies and ambiguities, and rhyme and alliteration, pictures in pure sound—everything, in short, Dylan needed to make him the poet he wanted to be.

Other Village folksingers were busy transforming folk music into poetry. Phil Ochs, at the time Dylan's peer, was a major source of topical protest lyrics and another repository of imagery, rhyme, alliteration, and hidden meaning (but not too hidden, since Ochs was writing protest songs). Paul Simon, English major, former rock-n-roller, part-time folksinger, was beginning to write his own poetic folk songs, very strongly influenced by the themes and techniques he had studied in college. And his partner, Art Garfunkel, was critiquing Simon's work in prose that sounded suspiciously like literary criticism.

I confess that *Bleecker Street* (finished in October 1963) was too much for me at first. The song is highly intellectual, the symbolism extremely challenging. The opening line in which the fog comes like a "shroud" over the city introduces the theme of "creative sterility." But it is the second verse which I find particularly significant:

Voices leaking from a sad cafe,
Smiling faces try to understand;
I saw a shadow touch a shadow's hand
On Bleecker Street.

The first line is a purely poetic image. The second touches poignantly on human conditions of our time.

In 1964 Simon wrote "Sounds of Silence," an elaboration of the failure-to-communicate theme broached in "Bleecker Street" and a (delayed) hit with the college set. In 1965, with "I Am a Rock," Simon was recognized as a folk rock poet.

By the time 1966 arrived, rock lyrics—well, *some* rock lyrics—were well on their way to being poems, and thus art. Ralph Gleason, soon to become a pillar of *Rolling Stone* magazine, wrote in the album notes to Simon and Garfunkel's *Parsley, Sage, Rosemary and Thyme* (1966):

> The New Youth of the Rock Generation has done something in American Popular song that has begged to be done for generations.
>
> It has taken the creation of the lyrics and the music out of the hands of the hacks and given it over to the poets. . . .
>
> That Simon and Garfunkel—and the other representatives of the new generation's songwriters, an elite which includes Bob Dylan, Phil Ochs, John Sebastian, Marty Balin, Dino Valenti, Tim Hardin, Al Kooper, Smokey Robinson, Mick Jagger, John Lennon, Paul McCartney, John Phillips and others—have succeeded in putting beauty and truth and meaning into popular song, fractures the stereotyped adult view that the music of youth is at best only trivial rhymes and silly teen-age noise, and at worst offensive.
>
> This generation is producing poets who write songs, and never before in the sixty-year history of American popular music has this been true.

Although others were willing to debate the issue—most notably Robert Christgau, "Rock Lyrics Are Poetry (Maybe)," which appeared in *Cheetah* in 1967—rock was clearly headed in the direction of poetry by the end of 1966. In fact, the Byrds had taken some verses from Ecclesiastes ("Turn, Turn, Turn"), Simon and Garfunkel had copped a poem from E. A. Robinson ("Richard Cory"), and Phil Ochs had set to music an Edgar Allen Poe poem ("The Bells"). Bob Dylan had written "Desolation Row" (1965), with its reference to Ezra Pound and T. S. Eliot fighting in the captain's tower and its imagery (mermaids singing below the sea) borrowed from Eliot's "Love Song of J. Alfred Prufrock." And he had written "Love Minus Zero/No Limit" (1965), with its fire and ice imagery borrowed from Frost's "Some say the world will end in fire, / Others say in ice."

> "The man is his *own* man, has his own statement to make and makes it. He's a universal poet. He's not trying to be white or colored. The man is just a great *poet*. And I admire him very much."—Nina Simone on Bob Dylan

(It is a little-known fact that in addition to his pilgrimage to Woody Guthrie, Dylan also made a
pilgrimage in 1964 to Carl Sandburg, retired in
North Carolina: "You're Carl Sandburg. I'm Bob
Dylan. I'm a poet too.")

Paul Simon had written "Dangling Conversation" (1966), with its reference
to poets Frost and Dickinson, and "A Simple Desultory Philippic," with
poets Bob Dylan and Dylan Thomas. Poet Leonard Cohen had set his poem
"Suzanne" to a folkish tune, and singer Judy Collins had recorded it on *In
My Life* (1966).

None of these borrowed poems and none of the references to literature
class poets seemed particularly out of place because rock lyrics had become
poems themselves or as like poems as to make the differences negligible.
The fact, of course, was not recognized at the time, and most art rock came
packaged somewhat inaccurately as folk rock. It was not widely played on
AM radio, so it did not crack many of the top-forty lists; however, it had an
enormous following on college campuses and among pop musicians, many
of whom *did* enjoy substantial AM air play and had collected vast legions of
fans. This mid-sixties art rock was influential out of all proportion to its record sales and—after the Beatles came over in 1966 and 1967—proved to be
the cutting edge of sixties rock.

Many of these songs of the late 1964 to late 1966 period remain even today some of the best art rock available. They are mature without being
overripe, artistic without being artsy, poetic without being overly sopho-
moric or overly opaque.

The best of it came from Dylan—*Bringing It All Back Home, Highway
61 Revisited*, and *Blonde on Blonde*: "Subterranean Homesick Blues,"
"Gates of Eden," "Mr. Tambourine Man," "Like a Rolling Stone," "Desolation Row," "Visions of Johanna," "Memphis Blues Again," "Sad-Eyed Lady
of the Lowlands," and a couple of dozen others that Dylan freaks know by
heart, long years after their release.

John Lennon once claimed that he didn't get most poetry, but he always
understood Dylan, there was never any shadow, it was all right there. And
this is true, even if it's surreal and beyond explanation on a "first this, and
then this, and then this" basis. But Dylan's lyrics from this time are also intensely personal. He belongs with the so-called confessional poets (Sylvia
Plath, Robert Lowell), who look in to look out. "Like a Rolling Stone" is
first and foremost about Bob Dylan. And "Maggie's Farm" and "Visions of
Johanna" as well. Dylan had left the protest movement, which was busy
pointing fingers at other people, and had begun to point a finger at himself.
He had departed from external reality for the landscape of his own soul, the
smoke rings of his own mind.

Most of these are songs of personal torment and frustration, loaded with
absurdist vision and strange apocalypse and obvious paranoia. They are

filled with hate, ridicule, and scorn, but it's all internally directed. For all the talk of departure and escape, there are too few moments of actual freedom, too little exaltation of the "Like a Rolling Stone" variety. Often the escape is into art ("the harmonicas play the skeleton keys" that spring Dylan in "Visions of Johanna"; the Tambourine Man's magic swirling ship is first and before all else a tambourine), and often it is only partially satisfactory.

More often there is no exit at all. "Better climb down a manhole," Dylan concluded in "Subterranean Homesick Blues." "Can this really be the end?" he asked desperately in "Stuck inside of Mobile with the Memphis Blues Again." In "Desolation Row" he had lost even the desire to escape.

As portraits of frustration, these songs were somewhat ahead of the times. It is true that the nation felt confusion and frustration following the assassination of President Kennedy: Lyndon Johnson was an unknown quantity, and the tremendous uplift Camelot had given the national psyche was neutralized in an absurd, totally incomprehensible instant. For one blinding, unnerving blink, the irrationality of things had been made unmistakably clear. Even strong men winced. Civil rights, the Peace Corps, all the other dreams of social reconstruction hung precariously. Chaos threatened.

But failed to materialize. Not in 1964. Not to the extent suggested by "Desolation Row" or "Stuck inside of Mobile." Next to 1968, 1964 was good times politically, socially, economically. The insanity of Dylan's lyrics, though certainly a foreshadowing of the apocalypse to come, stemmed more from his own personal problems as a reluctant and confused leader, and from the nightmare visions of the poets he was imitating, than from social realities.

Some rock artists of the 1964–1966 period imitated Dylan's dark vision. In 1966 Phil Ochs wrote "Crucifixion," an allegorical elegy on the death of John Kennedy, with obvious transmutation of politician into Christ figure.

Then his message gathers meaning, and it spreads across the land.
The rewarding of the fame is the following of the man.
But ignorance is everywhere and people have their way,
And success is an enemy to the losers of the day.
In the shadows of the churches who knows what they pray.
And blood is the language of the band.

So dance, dance, dance, teach us to be true.
Come dance, dance, dance; 'cause we love you.

In an allegory that swept across two thousand years of history, Ochs traced the process of co-option. His only consolation lay in the cyclical nature of this process: "Crucifixion" ends where it began, with the birth of a new hero and a new sacrifice.

(The critics were unimpressed. "To the land of the art song [Ochs] is certainly a stranger," chirped

> *Boston Broadside.* However, teachers of poetry
> rallied to "Crucifixion," including it in two or
> three late sixties anthologies of modern poetry.)

The most remarkable aspect of "Crucifixion," however, is the elaborate musical arrangement by Ian Freebairn-Smith and Joseph Byrd and the baroque production job by Larry Marks: atonality, electronic gadgetry, strings, brass—all the developing artiness of art rock. (And, shades of things to come, a significant step in the transformation of protest into art.) The music *sounds* cosmic, descending out of and then receding into the great recesses of the galaxy to reflect the concentration and then the diffusion of holy goodness in the sacrificial victim. "Crucifixion" *is* a good poem and an involving head trip.

Yet it was the Beatles who were crucial to the development and popularization of artiness in rock music. For better or worse, their conversion to art rock turned all of rock into self-conscious art around 1968, which is exactly why people who liked their music heavy, loud, and mindless, expressed ambivalence toward the moptops and their effects on rock-n-roll. Dylan commanded the musicians and the intelligentsia; the Beatles commanded *everyone*—in England, in America, around the world. And in the middle sixties they commanded absolutely: where they led, their audiences would follow without hesitation.

The albums *Rubber Soul* (December 1965), *Yesterday and Today* (June 1966), and *Revolver* (August 1966), and songs like "Nowhere Man" (February 1966), "Yellow Submarine" and "Eleanor Rigby" (August 1966), "All You Need Is Love" (October 1966), and "Strawberry Fields Forever" (February 1967) were seminal. Somewhere between game and earnest, the Beatles moved from the amateur, formulaic, lyrically and musically limited "I Want to Hold Your Hand" and "I'm Happy Just to Dance with You" to the realm of the serious song.

"The best of these memorable tunes," wrote Ned Rorem in the *New York Review of Books* in 1968, "compare with those by composers from great eras of song: Monteverdi, Schumann, Poulenc." "The remarkable song 'Tomorrow Never Knows,'" wrote Wilfrid Mellers in 1967, "begins with jungle noises very similar to Coleman's or Coltrane's 'free' jazz, and employs both vocal and instrumental techniques which we may find both in Ornette Coleman and in Stockhausen!" Richard Poirier summed things up for readers of the *Partisan Review* in 1968: "Well, sometimes they are like Monteverdi and sometimes their songs are even better than Schumann's."

> "Then I was consciously writing poetry, and that's
> self-conscious poetry."—John Lennon, 1971

The Beatles' thematic range had expanded immeasurably: from handholding and dancing they moved on to taxmen and paperback writers, nowhere men and pill doctors, and the (bittersweet) human condition. Love was more ambiguous, less naive, and certainly more than just holding hands. Lovers quarreled, girls teased, affairs came and went with all the magic and all the impermanence of "Norwegian Wood." Some people never loved at all, living like Eleaner Rigby and Father McKenzie within a world of each other. Philosophically the Beatles had grown up.

As their range of subjects broadened, the Beatles' technique—musical and verbal—also developed. Quickly. Instrumentation became increasingly exotic, increasingly arty. The sitar was introduced in "Norwegian Wood," the cello in "Eleanor Rigby." Rhythms and chord progressions became increasingly subtle, increasingly rich. Lyrics broke out of the simple stanza-refrain form, or the old Tin Pan Alley pattern of melody A, repeated melody A, melody B, and then melody A again. Lennon's "Joycean verbal play" (the phrase is Poirier's) became increasingly prominent and increasingly subtle ("She Said She Said"), with the result that "no one is ever in danger of reading too much into the lyrics of their songs" (again Poirier). Most obviously, the Beatles began offering explicit philosophizing on the one hand ("Turn off your mind; relax and float downstream") and hard, concrete, visual details on the other ("picks up the rice in the church where a wedding has been"). Early Beatles lyrics are noteworthy in their avoidance of concrete images, literary allusions (like, for example, the pennies on the dead man's eyes in "Taxman"), and heavy themes. Their songs from *Revolver–Rubber Soul* days are full of all three. The Beatles were writing poems, serious songs.

The Beatles themselves were not all that holy about their art, however, not even about the great songs like "Norwegian Wood" and "Strawberry Fields Forever" and "Eleanor Rigby." Or, to extend the narrative into the golden age of sixties art rock, about all those other complexities on *Magical Mystery Tour, Sgt. Pepper* and the white album of 1968. John Lennon:

> It's nice when people like it, but when they start "appreciating" it, getting great deep things out of it, making a thing of it, then it's a lot of shit. It proves what we've always thought about most sorts of so-called art. It's all a lot of shit. . . . It all becomes a big con.
>
> We're a con as well. They've given us the freedom to con them. Let's stick that in there, we say, that'll start them puzzling. I'm sure all artists do, when they realize it's a con. I bet Picasso sticks things in. I bet he's been laughing his balls off for the last eighty years.

"Being for the Benefit of Mr. Kite"—the Beatles tell us straight-facedly—came directly off a wall poster. "Good Morning, Good Morning" was a television commercial. "Lucy in the Sky with Diamonds" was from a drawing by John's son Julian. Hunter Davies's biography is full of stories of how Beatles lyrics supposedly got composed: John and Paul have a tune and a name, "A Little Help from My Friends." John sings, "Are you afraid when you turn out the lights?" Paul suggests a song that is a series of questions and adds, "Do you believe in love at first sight?" Then, "No, it hasn't got the right number of syllables. What do you think? Can we split it up and have a pause to give an extra syllable?" Then Paul comes up with "Do you believe in a love at first sight?" John sings it back and adds, "Yes, I'm certain that it happens all the time." Then they are stuck and they begin "larking around," stomping out "Can't Buy Me Love" and "Tequila." Then John's back with "What do you see when you turn out the light?" "I can't tell you, but I know it's mine" follows easily. Then more horsing around, and they call Ringo to tell him the song is done, which it is not, and off they go to the EMI studios. And that's how "With a Little Help from My Friends," a very important song in the story of Sgt. Pepper and his band, got composed.

> "Lennon and McCartney are the only rock song-
> writers who combine high literacy (as high as
> Dylan's or Simon's) with an eye for concision and
> a truly contemporary sense of what fits."
> —Robert Christgau, 1967

So the Beatles became artists. And if the collective wisdom of a genera-tion of pop critics is to be trusted, they became very good artists, maybe in spite of themselves, maybe just by sticking things in. And thus it was that the Beatles, and rock, and the sixties came to *Sgt. Pepper's Lonely Hearts Club Band*, released to an expectant world on June 1, 1967.

Sgt. Pepper was the album of the decade. It contained more instruments, more tracks, more concrete images, more word play, more metaphysics, more money and time (the first Beatles album took one day and £400 to record; *Sgt. Pepper* took four months and £25,000). The rhyme and meter and rhythm (and tone) are complicated, the old Tin Pan Alley AABA form warped far out of recognizable shape.

> For the benefit of Mr. Kite
> There will be a show tonight
> On trampoline.
> The Hendersons will all be there
> Late of Pablo Fanques Fair
> What a scene.
> Over men and horses hoops and garters
> Lastly through a hogshead of real fire!
> In this way
> Mr. K.
> Will challenge the world!

Perhaps most unusual, *Sgt. Pepper* is not simply a collection of hit singles or of potential hit singles: it has a beginning and an end and a middle, a central idea, a governing metaphor. It told a story. It was a concept album.

> "We realized . . . that someday someone would ac-
> tually be holding a thing that they'd call 'the
> Beatles' new LP' and that normally it would just be
> a collection of songs or a nice picture on the cover,
> nothing more. So the idea was to do a complete
> thing that you could make what you liked of; just
> a little magic presentation. We were going to have
> a little envelope in the center with the nutty things
> you can buy at Woolworth's: a surprise packet."
> —Paul McCartney

The notion of a concept album is self-conscious and artsy. But when the concept of the album is what everyone called "the Beatles' 'Wasteland'" a thematic and structural equivalent of Eliot's poem, there is less madness and more art in the wind.

In the waning months of 1967, throughout 1968, and on into 1969 came the whirlwind of art rock. The generation had come philosophically and musically of age and it was ready. (A few joints or a tab of acid didn't hurt any, either.) Rock exploded in lush images and lusher arrangements. Album covers turned to rococo ornamentation, and lyric poems were routinely printed either on jackets or on inserts. Here was Poetry with a capital P, Art with a capital A.

Some was good and some was bad. Some was good for rock and for the sixties; some was not so good because now the dangers of artiness showed more clearly than they had before.

The first and most obvious danger was that art lured some very solid folksingers or rock-n-rollers who just weren't cut out to be artists in the Beatles' or Dylan's or Simon's fashion and who fell disastrously, embarrassingly on their faces trying to be artsy. The Rolling Stones are an important case in point. Mick Jagger is not John Lennon, and the Stones chose to break from producer Andrew Loog Oldham and go it on their own at the very moment they chose to follow the Beatles into high art; the result was *Their Satanic Majesties Request*, a flop on all counts. Suddenly the songs are full of images and colors. The album jacket features a three-dimensional photo of wizard Jagger and his psychedelic companions among the flowers and the planets (more the fool on the hill than a mystical Sgt. Pepper). The air is thick with Eastern mysticism, a result of the Maharishi and a Taoist classic Jagger had been reading called *The Secret of the Golden Flower* (or was it simply debased George Harrison?).

The poetry is strictly junior high school; the jamming, mediocre. The cops from *Sgt. Pepper* are obvious on a first listening: the dubbed bits and electronic distortions of "On with the Show," the use of "Sing This Song Together" to open and close side one of the album (as the Beatles had used "Sgt. Pepper" to frame their album), similarities between "She's a Rainbow" and "Lucy in the Sky with Diamonds." And for a theme, the two human companies of the damned and the elect, a kind of "Eleanor Rigby"–"Yellow Submarine" set piece.

Jann Wenner, editor of *Rolling Stone*, called the album a culmination of "all the pretentious, nonmusical, boring, insignificant, self-conscious and worthless stuff that's been tolerated during the past year," and as far as the Stones' music was concerned, he was right. In the fall of 1968 they got themselves together and hired a producer and returned with *Beggar's Banquet* to the mother lode of rhythm and blues: "Love in Vain," "Prodigal Son," "Midnight Rambler."

> (The aftereffects, however, were some time in wearing off. "Street Fighting Man," from *Beggar's Banquet*, straddles a thin line between actual violence in the streets and violence sublimated into playing for a rock-n-roll band. It is coy the way earlier Stones songs are not coy.)

Joan Baez was another not really suited to high art. She was magic singing a folk song and starlight doing young Bob Dylan's protest songs. But *Baptism* (1968), subtitled "A Journey through Our Time," was not a good idea for either Joan or the times: a collection of songs and poems designed to be a collage of the age, a portrait-anthology in poetry. All the important names are there: Whitman, Ferlinghetti, Joyce, Blake, Rimbaud, Rexroth, Yevtushenko, cummings, García Lorca, even John Donne ("No Man Is an Island") and Countee Cullen. But it did not, could not generate the kind of reaction Baez's earlier work had produced. (Neither could *Any Day Now*, an album full of Dylan's songs, also released in 1968. The interpretation of songs like "I Pity the Poor Immigrant," "Sad-Eyed Lady of the Lowlands," and "Dear Landlord" is shallow, and it proved again that nobody sings Dylan like Dylan except maybe the Byrds.)

The second danger of increased artiness was obscurity.

Obscurity, of course, has been a problem in all modern art: people just do not understand modern art, and artists rebelling against being expected to be understood make it a point to defy understanding. Most poets—during the sixties especially—seemed to pride themselves on their obscurity. The imagistic poem made it particularly difficult at times to tell the difference between a work of genius and pretentious imitation. Until the end of 1967, art rock had been intent mostly on making a statement. It made its statements subtly, indirectly, with a sophistication absent in earlier rock-n-roll, but it made statements. After the close of 1967, art rock became more obscure.

This trend is fairly obvious in the work of rockers trying to be artists, say, the Rolling Stones in *Satanic Majesties*. It is less obvious in a song by, say, the Beatles, who generally made good sense. But the Beatles came increasingly to offend in this matter of obscurity, in albums like *Abbey Road* (1969) and in songs like "I Am the Walrus" (1967): "Crabalocker fishwife pornographic priestess boy you been a naughty girl." This makes no sense. Overdub it a few times with somebody chanting "everybody's a hunchback" or "everybody turn on" or "turn me on, dead man" or whatever he *was* chanting (a question the answer to which lies lost in the cistern of Beatles' history), and somebody else reading from Shakespeare's *King Lear* ("a serviceable villian, as duteous to the vices of thy mistress as badness would desire." "What, is he dead?" "Sit you down, father, rest you."), and somebody else mumbling God knows what about the English garden, and you have a small monument to sticking bits in. "I Am the Walrus" falls just short of being a parody of art rock because it demands we take it seriously. Which makes it closest of any major Beatles lyric to pure poetic pretense.

Just as obscure are songs like Cream's "White Room" (1968) and Procol Harum's "Whiter Shade of Pale" (August 1967), set to J. S. Bach's "Sleepers Awake."

> She said "There is no reason,
> And the truth is plain to see,"
> But I wandered through my playing cards
> And would not let her be
> One of sixteen vestal virgins
> Who were leaving for the coast
> And although my eyes were open
> They might just as well been closed.

This is all very literary, to be sure. So is Cream's "Tales of Brave Ulysses." And very subtle musically, with the Bach and all. Blood, Sweat, and Tears were musically sophisticated, too, with "Variations on a Theme by Erik Satie" (1969). But what was being said?

Maybe it would be more accurate to accuse the Beatles and Cream and Procol Harum and BS&T of pretension rather than deliberate obscurity. A lot of people considered the Doors pretty pretentious, especially when they took an old Morrison high school poem titled "Horse Latitudes" and *read* it to audiences and purchasers of their second album, released in October 1967. Or when they filled their lyrics with Freudian symbols and sexual imagery and Lennonesque word play ("She's a Twentieth Century Fox," oh yes she is . . .).

Most pretentious of all, however, was Van Dyke Parks, the king of sixties artiness, whose ambitious *Song Cycle* was released in November 1967 after seven months of production and plenty more money than Warner Records ever made from it. Parks had earned his shot at an album by writing and producing songs for Harper's Bizarre and by collaborating with the Beach Boys' Brian Wilson on the great lost album of rock music, reportedly highly artistic and slightly pretentious itself, tentatively called *Smiles*, never seen or heard except for a single tantalizing Wilson-Parks fragment, "Heroes and Villains," on the *Smiley Smile* album. Parks was a session man of undisputed talent, burdened with a certain musical and philosophical profundity. When he got his chance, he blew it big.

Song Cycle credits no fewer than sixty-five musicians, not including engineers, "musical advisor and conductor," "contractor," and sound effects men. It features a violin solo and a viola solo, a harp, four percussionists, a couple of dozen strings, half a dozen woodwinds, and reeds, brass, an accordian, a few balalaikas, drummers drumming, pipers piping, and a partridge in a pear tree. It's got everything you can think of, and it sounds as little like rock music as do the Moody Blues' offerings. If you listen closely you can pick out musical allusions to Beethoven, Debussy, Ives, Stravinsky, Bartok, Mahler, Stockhausen, "Nearer My God to Thee," "The Battle Hymn of the Republic," "The Star-Spangled Banner," saloon piano, silent movie music, Hollywood film music circa 1947, Hawaiian serenades, bluegrass and "Black Jack Daisy," sung by Steve Young of Gadsden, Alabama. Its lyrics are a verbal analogue of its music: neo–waste land, full of vaulting fragments, juxtapositions, ironies, and ambiguities. "Back to the academically beautiful," observed Sandy Pearlman, looking back at the album in 1970. "And we note that the ideal for this stuff's words is most of the poetry we had to learn in the seventh through twelfth grades. Perhaps that explains its high dullness potential."

(*Song Cycle* was Parks's first and last album.)

A third problem with art rock was that it tended to emasculate the movement for social reform. This is important because rock and folk protest traditionally had worked to strengthen social and even political revolution. Rock made you dance, and sometimes it made you smash things. Folk protest made you march and shout. It made you angry. But art rock tended to tangle you in complexities and engage your mind rather than your fists.

Paul Simon's "The Boxer," for example, is really a protest song, and a warning, and a demand that something be done. The poor boy has been kicked around, used and abused, bought off time and again for a pocketful of mumbles, lies, and jests. No job, no bread, no clothes, just the bleeding New York winters. And yet underneath the wiped out, docile, impotent exterior lurks a fighter who remembers every cut and every bruise and every embarrassment and is one day gonna even up the score. There is something totally unnerving in the "lie la-lie" chorus as it grinds to a tooth-rattling crescendo, and maybe for just an instant you sense what Simon is trying to say. But "The Boxer" is a subtle song and a work of art. It makes its point obliquely, and there is a very real danger that its point is missed entirely, and what happens then? (The same might be said of other songs on *Bridge over Troubled Water*, like "So Long, Frank Lloyd Wright" or "El Condor Pasa.") So if the protest is lost in the art, then isn't maybe an earlier, less artistic work like "Sparrow" or "Wednesday Morning, 3 A.M." a better song? Or one more useful to the movement for social reform?

The same argument, of course, could be made for Bob Dylan's art protest songs like "Subterranean Homesick Blues" and "Highway 61 Revisited." It could also be made about the Jefferson Airplane's *Sgt. Pepper*–influenced concept album *After Bathing at Baxters* (1968), in a song like "Rejoyce." "War is good business, so invest your son," sings Gracie Slick satirically, and it should be impossible to miss the point. Except that there is so much else going on in the song, most of it having to do with artiness, that the antiwar message gets lost in the explanation that "Rejoyce" means "re Joyce," that is, James Joyce, author of *Ulysses*, which contains characters named Stephen (that's the Stephen mentioned in the line "Stephen won't give his arm to no ghost on mother's farm") and Molly Bloom, who is having an affair with a man named Blazes Boylan (also mentioned) and who talks a lot about arms and legs (also mentioned) and whose husband sleeps at the bottom of the bed, which explains a line about all that, and isn't this truly an amazing song?

Artiness did not help movement singer Phil Ochs, either. In the old days of "I've got something to say, sir, and I'm gonna say it now" it was pretty easy to grasp what Phil was protesting against. Even "Crucifixion" is fairly direct, as are some of the later art protest songs like "I Kill, Therefore I Am" (cops) and "White Boots Marching in a Yellow Land" (Vietnam). In a song like "The Scorpion Departs but Never Returns" (1969), however, Phil tended to leave the real world of social struggle for the fantasy world of art. His theme is a subject he used earlier in another song, "The Thresher": the nuclear submarine that disappears into the void, not a trace, not a toothbrush, not a cigarette to be seen. Here the ship becomes a symbol for a new lost generation, the Vietnam dropouts.

> Radio is begging them to come back to the shore
> All will be forgiven, it'll be just like before
> All you ever wanted will be waiting by the door,
> We will forgive you, we will forgive you, we will forgive you.
>
> But no one gives an answer, not even one good-bye.
> The silence of their leaving is all that they reply.
> Some have chosen to decay and others chose to die
> But I'm not dying, no I'm not dying, tell me I'm not dying. . . .

There exists nowhere a more articulate statement of the painful choices that confronted sensitive young Americans in 1967 and of the anguish felt by everyone—establishment and counterculture—when large numbers of men chose to depart in silence. But what's dangerous about "The Scorpion Departs" is the way the real world turns poetically surreal; the song almost (but not quite) becomes a song about a song, not about draft evasion.

The schooner ship is sliding across the kitchen sink
My son and my daughter, they won't know what to think
The crew has turned to voting and the officers to drink. . . .

Isn't the problem with *Yellow Submarine* and all other art protest songs that they slip into fairyland? When you come face to face with the Blue Meanies in real life, they don't evaporate the way they do in the movie. You discover the hard way that it's *you* who's been living an illusion all along, the illusion of art. Then you must make a choice: either you opt for the world of social and political reform or you climb into the world of art. Ochs, at the close of the sixties, climbed into art. In "Rehearsals for Retirement" he took his tattered colors from the tournament and went home. A year or so later we find him in isolation at an imaginary rest home for artists.

I'll talk, I'll talk, they live by the sea
Surrounded by a cemetery.
If you have time stop by for some tea
With Bach, Beethoven, Mozart and me.

(The choice—and the decision—were those of another artist-revolutionary to whom Ochs alluded in one of the finest art rock songs of the sixties, "William Butler Yeats Visits Lincoln Park and Escapes Unscathed." Yeats was a leader of the fight for Irish independence and a major poet in whom Ochs saw parallels to himself. Building around Yeats's work the way Slick built around Joyce's *Ulysses*, Ochs recounted the disorders of Chicago, 1968, called indirectly for a revolution, tied the struggles of 1968 with the struggles of Ireland in 1917 and himself with Yeats. The song is a tour de force, but it is art, not revolution.)

Leonard Cohen released his own masterful album of art songs in January 1968. A poet and novelist of some reputation (and quality) before beginning his career as a singer, Cohen wrote songs that are legitimate works of art, real poems. "Suzanne," "Sisters of Mercy," "Stories of the Street," later "The Story of Isaac" and "Last Year's Man" and "Joan of Arc." His song-poems, moreover, are not as utterly removed from the scene of the sixties social and political reformation as are songs like "Whiter Shade of Pale" and most poetry of the decade. "The Story of Isaac" was especially on target in 1967 when it was written.

You who build these altars now
To sacrifice these children,
You must not do it any more.
A scheme is not a vision. . . .

The point is that like most poets, Cohen saw many sides of an issue and was therefore less absolutely, dead-on certain than your standard SDS ideologue. When it came to activism, Cohen—like most poets—passed. "He is frozen in an anarchist's posture, but unable to throw his bomb," wrote William Kloman in the New York Times. "At the time of the Bay of Pigs . . . he was unable to determine which side to fight on. Both sides were evil, both causes were holy." So Cohen didn't fight. In "Stories of the Street" he retreated from the issues in a medieval ascent to the spheres.

> We are so small between the stars,
> So large against the sky
> And lost among the subway crowds
> I try to catch your eye.

The last problem with art rock was that it tended to produce professionalism. Which discourages innovation, lay participation, and content while encouraging elitism and style. And that ultimately separates rock musicians from their audiences. Like rock-n-roll and folk music, rock never intended to be professional. Sophisticated, maybe, but professional, never.

Again, Dylan and the Beatles present cases in point, especially the Beatles because the white album that followed Sgt. Pepper and Magical Mystery Tour is so obviously professional. It is so professional that every one of its thirty songs is absolutely first-rate, and it is so ultimately disappointing because of its eclectic professionalism. You want a calypso? Okay. You want a country ballad? Okay, too. How about a heavy blues? We can do that as well.

Professionalism of any sort was death to the sixties. It meant a tighter reign on emotions and commitment, a cool remove. It meant more organization and delegated authority, it meant more system and more boxes for people to be put in, it meant more of everything the sixties—and rock—held suspect.

These tendencies that vitiated rock and the movement of the sixties may have been just what made Bob Dylan turn his back on artiness and professionalism and at the close of John Wesley Harding adopt the simplest, most hokey, most unpoetic and unprofessional music of all, country music. Along with its assorted metaphysical progressions through guilt, confession, atonement, and grace, and along with its musical progression from rock to country, came a farewell to high poetry. On side one of Harding Dylan sang one of the most metrically perfect, thematically and metaphorically clear poems in rock.

> I dreamed I saw St. Augustine,
> Alive as you or me,
> Tearing through these quarters
> In the utmost misery,
> With a blanket underneath his arm

And a coat of solid gold,
Searching for the very souls
Whom already have been sold.

"Arise, arise," he cried so loud,
In a voice without restraint,
"Come out, ye gifted kings and queens
And hear my sad complaint.
No martyr is among you now
Whom you can call your own,
So go on your way accordingly
But know you're not alone."

I dreamed I saw St. Augustine,
Alive with fiery breath,
And I dreamed I was amongst the ones
That put him out to death.
Oh, I awoke in anger,
So alone and terrified,
I put my finger against the glass
And bowed my head and cried.

After this kind of song what was Dylan doing when he closed *Harding* with "that big, fat moon is gonna shine like a spoon"? And on his next album sang: "Peggy Day stole my poor heart away, by golly, what more can I say." And: "I'd be sad and blue, if not for you." And all that absolutely sloppy, totally unprofessional singing on *Self-Portrait*—is it not a deliberate denial of art? A complete rejection of professionalism?

John Lennon would follow, at a distance of a couple of years, giving over "consciously writing poetry" for the simple, unpoetic, proletarian "Working Class Hero" and "Power to the People." A few others would follow as well, at even further remove, but a great deal of rock continued in the tradition of art rock, drawing itself and its audiences further and further from the arena of social and political activism. Looking back one has to admit that although great, great art came out of rock in the sixties (dozens of Dylan lyrics, Beatles lyrics, Leonard Cohen songs, albums like *Sgt. Pepper* and *John Wesley Harding* and Simon and Garfunkel's *Bookends*), in the long run art was not good for rock. Poetry was not good for rock. The sixties were too real for poetry.

Another art form that attracted rock toward the end of the sixties was theater. Of course rock had had theatrical aspirations ever since the days of Alan Freed, Jerry Lee Lewis, and Elvis. The Beatles were told in Hamburg to "make show." They did and they got famous. The Stones always made show because they were imitating black high strutters who made show. There was *no* show like that made by soul brother number one, James Brown. Little Richard was the granddaddy of show. Even folksingers and the San Francisco groups that made a show of not making show were acting out very rigidly defined roles. So you had to dress it up a little, to get people interested, to get the message out. Otherwise you were lost.

The danger is obvious: the same substitution of style for content worked by poetry. But the risks of show are infinitely greater because for every American conned by poetry and classical music ten are conned by Las Vegas flash. Donovan got further with his flower power spectaculars, and Elvis and Sinatra infinitely further with their floor show theatrics, than did Van Dyke Parks with his two dozen violins or Phil Ochs with his allusions to Yeats and Whitman. Those who got the furthest were those who took rock directly to big theater: the Who with *Tommy*, Broadway with *Hair*, *Godspell*, and *Jesus Christ Superstar*, Alice Cooper with rock theater.

The marriage of rock and theater—real theater now, not just making show—began with Jim Morrison and the Doors. Morrison was an artsy sort, UCLA drama and arts department, specialty in the classics. One volume of published poetry, another circulating in manuscript among intimates. "Very serious about being a poet," a friend recalled. Also about film. But above all about avant-garde, Living Theater–type drama: characters out of Jung and Freud developing relatively free-form performances out of shorthand scripts, moving as the occasion and the audience and the spirit allowed, a drama of psychological rather than narrative truth, a drama of myth and idea more than story and character. A drama close to the primeval roots. Morrison wrote:

> In its origin the Greek Theater was a band of worshipers, dancing and singing on a threshing floor at the crucial agricultural seasons. Then, one day, a possessed person leaped out of the crowd and started imitating a god. At first it was pure song and movement. As cities developed, more people became dedicated to making money, but they had to keep contact with Nature somehow. So they had actors do it for them. I think rock serves the same function and may become a kind of theater.

In 1967 the Doors gave rock the semitheatrical "The End," a ritual enactment of the oedipal complex, performance of which resulted in the group's expulsion from the Whisky-a-Go-Go. In 1969 it was the Freudian "Soft Parade." In 1968 Morrison and the Doors came up with the epitome of rock as serious theater, "Celebration of the Lizard," subtitled "Lyrics to a Theatre Composition by the Doors."

> I am the Lizard King
> I can do anything
> I can make the earth stop in its tracks
> I made the blue cars go away
>
> For seventeen years I dwelt
> In the loose palace of exile,

Playing strange games
With the girls of the island.

Now I have come again
To the land of the fair, & the strong, & the wise.

Brothers & sisters of the pale forest
O children of Night
Who among you will run with the hunt?

Now Night arrives with her purple legion.
Retire now to your tents & go to your dreams,
Tomorrow we enter the town of my birth.
I want to be ready.

Even today these pieces come off as plot summaries for improvisational performances in some weird, psychomythic theater. But for them really to come alive you needed Morrison himself "in a blue flame (all right, so it was only a blue light shining on him!) above the audience's head on the scaffold left over from the *Hair* set," as Harvey Peer of the *Los Angeles Free Press* remembered him in 1969 or "along the misty littoral of Southern California, facing the setting sun leading a hippie tribe in their shamanistic rites," as Albert Goldman pictured him. Offstage and on record there was too little of either rock's joy or theater's catharsis to make the song-dramas work.

The best of rock theater was undoubtedly the Who's *Tommy* (1969), although it's been gummed up since by a symphonic performance, a Broadway musical, and most recently a superflick produced at a cost of $3.5 million with a cast of Eric Clapton, Elton John, and Ann-Margret.

Pete Townshend had been moving toward opera-theater for some time. *Tommy* can be traced ultimately to "La-La-La-Lies" on the *My Generation* album (1965), a dramatic monologue recounting an abortive seduction. Then came "A Quick One While He's Away" in 1967, heralded by Lillian Roxon in her *Encyclopedia* as "a very complicated twelve-minute rock opera." "A Quick One" is the story of Ivor the engine driver, an illicit child, and a quick one while hubby's away. Hubby returns, of course, in the middle of things, but all is forgiven. *Tommy* fans will recognize the germ of Tommy's story in this scenario, and from "A Quick One" to *Tommy* was largely a matter of time and scale.

So along came *Tommy*, with overture and recitative and chorus and all the trappings of classical opera. Mod made the Met in New York, and the way was opened for the aforementioned Broadway play and the cinematic spectacular, and the ascension of the Who into the establishment's artistic heaven.

> "Most people's pinball machines are their cars . . .
> it's the same fascination with machines."
> —Pete Townshend

But *Tommy* did not start out on the inside; in fact, for all the ballyhoo about opera, there is infinitely more mod than Verdi in *Tommy*, and more Who and more rock and more social commentary. These elements, rather than the artsiness and the heavy man's-inhumanity-to-man or lack-of-communication themes, explain *Tommy*'s success: flash and bash and cash, the apotheosis of pinball, the vibrations, and the "Sensation."

There is much less of this in *Hair* and even less in *Superstar*, the two other major sixties productions in rock theater. *Hair* actually predated *Tommy*, opening on October 17, 1967, in the old Astor Library in the Village, thence to the Cheetah discotheque, thence to Broadway's Biltmore, and thence to the world. It was enormously popular: cast albums alone sold over five million copies. And it had enough of the counterculture flavor to elicit the usual put-downs: no point, no quality, no sophistication, no acting, no art, the end of musicals, of stage, of art, of civilization. For some, at least, *Hair* was an exit, but most of those who thronged to the Biltmore were suspiciously paunchy and damnably affluent. Children of the sixties found *Hair* but one more co-option of countercultural forms and life styles, suitably sanitized by the establishment mostly to make money. (As for the music, as Tom Topor noted in *Rolling Stone*, Galt MacDermot's tunes are no more rock than the music of a toothpaste commercial.)

Superstar was even further from home. It has one major moment: "I Don't Know How to Love Him," sung by groupie Mary Magdalene. Though purporting to be a fresh way of looking at Christianity, *Superstar* is bad theology and worse rock. And unlike *Tommy* it failed to confront any of the many complex, pressing issues facing rock, the movement, the country in the sixties.

Godspell, composed by John-Michael Tebelak in a nonstop frenzy after a boring, pro forma Easter vigil at Pittsburgh's Anglican cathedral, is infinitely better theology, music (not really rock either), and theater.

Well, once opened, the door to rock opera and rock theater let pass the rock *Two Gentlemen of Verona* and *Inner City*. And also *Iphegenia, Ain't Supposed to Die a Natural Death, Company, Follies, The Survival of St. Joan, Tarot, Stomp, Blood, The Me Nobody Knows, Salvation, Your Own Sweet Thing, Sambo, The Last Sweet Days of Isaac*. Do you remember Jethro Tull and *Passion Play*? Some of this was good news; some, bad. *Tarot* even used real rock musicians from the Grateful Dead and Country Joe's Fish. But if rock was ever going to make it as Broadway theater, then somebody had to lie: rock wanted to assault audiences, to take them out of their seats and everyday lives and habitual modes of thinking and acting. Broadway theater had by the late sixties become too much a reinforcement of habit to coexist with real rock. The result was that real rock theater drew no audience, and the rock theater that did make a go of it was inevitably pop shlock. "Nobody wants rock theater," observed Richard Fields in 1972.

He threw over *Tarot* (it folded in six weeks) to return to *1776*-style Broadway musicals.

The solution was a new kind of theater, an antitheater, that had little to do with rock music but that embodied, as did rock, countercultural formlessness, sexuality, spontaneity, and direct frontal assault on the establishment (in this case usually the audience). *Hair* was a pale, musical, commercial version of this theater, just as it was a commercial version of rock. The real stuff was *Futz*, or *Dionysus in 69*, or the San Francisco Mime Troupe's brand of guerrilla theater, or the Living Theater.

All were attempts to break the barriers between actor and audience, between play and life, and to level the other unwritten assumptions about theater. "The drama," wrote Eric Bentley, "is felt to be dead, and the new theater is looking elsewhere for its ideas: to action paintings, to light shows, to street happenings, to tape-recordings, to movies and TV, and then again to social events outside show biz altogether." The result was that "life is all one. Group therapy, parties, and theater have merged."

And so along came *Futz*, the farmer who loved his pig, complete improvisation, nudity, audience participation, obscenity, scurrility, mimed sex acts, action, and general mindlessness. And along came *Dionysus in 69*: artier, with large doses of Euripides, and an audience set to watching the show from the rough-hewn towers of Thebes or participating in the show itself, and nude Pentheus getting it on (or as far on as she'd allow) with a woman from the audience, obviously impromptu, a "visual-verbal participatory game," a "form of communal celebration." (A combination of parodied SDS participatory democracy and Jim Morrison's primeval theater of communal celebration.) And along came *Oh! Calcutta!* a nude revue, which made the most money, although most of its coin was minted off what Lenny Bruce called "tits and ass," scarcely revolutionary in 1969.

The Living Theater's *Paradise Now* was a mixture of propaganda, art and encounter group. First a haranguing, chanting, shouting recitation of everything that ails the establishment ("I can't travel without a passport," "I can't take my clothes off," "I can't stop the war"), then a gentle laying on of hands ("holy forehead," "holy thigh," "holy breast," "holy ass"), then a bit of pot, then acrobatics as the troupe spelled out bodily "anachronism," then audience participation—complaining, disrobing, political argument, confrontation, coaxing, more haranguing, feeling, acting, and reacting. Jack Richardson, *Commentary*'s theater critic, most remembered a bare-assed and free seventeen-year-old blonde girl being fondled by a dirty old midget, raincoat folded over his groin. Says liberated blonde to midget, "Don't pinch now." There was one sense of the sixties in a phrase.

More formal (they used scripts) and more political than the Living Theater was the San Francisco Mime Troupe, which set out to straighten American heads through radical, didactic, propagandistic theater performed in Bay area parks, streets, schools, shopping malls, and factories throughout the sixties. In 1967, *L'Amant militaire*, a 105-minute, antimilitaristic grotesquerie transformed the U.S. presence in Vietnam to the Spanish Imperial Army in Italy and preached from there. Standard antiwar gags included a would-be deserter who dresses himself in women's clothes only to be arrested as a fairy and a pervert; GIs going through rifle drills on crutches; and a puppet leading chants (audience participation) of "Hell no, we won't go."

Later came *Olive Pits*, an attack on agribiz. And *Viet Rock, America Hurrah, Modern Minstrel Show: Civil Rights in a Cracker Barrel, BART* (the Bay area subway system), *The Independent Female*, children's theater pieces, and *Meter Maid*, in which the troupe demonstrated how to use aluminum can tab tops to rip off free time from parking meters and to sabotage them. And *Ripping Off Ma Bell*, in which the troupe demonstrated how to bill long-distance phone calls to the Bank of America by giving a very real, working, genuine credit card number.

[Man dials operator]
May I help you?
Yes, operator, I'd like to place a long-distance call to Zap, North Dakota, station-to-station.
Please deposit three dollars and 95 cents.
Three dollars and 95 cents?
Yes, sir, for the first three minutes, sir.
But operator, I'm calling my Guru!
Your Guru, sir?
Yes, operator, he's very sick. And I don't have that kind of change.
Perhaps you could place the call from your home phone, sir.
I don't have a "home phone sir."
Would you care to reverse the charges?
That might kill him!
Oh, sir, don't you have a credit card?
A—credit card?
Yes, sir. With a credit card you could place the call at your employer's expense.
I could?
Yes, sir. Suppose for example you worked for the Bank of America here in San Francisco. When the operator came on the line you would simply say, "Operator, I wish to make a credit card call. My credit card number is S-756-0400-158." And the call would go through without any further ado.
What was that code again, operator?
S as in Sabotage, 756-0400-158.

(*Ripping Off Ma Bell* was published in *Ramparts*, August 1970, and distributed across the country. They do not make magazines like that any more.)

Throughout the United States hundreds of groups like the San Francisco Mime Troupe were presenting similar guerrilla theater. They were subversive, or tried their best to be. According to Henry Lesnick in *Guerilla Theater* the idea was to educate: "Through theater we seek to unite all people against a system of profit and racism which exploits the earth and the people." Whether the challenge was political agitation, political confrontation, audience participation, or simply the demand that people do something for a change, the new theater sought to shake audience presuppositions and public lethargy.

The ultimate danger was the confusion of life and theater, so that while theater became increasingly "real," real life became increasingly theatrical, and the whole confused mass turned into an absurd playground in which anything was possible as long as it was done in play. Though the confusion may have revitalized theater, it undermined serious attempts to reform America.

The scene is 1969, college campus, politicized, largely antiwar, a witch's brew of Young Americans for Freedom, Students for a Democratic Society, ROTC cadets, hippie and Yippie crosscurrents. The local guerrilla street theater company is about to do a number on the ROTC boys as they march from lecture hall to parade ground. Masked to resemble pasty Richard Nixons, half the company has deployed itself in the shrubbery lining the walk; the rest are three stories up, just inside the open windows of a vacant classroom. As the boys in green march by, the toy Nixons leap suddenly from concealment brandishing toy machine guns, dancing madly about the surprised cadets like so many voodoo doctors intent on exorcising a demon, and shouting "ambush, ambush" and "akk akk akk" and "surprise, surprise!" Their confederates release a shower of paper scraps bearing the single word "Napalm." The green lines hesitate, flush, then continue determinedly—and virtually unaffected—toward the drill field.

They have just survived their first ambush, complete with napalm. It was painless. As painless as the nightly television news reports that have so numbed the sensibilities of the country that the unthinkably inhumane has become a matter of national policy. The guerrillas consider this piece of radical propagandizing (repeated, with variations, all across America during the late sixties) a strategic victory because it "brings the war home." In fact, it makes the war even more surreal, more fictional than it has already become.

Other street theater pieces attacked sexism, racism, slum landlords, and robber barons. In *GI*, the San Francisco Red Theater left the verdict on arch villain Uncle Sam to the audience. A simple thumbs down would end U.S. militarism instantly. Talk about deception! *Paradise Now* offed clothing and the war and audience hang-ups inside the theater, but the evening proved a game: people left the Brooklyn Academy of Music with their clothes (and hang-ups) back on.

(Even more vitiating to the sixties movement was the happening because it lacked all political and social activism. As Gerald Weales observed in *The Jumping-Off Place*, "The happening, in its attempt to bring life into art, tends . . . toward dehumanization.")

The inverse of theater-as-life was life-as-theater, performed by the Chicago Eight in the courtroom of Judge Julius Hoffman.

Judge Hoffman: "That is the best statement I have heard here during the trial. You said you enjoyed being here."
Jerry Rubin: "It's good theater, Your Honor."

The sense of the absurd, along with artiness and excess, helped bring down the sixties and rock. The sixties grew up with an awareness of life's absurdity. Every age creates its own apocalypse, which it either outlives or outgrows. If it's not the Romans who are coming, it's the Ostrogoths, or the Mongols, or the Danes, or the Catholics, or the Moors, or the Chinese, or the Germans, or the communists, or the plague. Each cataclysm so threatens society with instant, complete, and undeserved annihilation as to make all the carefully constructed systems of cause and effect, rules, rewards and punishments seem absurd. Modern doctrines of absurdity were developed largely to explain the paradoxes of World War II, to provide metaphysical sustenance during a nasty and chaotic time.

The apparent absurdity of life is always with us.

But in the twentieth century the accelerated pace of technological development has vastly increased the speed and the thoroughness with which the world could be leveled. The possibilities are limited only by the fertile imaginations of scientists.

"'How—how *does* the Universe end?' said Billy. 'We blow it up, experimenting with new fuels for our flying saucers. A Tralfamadorian test pilot presses a starter button, and the whole Universe disappears.'"—Kurt Vonnegut, *Slaughterhouse Five*

Mostly we continue playing at stock options, graduate degrees, and social security as if the cloud were not there. But at times we are compelled by the thought that tomorrow may be too late. At times we are reduced to a dark laughter at our own high seriousness. The important thing, we tell ourselves, is not to be uptight and not to give a fuck because in the end it doesn't matter anyhow. At times we are overwhelmed, blasted not to dignity or humane decency or heroic stoicism but to nervous exhaustion.

The sixties watched John Kennedy in Dallas in 1963. There followed ten years of absurd shootings, of the election of goons to high office and the incarceration of men of conscience, of the stupefying spectacle of Americans traveling thousands of miles to swat at flies with sledgehammers—and missing—flattening whole forests, subcontinents, peoples, lest Vietnam fall, and thus Laos, all of Southeast Asia, and thus Japan, and Hawaii, and they'd be right off the coast of southern California. Was there any absurdity more Catch-22 than "we have to destroy it to save it"? Than Mayor Daley's "the policeman is not there to create disorder, he is there to *preserve* disorder"?

> "Would I rather be a Vietnamese who was being 'saved' by the American Army, or a Czech who was being 'saved' by the Russian Army? Of course I would rather be the Czech."—Arnold Toynbee

(Black Americans, of course, had known only too well and too long the absurdity of America. I think immediately of Ellison's *Invisible Man*, a book discovered by the sixties: young blacks titillated and humiliated by a naked, blonde stripper, encouraged to pound each other senseless in a boxing ring, then to scratch and claw for money on an electrified rug, all for the entertainment of paunchy whites at a stag party. At the end of the evening, the Invisible Man presents a speech on humility as the key to racial progress, still spitting blood from the boxing match. He receives from the whites a scholarship to the state college for blacks.)

Blow-Up was the first film by a major foreign director to enjoy immediate national distribution and popularity in America. This made it the first art film many young Americans ever saw, so *Blow-Up* was the subject of unending hours of analysis, interpretation, viewing and reviewing. It opened the door to a phenomenon largely unknown in the United States: a popular film with artistic quality and intellectual bulk.

Through photographer Thomas, *Blow-Up* captures the essence of one sixties scene: hip, cool, trendy London, very much on the surface of things. The party at which Thomas stumbles through doped-up guests trying to get his doped-up host to come with him and verify a murder is pure sixties. So, too, is the nude romp with the aspiring models. And the camera's lens, through which Thomas sees life with arty detachment, becomes a perfect metaphor for the distance that fine art interposed between the movement and some sixties heads.

The most overpowering element in the film is the statement it makes on the way reality disintegrates into ambiguity and, finally, into absurdity. Each detail of the movie cuts relentlessly into the smooth, bright, careless surface of camp London to expose the dark, ambiguous, terrible underside of the sixties.

The story is an accident, really, unfolding out of some photographs Thomas takes in a park: a romantic interlude, intended to give a light ending to an otherwise heavy volume of pictures, develops upon successive enlargements into a murder. Apparently. A gun protrudes from behind the park fence; there is a look of terror in the woman's eyes as her middle-aged companion slumps heavily against her. But constant enlargement transforms the crisp black and white photographs into something resembling the abstract painting Thomas tried to buy earlier in the film from his artist-neighbor. Details are fuzzy and the hard evidence isn't so hard. "It's like one of Bill's paintings," a voice observes. "You can't recognize anything."

Thomas acts to confirm that what he saw was what he saw, that he photographed what he thought he photographed. He rushes back to the park and, sure enough, in the moonlight he sees the corpse, palpable, real, conclusive.

From this point, however, reality disintegrates until Thomas no longer knows truth from illusion. When he returns to his studio, Thomas finds that the blow-ups have been stolen, along with the original pictures and the negatives. The telephone number the woman has given him turns out to be phony. Thomas determines to photograph the corpse and rushes off to fetch a writer-friend to go with him. But he is diverted first by—he thinks but is not sure—the woman, whom he follows into a discotheque before losing her in a small riot, and then by his friend's party. There he lingers among the marijuana and the music and the other accoutrements of mod London, falls asleep, and awakens only the next morning. By the time he returns to the park of course the corpse is gone. The grass looks completely undisturbed.

Now, something serious obviously has happened. Thomas thinks, we think, everyone thinks something has happened. But whatever it was, it is now beyond verification. Every shred of evidence is gone, lost in the campy, op art photos Thomas takes of plastic girls, in his nude romp with the young hopefuls, in the talk and the running about, in the pot party, in Thomas's own cavalier attitude that turns—or attempts to turn—every personal encounter into a cliché. And it has been so utterly lost that we're not entirely sure in retrospect it happened to begin with.

Blow-Up ends with a return of the clowns who careened madly across the screen in the film's opening scene. This time they are playing a pantomime game of tennis. Thomas—and the movie audience—watch the make-believe ball as it bounces from one side of the net to the other. Then a stray shot flies over the fence and rolls toward Thomas. The camera tracks this invisible sphere, bouncing, rolling to Thomas's feet.

The mimers turn, look at the photographer expectantly. In an act of acquiescence to this make-believe, to ambiguity, to absurdity, Thomas picks up the nonexistent ball and tosses it to the players. The camera pulls back for a long shot, and Thomas dwindles into nothingness.

The vision of *Blow-Up* was also found in rock music, both in rock's critique of the establishment and in its conceptualization of the possible. At its best, a sense of the absurd fathered all the virtues Camus and Sartre expected it would: "Something inside of me gets greatly disturbed at seeing this absurdity; and this is probably the root of my songs. . . . The reward is the act of the struggle itself. In other words, even though you can't expect to defeat the absurdity of the world, you must make the attempt. That's morality, that's religion, that's art, that's life." (Phil Ochs, with "Crucifixion" and "Outside of a Small Circle of Friends," made the attempt.) The Fugs, masters of the absurd, did the same thing with "Kill for Peace," on their second album. Bob Dylan did the same thing in "Highway 61 Revisited."

> Now the rovin' gambler he was very bored
> He was tryin' to create the next world war
> He found a promoter who nearly fell off the floor
> He said I never engaged in this kind of thing before
> But yes I think it can be very easily done
> We'll just put some bleachers out in the sun
> And have it out on highway 61.

A sense of the absurd could also mean just plain fun, as in Dylan's early "I Shall Be Free No. 10."

> Well, I set my monkey on the log
> And ordered him to do the Dog
> He wagged his tail and shook his head
> And went and did the Cat instead.
> He's a weird monkey, very funky.

> I sat with my high-heeled sneakers on
> Waiting to play tennis in the noonday sun
> I had my white shorts rolled up past my waist
> And my wig-hat was falling in my face
> But they wouldn't let me on the tennis court. . . .

> Now you're probably wondering by now
> Just what this song is all about
> What's probably got you baffled more
> Is what this thing here is for.
> It's nothing.
> It's something I learned over in England.

As in the Beatles' "Norwegian Wood." And in their "Happiness Is a Warm Gun."

> The man in the crowd with the multicoloured mirrors
> On his hobnail boots
> Lying with his eyes while his hands are busy
> Working overtime

A soap impression of his wife which he ate
And donated to the National Trust.

As in Arlo Guthrie's delightful "Alice's Restaurant" and the less known but
equally delightful "Motorcycle Song" ("I don't want a pickle, just want to
ride on my motorcycle").

> (At the other end of the decade, Iggy Pop and
> Alice Cooper were presenting absurdist happen-
> ings promoted as rock concerts. As theater they
> were mediocre, as rock they were worse. As ab-
> surdity they were mostly asinine.)

But for all its virtues, for all its fun, the absurdist vision could be a turnoff, especially when it expressed itself in satire, where it leveled indiscriminately. The Mothers of Invention (the mother lode of absurdist vision in
so-called rock) are a case in point. The dozen records that Zappa and the
Mothers packed into the years between 1966 and 1972 are absurdist albums
that leave virtually nothing to believe in. Zappa suffered few illusions and
made fewer commitments, which was not really very sixties, but it allowed
him to throw darts in all directions at once. "Those kids don't love each
other," he once told an interviewer when accused of being part of the hippie
revolution. "They're in that because it's like another club—it's like the modern day equivalent of a street gang. It's clean *pachucoso*, a little hairier perhaps. But it's not right." And again, "The whole hippie scene is wishful
thinking. They wish they could love, but they're full of shit."

So what was not full of shit? So what was right? Zappa left no ground
on which to stand. You couldn't even be a Mothers fan—they sent you a
cheesy mimeographed letter that pimped you around. And if you persisted,
you heard Zappa saying things like this about you: "I got tired of beating
my head against the wall. I got tired of playing for people who clap for all
the wrong reasons."

Where do you clap in "America Drinks and Goes Home"?

It's now time to close! . . . I hope you've had as much fun as we have!
Don't forget the jam session Sunday! . . . Mandy Tension will be by,
playing his xylophone troupe! It'll be a lot of fun! Monday night is
the Dance Contest Night . . . Twist Contest. . . . We give away pea-
nut butter and jelly! . . . I hope we've played your requests . . . the
songs you like to hear. . . . Last call for alcohol! . . . Drink it up,
folks. . . . Wonderful! . . . Nice to see you . . . oh, "Bill Bailey"? . . .
we'll get to that tomorrow . . . "Caravan," with drum solo? . . .
Right! . . . We'll do that! . . . Wonderful! . . . Nice to see you again!
. . . Yeh! . . . la, la, la . . . Down at the POMPADOUR A-GO-GO."
. . . Vo-do-de-oo-pee-pee . . . Shoobe-doot 'n-dadada, ada-da-daahh
. . . Nya-da-da, nya-da-da . . . 'NITE' ALL!

There is, in fact, no right reason to clap, no right place to clap, for every reason and every place is wrong. Straight or hip, you had your earnestness thrown in your face and if you had no earnestness, that was held against you, too: "If the kids who are destined to take over the country could somehow acquire the sense of responsibility . . . they could tell everybody where it's at, but they won't." The whole entire world was absurd, everything was a freak-out. Which, after a very short while, can get to be a drag.

The most memorable of all promoters of the absurd, however, used neither cinema nor record. They used life. They were Abbie Hoffman and Jerry Rubin's followers, members of the Youth International Party, Yippies. Here was absurdity as fun, absurdity as protest, and—slightly beyond the end of the sixties—absurdity as turnoff. Here was all the distinctive flavor of the crazy late sixties: *Steal This Book, Revolution for the Hell of It,* and *Do It!* Far out!

Abbie Hoffman grew with the sixties. His first demonstration was at Caryl Chessman's execution in 1960—a polite, genteel, coffee and doughnuts with the warden affair. (By coincidence, William Kunstler, who would defend the Chicago Eight in 1969, wrote a book about the Chessman trial, *Beyond a Reasonable Doubt?*) Later Hoffman spent time organizing Friends of SNCC groups up north and then involved himself with the Poor People Corporation of Mississippi. His moment of radicalization came when ten drunk cops unloaded on Poor People organizers, their booth, Abbie's skull.

He worked for a while doing sales promotion for pharmaceutical houses, paying doctors for endorsements, "five year studies that took five minutes," which were written up and published in "medical journals" and taken around by Hoffman to show other doctors that his company's product was better than other companies' products. The job took maybe four or five hours a week, and he augmented his $15,000 a year salary by "stealing like crazy" and forging motel receipts. It was fun, profitable, and an opportunity for Hoffman to exercise his imagination.

But it was not revolutionary, and Hoffman was turning cynical and corrupt. He grew restless and left the wife and kids and a job in the suburbs and dropped out into New York's Lower East Side.

Then Abbie read Cohn-Bendit's *Obsolete Communism: The Left-Wing Alternative.* "The revolution will come through joy and not through sacrifice," it said, and the pieces all fell into place. The moments of radicalization and dropout were followed by the moment of Yippie! "There ought to be fun in revolution," Hoffman thought. "If fun was subversive, if we could define what fun was, if it wasn't going to the golf course or drinking a martini, if we could redefine what fun really was, in terms of fun being fighting for what you believe in, and fighting for the future—if that could be fun—wow!" The first revolutionary fun act (long before the official founding of the YIP) was to throw money among the money brokers at the New York Stock Exchange, a demonstration that moved the exchange to enclose itself in a $20,000, bulletproof glass cage "because they were afraid we'd come back and throw money out again." It was followed by others, each scheme more outrageous than the last, until Hoffman and Rubin and other Yippies mailed out thirty thousand Valentines on Valentine's Day, 1969, to persons unknown—each containing a joint. Terrific holy goof protest. Terrific sense of absurdity (and theater).

> "In New York at about the same time, April 1968, I was present at a yippie meeting in Union Park at which a department store loot-in was being planned. 'We'll choose a shop. About twenty of us will go in, select the stuff we want, hand the cashier a flower and head towards the door.'"
> —Richard Neville

The crowning achievement of Yippie absurdism was the Festival of Life at the 1968 Democratic national convention and the subsequent trial of the Chicago Eight.

> 22,000 feet over Hazed square Vegetable planet Floor
> Approaching Chicago to Die or flying over Earth another 40 years
> to die—Indifferent, and Afraid, that the bone-shattering bullet
> be the same as the vast evaporation-of-phenomena Cancer
> Come true in an old man's bed. Or Historic
> Fire-Heaven Descending 22,000 years End th' Atomic Aeon. . . .
> —Allen Ginsberg, "Going to Chicago"

"Join us in Chicago in August," the underground invitations ran. Some came to oust Johnson-Humphrey and to cheer the White Knight from Minnesota. Others came with other ideas, in response to another invitation.

> Rise up and abandon the creeping meatball! Come all you rebels, youth spirits, rock minstrels, truth seekers, peacock freaks, poets, barricade jumpers, dancers, lovers and artists. . . ! A new spirit explodes in the land. Things are bursting in music, poetry, dancing, movies, celebrations, magic, politics, theater and life styles. All these new tribes will gather in Chicago. We will be completely open. Everything will be free. Bring blankets, draft cards, tents, body paint, Mrs. Leary's cow, food to share, music, eager skin and happiness. The threats of LBJ, Mayor Daley and J. Edgar Freako will not stop us. We are coming! We are coming from all over the world!

Here would be an answer to the death dealers and the politicos, a real freak-out revolution, acid in the drinking water, chants, songs, peace symbols, wandering tribes of hippies, the nomination of a pig for president (with the aid of Phil Ochs, who—with the MC5—was the only rock singer to make the scene), the whole of the counterculture dumped on Johnson's (Humphrey's) front lawn and plastered across the television screens of millions of American homes.

Well, we all remember the story. How the underground pulled back, how the singers stayed away, how the projected fifty thousand Yippies turned out to be "only" a few thousand Yippies, hard-core radicals, and Mc-Carthy supporters. But it didn't matter, really. There *was* a spirit loose at the convention that Mayor Daley and the Chicago cops could not help sensing: speeches, dope, irreverence, high jinks, freedom. And of course they could not cope, and of course there was a police riot, great clouds of orange teargas flaring in the police spotlights, the Blue Meanies clubbing everything that moved, and a lot of demonstrators swatting back at the Meanies (and at streetlights and windows), and chaos everywhere, all plastered across the television screens of millions of American homes, and the fumes drifting into the houses of sleeping families on State Street, and wafting into the posh Pump Room down along the Gold Coast, and Chicago's most noted citizen, Hugh Hefner, unrecognized in the street, suffering with the flower children and the radicals and the McCarthy people and the Yippies, the situation outdoors completely out of control, the Democratic party conducting business as usual indoors.

But the absurdity of 1968 was only a prelude to the absurdity of 1969, when the federal government charged a grab bag of undesirables with violation of (ready for this?) a section of the 1968 Civil Rights Act. These eight, the government claimed, did "combine, conspire, confederate and agree together on or about April 12, 1968 . . . to travel in interstate commerce with the intent to incite, organize, promote, encourage, participate in and carry on a riot." The trial, as everyone realized even then, was a joke. The ultimate triumph of the YIP was the reduction of the American system of justice to complete absurdity in the proceedings against the Chicago Eight. Nobody was serious, except for Judge Hoffman and prosecutors Foran and Schultz.

> "For *Abbie* and *Jerry*, on the other hand, the courtroom was a new theater, perhaps a purer kind of theater than anything in previous Yippie history. More than any of the other defendants, they wanted to create the *image* of a courtroom shambles." —Tom Hayden, *Trial*

There was Bobby Seale, tied to his seat, his mouth taped, an incredible image of what it means to be black in America, and the judge assuring reporters and jury that "the steps taken here are to insure a fair trial." There was Jerry Rubin, frisking the court marshals who had just frisked him. There was Abbie Hoffman, giving "the Woodstock Nation" as his place of residence and, when asked where that might be, replying that it was a state of mind. There was Julius the Just, reduced unwittingly, almost acquiescently, to just Julius, a fumbling and rather pathetic figure in a courtroom melodrama completely out of his control, handing out contempt of court sentences like the Red Queen calling for heads (and with much the same effect). There was the defense, asking prospective jurors whether their female children wore brassieres all the time, whether they considered marijuana to be habit forming, and whether they knew who the Jefferson Airplane, Phil Ochs, and Country Joe MacDonald and the Fish were. Seale, short-circuiting the usual courtroom procedure and directly addressing the court and just Julius: "I would like to speak on my own behalf. How come I can't speak in behalf of myself? I want to defend myself." And Dellinger, calling the judge "Mr. Hoffman" and observing, "I believe in equality, so I prefer to call people Mister or by their first name."

> The Witness (Abbie Hoffman): Everybody dressed as Keystone cops
> and we went to Stony Brook to arrest all the whiskey drinkers.
> Mr. Schultz: Objection.
> The Court: I sustain the objection.
> The Witness: You missed a good story.

The defendants, observing the Moratorium of October 15 with NLF flags on the defense table and an attempt to read the names of the war dead. The birthday cake for Bobby Seale, with "Free Huey. Free Bobby" in icing across the top. Hayden, in parody, directing the court stenographer, "Let the record show the judge is laughing." And Jerry Rubin, "Let the record show that Foran is a Nazi." And Judge Julius shouting, "Everything you say will be taken down," and Davis hooting, "This court is bullshit." Allen Ginsberg, chanting to the court in tennis shoes, leather vest, and jeans, "Hare Krishna, Hare Krishna, Krishna, Krishna, Hare, Hare," playing his harmonium, and reciting his own poetry and Whitman's.

> The Court: Mr. Ochs, just answer the questions directly. You are a
> singer, but you are a smart fellow, I'm sure.
> The Witness (Phil Ochs): Thank you. You are a judge, but you are a
> smart fellow too.

The appearance in court of Mayor Richard Daley, blue-suited and stone-faced, followed by the forces of life: Judy Collins, Arlo Guthrie, Pete Seeger, Phil Ochs, Country Joe singing "and it's one two three, what are we fighting for? Don't ask me, I don't give a damn. The next stop is Vietnam. And it's five, six, seven. . . ." And the whole trial capped by one Hoffman telling the other he was a disgrace to the Jewish race and would have served Hitler better, accusing him in Yiddish of behaving disgracefully in front of gentiles, and shouting in the government's face, "You know you can't win this fucking case! The only way you can win is to put us away for contempt. We have contempt for this court and for you, Schultz, and for this whole rotten system!"

It was a trial straight out of *Alice in Wonderland.*

"Good theater, Your Honor," as Rubin had put it.

Yet it was the beginning of the end. After surrealism, the next stop is anarchism. After the absurdity of the convention and the trial, what was left but chaos? If you follow absurdist thought to its logical conclusion, you either leap off the edge or turn around.

Most Americans were not about to leap off the edge, which is why a little bit of the absurdist vision can go a long way. Which brings us to the third trend that weakened the sixties from within: excess—excess of protest, excess of art, excess of absurdity, excess no and excess yes, excess dope, excess sex, excess violence, maybe even excess music.

Within a movement excess creates problems as the vanguard gets too far out in front of the troops: suddenly you discover you're out there alone, naked, with nobody behind or around you, and you get yourself picked off. When whole movements turn to excess, they tend first to shrink and then to isolate themselves from the rest of society. Isolation in turn breeds impotence. Always. The lesson cannot be overstressed because it is a lesson the sixties bought dearly. And when there is an excess of causes, or an excess of reform, or an excess of criticism, you get reaction. Some people you overwhelm, and they shrug their shoulders and ask, "What's the use?" Others you irritate to the point of counterrevolution or active resistance.

One of the reasons the sixties fell apart is that the movement went too far too fast. The front got way ahead of the main body, and communications became a problem. Increasing numbers of Americans, young Americans, wrote movement leaders off as wild, excessive, crazy people. Increasing numbers of Americans found themselves worn out, burnt out, exhausted.

The sixties never learned the art of temperate, deliberate growth. It's not characteristically American to begin with, not characteristically romantic, not characteristically young. It certainly was not characteristic of the times, which thought of themselves as born to be wild. "We want the world and we want it now." Tomorrow was not a part of the sixties mentality.

Excess is encouraged by the mass media. Our co-optive system exploits through its electronic and news media whatever it can grab: ideas, movements, talent, fads, styles. Allow a year for discovery of an idea or a talent, a year for promotion, and two years for exploitation. This process moves you along quickly, and if you want to hang in there you soon learn that you need to go further and further to keep in the public eye. Every artist, every television personality, every public figure understands this game.

People in rock and in the movement understood it as well, and to promote the revolution they cleverly attracted media attention through increasingly outrageous behavior. "That rock was commercial seemed only a benefit," *Rolling Stone*'s Michael Lydon observed looking over his shoulder: through the establishment's media the movement would subvert the establishment. But life in the media put political revolutionaries, rockers, hippies, and Yippies in a tight spot: on the one hand, absorption; on the other, the excess needed to maintain visibility. If the right one didn't get you, then the left one did.

What undid most parts of the sixties that successfully resisted absorption and artiness and absurdity was media-fueled excess: more and more radical postures, finer and finer art, kinkier and kinkier scenes, larger and larger crowds, more and more causes, transcendence from the beautiful to the sublime, from the sublime to the ridiculous, from the ridiculous to the desperate.

"I want to take you Higher!!!"—Sly Stone

How quickly, in retrospect, the movement came and went, and how superficially. It never had the time, really, to deal with much other than its own growth, its own being. The tiny band gathered against Chessman's execution or HUAC's Berkeley session in 1960, the sit-ins and the freedom rides, even the first ban the Bomb marches—these were very small-scale, isolated acts of four, a dozen, maybe a hundred or a few thousand people. They were mighty, important, and symbolic, but they engaged the active participation of but a fraction of a percent of the population. There was little premeditation and virtually no need for coordination across the country.

Then, so quickly, the rush of people and of ad hoc organizations. An explosion of numbers: 5,000 demonstrating against nuclear testing in Washington, D.C., 1962; 200,000 there the following year in the civil rights march; 6,000 students involved to varying degrees in the SDS-led Berkeley free speech movement, 1964; 25,000 in the SDS-led protest against Vietnam in 1965. And in November 1965, 200,000. In New York 250,000 came together in April 1967 at a rally sponsored by the Spring Mobilization Committee. Not one, not two, but dozens, scores of college campuses went up in 1968 and 1969. In 1968 unnumbered thousands of Americans milled about the Pentagon and demonstrated in New York and Chicago and Washington and Boston and the world—supporting black power, student power, gay power, Black Panthers and White Panthers and Grey Panthers and Lavender Panthers, and women's liberation, for every cause a dozen organizations: CORE, NAACP, SCLC, SNCC, AFSC, CCCO, SLA, CNVA, SANE, FSM, National Coordinating Committee to End the War in Vietnam, Emergency Civil Liberties Committee, Another Mother for Peace, National Committee to Abolish HUAC, May Second Movement, North American Congress on Latin America, Sexual Freedom League, New University Conference, United Farmworkers Association, Freedom and Peace Party, National Conference for New Politics, Peace and Freedom Party, Weathermen, Witches, hippies, and Yippies.

This list overwhelms us with letters and causes and names and places. It is unmanageable. It is incomprehensible. It is excessive.

It also made fairly stale copy unless each demonstration, each new organization pressed a little further toward the edge. And in a very short time we came very close to the edge. "We want freedom for all black men held in federal, state, county and city prisons and jails," demanded the Black Panthers (with one eye on the media). "We want free birth control, free pregnancy leave for working women, and free child care centers," demanded the women. "We want academic credit for 'life experiences,'" demanded college students. "We want the state of Maine," demanded the American Indians in the early seventies with perhaps the most justification of all.

> "And we *were* motherfucking bad. We were dirty, smelly, grimy, foul, loud, dope-crazed, hell-bent and leather-jacketed. We were a public display of filth and shabbiness, living in-the-flesh rejects of middle-class standards. We pissed and shit and fucked in public; we crossed on red lights; and we opened Coke bottles with our teeth. We were constantly stoned or tripping on every drug known to man. We were the outlaw forces of Amerika displaying ourselves flagrantly on a world stage. Dig it! *The future of humanity was in our hands!*"
> —Jerry Rubin

About this time the numbers started dwindling. The movement had grown big and quarrelsome. Leaders were too far in front of followers. More and more people started thinking, "This is crazy." And off they walked to feel their way back toward some kind of normalcy.

Carl Oglesby, onetime president of the SDS, made just that point in writing about the candidacy of Eugene McCarthy. You have to be careful or you lose your following.

> It is just that Left politics in America is hard. There is not much room for movement in that direction. Not much is possible. Play to secure the marginal victory and avoid central defeat.
> So it comes down to the famous bird in the hand. . . .
> Don't demand the final salvation of the whole world tomorrow.
> Demand, instead, the end of the War today.
> Don't demand socialism tomorrow.
> Demand, instead, that capitalism, starting today, begin creating for itself a more human heart.
> Don't demand for tomorrow that real democracy establish itself in our society.
> Demand, instead, that the old elites at once start behaving better.

That is how Oglesby, romantic revolutionary, outlined the compromise position. And then Oglesby, romantic revolutionary being true to himself, rejected the compromise position. He wanted the whole loaf, and a big loaf. No compromises anywhere. The result was that the left went down in flames, and Gene McCarthy got dumped, and the Hump got dumped, and America and the movement and rock and the world got Richard Nixon and

Spiro Agnew because people looked at their television sets and said to themselves, "Things may be terrible, but this is fuckin' crazy."

The excess that undercut protest during the sixties had been undermining fine art for some while, and it finally filtered into rock music—the music of the revolution and of the people—and rock found itself losing altitude and audience quickly.

Evidence: the disintegration of form in Beatles songs, from the exciting, riotous experiment of *Sgt. Pepper* to the baroque overripeness of "Hey Jude" to the glorious collage of meaningless fragments, many of them half finished, on the flip side of *Abbey Road*.

> "We did it this way because both John and I had a number of songs which were great as they were but which we'd never finished."—Paul McCartney

Evidence: the Mothers of Invention song "Son of Suzy Creamcheese," with four bars in 4/4 time, one bar in 8/8, one bar in 9/8, then 8/8, 9/8, 8/8, 9/8, 8/8, 9/8, 8/8, 4/8, 5/8, 6/8, and then 4/4 again. And their concerto for farts and violin. And "Lumpy Gravy," strictly instrumental with a cocktail bar flavor and weird voices weaving their way through piano strings in the style of the Beatles' "Revolution 9" and the Stones' "On with the Show."

Evidence: the Moody Blues, with the London Festival Orchestra and a lot of pseudopoetry, on one musical sojourn after another: *Days of Future Passed, In Search of the Lost Chord, On the Threshold of a Dream, To Our Children's Children, A Question of Balance, Every Good Boy Deserves Favour* (a mnemonic children use to remember lines of the G clef, E G B D F), and *Seventh Sojourn.*

Evidence, King Crimson (read Robert Fripp), who had little background in pop rock and was artsy from its first album, *In the Court of the Crimson King* (1969), an "observation" on the state of the world in five lengthy, relatively tuneful songs, full of metaphors and symbols and heavy themes, behaving the way students of the sixties thought poetry ought to behave, in basic Paul Simon, Leonard Cohen, Jim Morrison manner. And some bluesy rock mixed in with the then popular allusions to jazz and the mighty mellotron.

But Fripp flipped, and before you could say King Crimson three times the group was beyond the edge of night. Experimental, full of long, rambling solos on the mellotron, overproduced, impossibly obscure.

Go Polonius or kneel
The reapers name their harvest dawn
All your tarnished devil's spoons
Will rust beneath our corn.
Now bears Prince Rupert's garden roam
Across his rain tree shaded lawn

Lizard bones become the clay
And there a swan is born.

The end was reached in 1973 with *Lark's Tongues in Aspic*, an album strictly for the musical gourmet, indistinguishable from "classical" music, an excess far removed from rock. Not even head food.

Further evidence: Paul Simon's first solo album, so completely and so subtly artistic as to be entirely misunderstood. "Everything Put Together Falls Apart," Jon Landau headlined his *Rolling Stone* review and bombed the album. And nothing proved the fact more than the review, which Simon claimed completely misinterpreted his songs. "A lot of the lyrics they thought depressed and pessimistic are really ironic and funny," a Columbia Records spokesman told a *New Yorker* reporter interested in meeting Paul "to clear up some of the lyrical confusion." "Armistice Day" appears to be a protest number in the style of early Phil Ochs. But not so, said Paul. "'Armistice Day' is *not* a protest song—protest songs are a little trite at the moment." And you thought "Mother and Child Reunion" is a witty, wistful, impressionistic throwaway. Turns out it's about death!

So the album confused Landau and the *New Yorker*, and it baffles me even today. Art—especially that old favorite of the literati, irony—had become so subtle that what appears to be is not, and what appears not to be, is. Message had been lost, sophistication gained. But so much sophistication that some very intelligent people could not make heads or tails of the album.

Further evidence: Deep Purple (which in 1970 at the Royal Albert Hall recorded *Concerto for Group and Orchestra*, the orchestra being the Royal Philharmonic), Emerson, Lake, and Palmer, Jethro Tull, and the group Yes.

Further evidence from this side of the Atlantic: Lou Reed and the Velvet Underground, which made its name touring with Andy Warhol's Exploding Plastic Inevitable. Though the Underground avoided the Victorian heaviness of King Crimson, the Moody Blues, and Emerson, Lake, and Palmer, it could not escape the equally manneristic, avant-garde pop world.

> "You're not powerful enough. You're just an idiosyncratic fringe group like the Anabaptists. You don't have the capacity even to close down the universities."—Paul Goodman to the Theater of Ideas

Excess swells the numbers and confuses the focus. It pushes leaders on out front, and then the middle ground gets lost. "The cities they are broke in half, and the middle men are gone," lamented Leonard Cohen, and he was right. Given the choice, at the close of the sixties, between political radicalism or conservatism, between art rock and shlock, between complete freedom (anarchy) and complete repression (tyranny), between Abbie Hoffman and Richard Daley, many thoughtful sixties types did just what you'd expect them to do: they walked away. They made no choice. They dropped out.

The field was left to the generations of the fifties and the seventies, which opted without delay for conservatism and shlock. The centrifugal forces of the sixties are the main reason for the centripetal forces at work during the seventies.

> "Now I'm doing my level best as a saboteur of values, as an aider of change, but when it comes down to blood and gore in the streets, I'm takin' off and goin' fishin'." —David Crosby

It was fashionable by 1972 to claim that rock, like the movement and the sixties, was dead. Several emblems of death by decadence stick in the minds of everyone who endured the painful transition from sixties to seventies: the Lincoln Park massacre, the trial of the Chicago Eight, the shootings at Kent State, the wedding of Tiny Tim on the *Johnny Carson Show*, the Charles Manson insanity, with its perverse guru and misled flower children, the deaths of Jimi Hendrix and Janis Joplin, the Rolling Stones' concert at Altamont.

As emblems of death by excess, Joplin and Altamont make the best claim to purity: both were counterculture conceptualized and counterculture executed. Both were very clearly dysfunctions of the counterculture itself. There could be no finger-pointing and no debate. Even the most passionate partisan had to admit defeat.

Janis Joplin *was* the motion of the sixties. Action. Dynamics. Efflorescence. Change. For three short years, between Monterey in 1967 and her death in October 1970, a constant blur. "No two pictures of her ever looked the same," said Bruce Steinberg. "Not only was her normal, conversational face dynamic and constantly changing, but even statically she just *looked* completely different from any new angle." A Roman candle, an explosion. "A symphony of violence, the great Southwest unbound," wrote Mimi Fariña in her elegy, "In the Quiet Morning."

Excess. Loud, ballsy, aggressive, liberated, screaming and yelling, inciting, *demanding* that the audience join in her riotous assault on life. "When they reach a certain level, you know they want to be lifted but they're scared. Then all you gotta do is give the old kick in the ass, a big fucking kick in the ass, man." Janis drumming time in front of her, harrying her mortality lest it harry her. "All my life I just wanted to be a beatnik, meet all the heavies, get stoned, get laid, having a good time, that's all I ever wanted." Dope, Southern Comfort, loud music, sex.

"You ought to watch it in the next couple years."
"Oh, man."
"The pace. Slow down, you finally realize you're doing yourself in."

"I figured that out a long time ago. I also figured this out: I gotta go on doin' it the way I see it. . . . I am here to have a party, man, as best as I can while I'm on this earth. I think that's your duty too."
—Interview with Janis Joplin

Superwoman Janis, with the old kozmic blues, challenging the whole goddam world to have another little piece of her heart, driving ahead full tilt boogie lest in her time of dyin' she discover that she'd never lived, trading her tomorrows for a few todays. A hard life, an earthy life, a Rabelaisian life she'd created piece by piece, vice by vice, liberation by liberation out of the fifties and out of Port Arthur, Texas, where she'd grown up, out of her own fragile, straight self.

A new myth.

"I used to ask guys I was balling, 'Do I ball like I sing? Is it really me?' That's what I wonder sometimes when I'm talking. Is this person that's talking me?"

Ultimately Janis turned into her own carefully cultivated myth of constant motion and in so doing became the personification of the sixties.

"Yeah, I get tired of being in the same place. I hate boredom."

A wave of electrical sound, Country Joe MacDonald called her, "a flashing light."

The light flashed, the music went round and round, and Janis rocketed from place to place and lived harder and harder and harder until on October 4, 1970, the motion stopped, and the woman who had lived on the outer edge of probability overdosed on heroin. "In the quiet morning there was much despair," Mimi Fariña wrote.

> "Jagger screams 'Hello!,' springs into the air and slams down in a split, as the Stones start bashing out 'Jumpin' Jack Flash.' The audience, recoiling in audiovisual shock, not only screeeeeeeeeeams, but starts climbing the furniture, dancing in the aisles and charging the unguarded stage. Tasting the crowd's warm, salty blood, Mick the Jagger goes mad, tears off his belt, flogs the stage floor, incites the mob to riot and offers himself as their superhuman sacrifice."—Albert Goldman, November 8, 1969

The most disheartening blow of all, however, was the Rolling Stones concert at Altamont Speedway on December 6, 1969. Mick Jagger was one of us. We knew him, we loved him, we *revered* his satanic majesty, the role he played between game and seriousness. The Rolling Stones were no pack of crazies out there in the desert, and they were not uniformed National Guardsmen on an Ohio college campus or establishment pigs along Lake Michigan. They were counterculture. So were their fans, who reveled in this taunting, androgynous personification of the good in evil and the evil in good. This was ritual theater, good game, great show, super music.

And the Hell's Angels, playing security guard for $500 worth of beer, were the very embodiment of the angry no that the counterculture had espoused from the beginning, grown-up greasers, teds, rockers—mythic heroes to angry young men, protesters, and dropouts. They were misunderstood rejects of society who would, given any chance at all, prove their innate decency. So what were they doing up there clubbing people with pool cues, smashing the head of Marty Balin of the Jefferson Airplane, kicking and stabbing Meredith Hunter to death? Four dead, a hundred injured, thousands freaked out on bad acid, bad vibrations, the whole bad scene.

> "There were kids being stabbed and heads cracking the whole time. We tried to stop it the best we could by not playing, but by the time we got into our fourth song, the more we got into it, the more people got into their fighting thing."—Carlos Santana

The Airplane, stopping "up against the wall, motherfucker" to tell the Angels to cool it, and Marty getting smashed, and Paul Kantner nearly getting whacked, and then back to "up against the wall"—talk about absurdity!

Tim Leary, stoned out of his head, watching bad trips all around him in complete passivity.

A hundred Angels in total control of the stage, utterly intimidating the audience, which hated them, arrogant, indecent, indifferent, violent. Even to Jagger, whom they'd been hired "to protect." "Hey brothers and sisters, come on now. Cool it. Everybody cool down." Then "Sympathy for the Devil." Then an abrupt stop and "Hey, we need a doctor here." Then more "Sympathy for the Devil," as Hunter was stabbed to death in front of the stage.

"The violence seemed just another stage setting for the Stone's routine," wrote Sol Stern in "Altamont: Pearl Harbor to the Woodstock Nation." "They continued to play, mostly uninterrupted, while the fights flared again and again across the front of the stage." The truth is that Jagger was himself terrified, helpless, threatened as anyone else by events absolutely and completely out of his or anyone else's control, the whole scene gone berserk, a game become suddenly, threateningly, terrifyingly earnest.

The socially conscious, the politically active, the music freaks and the drug freaks, the hippie apostles of the new love and freedom, the mean-mother Angels, the young of youthful California, the rebels, the redeemed, the elect—everybody was there, everybody was a part, everybody contributed to the death of the Woodstock myth.

What made matters worse, of course, was that Altamont was to have been the cinematic high point of the Stones' American tour, a Mick Jagger

Woodstock that could be staged cheaply and earn bundles. Throughout the murder of Meredith the cameras rolled; in fact, you almost got the impression that it was *for* the cameras that all the rest rolled, all the satanism and the taunting and the bad vibrations. Not enough planning, not enough medical help, not enough legitimate security, too much inducement, too much show, too much commercialism. "The Stones Have Not Acted Honorably," charged *Rolling Stone*, accusing them of refusing to face up to their responsibility for the disaster.

> (All the bad vibrations showed right on through *Gimme Shelter*, the film released with no apparent remorse in 1972. That may have been the most dishonorable act of all.)

"We're finally on our own," Neil Young had exulted after the shootings at Kent State, as if he expected to dispel any lingering illusions about the intentions of the establishment and to send the counterculture off into a new America. But those four deaths did not liberate anyone. Neither did the deaths at Altamont. This is the kind of excess that freezes motion in iced terror, that elects a Richard Nixon to keep the peace, that of necessity reestablishes rules and regulations, that kills rock concerts and festivals, that forces the world to conclude that "this is fuckin' insane." That runs the freewheeling, wild, magnificent sixties into the sober, circumspect, temperate seventies.

Onstage in 1974, Phil Ochs (left) and Bob Dylan share a moment of fun reminiscent of the innocence and joy of the early sixties. *Photo by Chuck Pulin. Used by permission.*

| 7 | The Seventies: Looking Back, Looking Ahead

> "It may not be the Sixties, but nothing's the Sixties any-more."—Paul McCartney, June 1976

If partisans of the fifties found the sixties chaotic, barbaric, un-settling, a slum of a decade almost beyond endurance, sixties people have found the seventies virtually uninhabitable: law and order, structure, the death penalty, short hair, Anita Bryant, Proposition 13, Bakke, Nazis marching in Illinois, Guyana, punk rock, Performance with a capital P: im-age without substance, illusion, formula. Precious little imagination, except in the direction of orthodoxy. Less eccentricity and more uniformity. Less spontaneity, madness, vision, experimentation. Lowered expectations and lowered accomplishments.

Less motion.

The Voidoids described the generation of the seventies on an album of the same title as a blank generation. The Rolling Stones took one long look at the seventies and concluded their 1978 album *Some Girls* with a declara-tion of bankruptcy: "What a mess, this town's in tatters. . . . My brain's been battered. . . ."

> "Now the things [the Beatles and Bob Dylan] sang about—love, peace, and the courage to explore our own minds—so often seem to have passed into suspension."—*Rolling Stone* on the occasion of the concert for Bangladesh, 1971

> "Now there's just so much crap going down. I don't enjoy any of it. I've always thought that the next thing that's gotta happen—I think it could possibly be a singer or a group—in '74 is going to be that start of a new band, a new Elvis, Beatles . . . it's been long enough."—Ringo Starr, 1974

There are critics, of course, and there are still countercultural freaks. There are Paul Goodman's "early resigned" and "early fatalistic." But they are underground and you have to go looking for them. Social and political criticism is found mostly in the comedy of *Saturday Night Live*. We are, in the words of Jethro Tull's Ian Anderson, "too old to rock-n-roll, too young to die."

> And the ashes of the dreams
> Can be found in the magazines,
> And it seems that there are no more songs.
> —Phil Ochs, "No More Songs"

The guardians of the old order approached the seventies with trepidation. In December 1968 the Ford Foundation sponsored a symposium at Princeton, with George Ball, Daniel Bell, Sam Brown, John Kenneth Galbraith, Henry Kissinger, Allard Lowenstein, Norman Podhoretz, and eighty others. The record of that conference, published in 1970 as *The Endless Crisis: America in the Seventies*, is a mirror of establishment anxieties: "All life is balance," argued François Duchêne in summarizing three days of discussion and argument, "and there are dangers even in progress: broadly speaking, the current ones seem to be those of undirected anarchy capable of leading, if unchecked, to the disastrous habits of self-assertion of the early twentieth century." What was feared was world war on the one hand, repressive fascism on the other.

> "The danger is that once a revolutionary state has been created, a new conservative bureaucracy tends to form around it."—Robin Blackburn in interviewing John Lennon

Benjamin DeMott, in *Surviving the Seventies* (1971), spoke for the common folk, but he voiced the same numbed confusion: "How much New Thought can actually go down in a stable middle life? How can a human being (as opposed to History in the large) cope, in his own local, limited head, with the tilts of assumption and belief now occurring regularly in all corners of culture?" What do we do when our world is unraveling, when the dislocations continue, extended and accentuated?

Sometime around 1970 the public climate in America began a prolonged retreat to normalcy, which for children of the sixties amounted to a great turning out of lights, a profound sleep. It is, in fact, this sharp shift in the social climates of the sixties and seventies that complements our own "passage" from youth to middle age. The war was winding down, Nixon was in the White House, students had graduated and were job-hunting, and the pendulum had swung from activity to reflection.

Witness Paul Simon's 1973 statement, "American Tune," the melody of which comes from the Good Friday hymn, "Oh Sacred Head Now Wounded."

> Many's the time I've been mistaken
> And many times confused
> Yes, and I've often felt forsaken
> And certainly misused

But I'm all right, I'm all right
I'm just weary to my bones
Still, you don't expect to be
Bright and bon vivant
So far away from home, so far away from home

And I don't know a soul who's not been battered
I don't have a friend who feels at ease
I don't know a dream that's not been shattered
Or driven to its knees
But it's all right, it's all right
We've lived so well so long
Still, when I think of the road
We're traveling on
I wonder what went wrong
I can't help it, I wonder what went wrong

And I dreamed I was dying
And I dreamed that my soul rose unexpectedly
And looking back down on me
Smiled reassuringly
And I dreamed I was flying
And high up above my eyes could clearly see
The Statue of Liberty
Sailing away to sea
And I dreamed I was flying

We come on the ship they call the Mayflower
We come on the ship that sailed the moon
We come in the age's most uncertain hour
And sing an American tune
But it's all right, it's all right
You can't be forever blessed
Still, tomorrow's going to be another working day
And I'm trying to get some rest
That's all I'm trying to get some rest

Paul Simon's explanation had much currency early in the decade. A little weary now, holding on, knocked around, gathering strength, he suggested, just resting up for another working day, for tomorrow. "All I need is someone to awaken me," Graham Nash sang in *his* sixties retrospective, *Wild Tales*: "Much of me has gone to sleep and I'm afraid to wake up."

"We all get tired and feel the need to relax a bit."
—John Lennon

The three men I admired most,
The father, Son and Holy Ghost,
They caught the last train for the coast
The day the music died.
—Don McLean, "American Pie"

"At this time I feel I can no longer refuse myself the time and the leisure and the privacy to which any man is rightfully entitled."—Bill Graham in closing the Fillmores

"I've just been lazy, Jann. I've been just getting by, so I haven't really thought too much about putting out anything really new and different."—Bob Dylan, to *Rolling Stone*'s Jann Wenner in 1969

"I just don't have the energy to do it, to say it sucks."—Tom Smothers

In England the Who's observations arrived in a long, brilliantly conceived and executed successor to *Tommy* titled *Quadrophenia*. Far too reflective for 1973, *Quadrophenia* asks what is the impact of time on a philosophy and life style built upon youth and motion? What options are available to aging radicals and burnt-out rebels?

The issues are raised and alternative resolutions explored in the course of the Who's tale about Jimmy, an aging mod, a misunderstood son, a rebel without a cause, a bummed out teenager of early seventies England. A lad of multiple personalities, as the title *Quadrophenia* suggests, Jimmy is most of all a British mod, dedicated to pills and scooters and dance halls and Who concerts and the whole rich sixties scene. It is (was) magic while it lasts, but as the Who understand, it cannot possibly last. Jimmy grows old, and his world breaks into pieces around him. He confronts his parents and is bummed out. He tries working and is bummed out. He catches his girl with his best friend and is bummed out. So he totals his scooter in frustration and takes off on the train for the beaches of Brighton, where all the mods used to hang out. We catch a glimpse of him—high as a sunflower and sandwiched between two banker types—on the train, returning to the old mod vibrations along the coast.

This trip proves to be the ultimate bummer because the magic is gone. Quite by accident, Jimmy meets the leader of yesteryear's rebellion, the geezer with the sawed-off shotgun under his jacket who once took on two rockers and pounded them both, the guy who actually smashed the doors of the Brighton Hotel in a riot reported on earlier in the album. And there is this character, the head mod as it were, working as a bellboy at, would you believe, the same Brighton Hotel: Telling Jimmy that he could learn a lot from a case such as his, intimating that Jimmy, too, should sell out and join the system. "Me folks had let me down," Jimmy recalls. "Rock had let me down, women had let me down, work wasn't worth the effort, school isn't even worth mentioning. But I never thought I'd feel let down by being a mod." He tries suicide.

Over the course of the opera, Jimmy confronts parents turned hostile, friends turned faithless, rock gone sour, a life style worn out, a rebellion ended—the world of the sixties become the world of the seventies—and he wonders where to go. The Who offer several options open not only to Jimmy but to all society. (Jimmy's problems, *Quadrophenia* makes clear in "Is It in My Head," are the problems of the country). In "The Punk Meets the Godfather (A Mini Opera with Real Characters and Plot)" they suggest that everything, even rebellion, is a sellout. The Who, leaders of the mod rebellion, are the song's phony leaders. The Who are a con. Rock is a con. Mod is a con. The sixties were a con. Jimmy and the rest of us might just as well face the fact, turn cynical, and pull in the horns. During the sixties we were being naive; now we have lost our innocence, and so much the better. Be cynical.

"Helpless Dancer" suggests that if it's all a sellout and you *know* it is, you can't win by fighting and you can't win by joining. The only thing you can do is quit: "You stop dancing." You drop out.

Another alternative is suggested in "Dirty Jobs." You can't quit, imply the Who: always battle, never give in. You must remember how you used to fight and keep on fighting. If you get screwed again, you've got only yourself to blame. Keep the faith.

In the final voice of the album, Pete Townshend suggests something quite different from anything the Who suggested during the sixties. Borrowing, as did the Beatles in *Sgt. Pepper* and Bob Dylan in "Desolation Row," from T. S. Eliot's "Waste Land," the Who turn the waters of Jimmy's suicide into the waters of rebirth, a baptism that transmutes anger and aggression into internal spiritualism and love.

> On the dry and dusty road
> The nights we spent alone
> I need to get back home to cool cool rain.
> The nights are hot and black as ink
> I can't sleep and I lay and I think
> Oh God, I need a drink of cool cool rain
>
> Only love
> Can make it rain
> The way the beach is kissed by the sea.
> Love, reign o'er me.

Some rebels (not many) continued to protest. Some turned cynical and dropped out. And some transcended the struggle retreating into a personal ethic of love. And that, the Who imply in *Quadrophenia*, is what became of the sixties.

Sixties people have become private persons and have busied themselves with private affairs. Many sixties people came to that outer edge and stepped neither over it nor back from it but through it. They internalized the revolution and ceased to care enough about externals even to protest against them. Instead of demanding humane social, political, and economic structures or sensible educational programs or a just legal system, they determined to live humane, sensible, just lives themselves and try to bend the system from within to their own personal visions.

Faced with the exigencies of adulthood and survival, they looked for jobs within the system that were not sellouts—that would give them the most latitude for self-discovery, growth, compassion and community concern on a private level. Many a Vista worker is now working for a city-funded agency helping neighborhoods control and revitalize their own housing. Many a secretary chooses her job by the amount of time it gives her to write songs. Many an accountant chooses the relatively low-paying public accounting over corporate tax accounting because she likes "working with people and having every day be different." Jane Fonda has built a brilliant and profitable career within the movie industry, but she maintains a low-keyed life-style, funding projects that reflect her social and political values.

The mentality of the sixties remains buried in the psyches of a million individuals. The values remain, but they are no longer as public as they once were. The times are dull; not the individuals.

> "The task of the new generation is to see the humanity in all men, and to work for the renewal, the rebirth, the return to life, of all men."
> —Charles Reich, *The Greening of America*

The legacy of the sixties—experimentation, vision, generosity, candor, and impatience with injustice—is still with us. What is gone is the sense of public motion that made the generation act together, made them march and say decisively "Now."

> "For me, it's just reinforcing those images in my head that were there, that don't die, that will be there tomorrow, and in doing so for myself, hopefully, also for those people who also had those images . . . the same electric spark that went off back there could still go off again—the spark that had to be moving."—Bob Dylan

We can remain, as Paul Simon put it, "still crazy after all these years"; in Bob Dylan's words "forever young."

> "What I'm asking you to do is take some risks. Stop paying war taxes, refuse the armed forces, organize against the air war, support the strikes and boycotts of farmers, workers and poor peo-

ple, analyze the flag salute, give up the nation state, share your money, refuse to hate, be willing to work . . . in short, sisters and brothers, arm up with love and come from the shadows."
—Joan Baez, *Come from the Shadows*

"It's been a long and lonely winter"—the Beatles

"Here Comes the Sun"

Suggested Recordings

The following albums represent the simplest, most direct, and most enjoyable route into the consciousness of the sixties. In making selections I excluded fifties artists who did not prefigure or influence the sixties, sixties shlock, and all seventies music except that which comments upon or directly reflects the mindset of the sixties.

Joan Baez, *Joan Baez*, Vanguard VSD 79078—*Come from the Shadows*, A&M SP 4339

The Band, *Music from Big Pink*, Capitol SKAO 2955—*Rock of Ages*, Capitol SABB 611045

The Beach Boys, *Close Up*, Capitol SWBB 253—*Pet Sounds*, Capitol DT 2458

The Beatles, *Meet the Beatles*, Capitol T 2047—*Rubber Soul*, Capitol ST 2442—*Revolver*, Capitol ST 2576—*Sg. Pepper's Lonely Hearts Club Band*, Capitol MAS 2653—*Magical Mystery Tour*, Capitol MS 2835—*The Beatles* (the white album), Apple SWBO 101—*Abbey Road*, Apple SO 383

Chuck Berry, *Chuck Berry's Golden Decade*, vol. 1, Chess 2CH 1514

Big Brother and the Holding Company, *Cheap Thrills*, Columbia KCS 9700

Blood, Sweat, and Tears, *Blood, Sweat and Tears*, Columbia KCS 9720

James Brown, *Nothing But Soul*

Buffalo Springfield, *Retrospective*, Atlantic SD 33-283

The Byrds, *Greatest Hits*, Columbia CS 9516

Ray Charles, *Yes Indeed*, Atlantic 8025—*What'd I Say*, Atlantic 8029

The Coasters, *Greatest Hits*, Atlantic 33-111

Joe Cocker, *Joe Cocker!*, A&M SP 4224

Leonard Cohen, *Songs of Leonard Cohen*, Columbia CS 9533—*Songs from a Room*, Columbia CS 9767

Judy Collins, *Who Knows Where the Time Goes*, Elektra EKS 74033

The Concert for Bangla Desh, Apple STCX 3385

Country Joe MacDonald and the Fish, *Greatest Hits*, Vanguard VSD 6545

Cream, *The Best of Cream*, Atlantic SD 33-291

Creedence Clearwater Revival, *Cosmo's Factory*, Fantasy 8402

Crosby, Stills, Nash and Young, *Déjà Vu*, Atlantic SD 7200—*So Far*, Atlantic SD 18100

Bo Diddley, *Have Guitar Will Travel*, Checker 2974

Fats Domino, *Million Sellers by Fats,* Imperial 12195

The Doors, *The Doors,* Elektra EKS 4007—*L.A. Woman,* Elektra EKS 75011

Bob Dylan, *The Freewheelin' Bob Dylan,* Columbia CS 8786—*The Times They Are A-Changin',* Columbia CS 8905—*Another Side of Bob Dylan,* Columbia CS 8993—*Bringing It All Back Home,* Columbia CS 9128—*Highway 61 Revisited,* Columbia CS 9189—*Blonde on Blonde,* Columbia K2S 841—*John Wesley Harding,* Columbia CS 9604—*New Morning,* Columbia KC 30290—*The Basement Tapes,* Columbia CBS 88147—*Blood on the Tracks,* Columbia PC 33235—*Desire,* Columbia PC 33893

The Everly Brothers, *The Everly Brothers' Original Greatest Hits,* Columbia BGP 350

Aretha Franklin, *Aretha's Gold,* Atlantic SD 8227

The Grateful Dead, *Workingman's Dead,* Warner WS 1869

Arlo Guthrie, *Alice's Restaurant,* Reprise RS 6267

Woody Guthrie, *The Greatest Songs of Woody Guthrie* (performed by various artists), Vanguard VSD 35/36

George Harrison, *All Things Must Pass,* Apple STCH 639

Jimi Hendrix, *Are You Experienced?* Reprise RS 6261

Buddy Holly, *Buddy Holly: A Rock and Roll Collection,* Decca DXSE7-207

Jefferson Airplane, *Surrealistic Pillow,* RCA LSP 3766—*After Bathing at Baxter's,* RCA LSP 4545—*Crown of Creation,* RCA LSP 4058—*Volunteers,* RCA LSP 4238

Janis Joplin, *Pearl,* Columbia KC 30322

B. B. King, *B. B. King Live at the Regal,* ABC-Paramount ABC S-509

King Crimson, *In the Court of the Crimson King,* Atlantic SD 8245

The Kinks, *Greatest Hits,* Reprise R 6217

John Lennon, *Live Peace in Toronto,* Apple SW 3362

Jerry Lee Lewis, *Original Golden Hits,* vols. 1 and 2, Sun 102/103

Little Richard, *Little Richard's Greatest Hits,* Columbia OKS 14121—*Little Richard's Grooviest 17 Original Hits,* Specialty SPS 2113

Mamas and Papas, *Farewell to the First Golden Era,* Dunhill 50031

MC5, *Kick Out the Jams,* Elektra EKS 74042

Joni Mitchell, *Clouds,* Reprise R 6341

Moody Blues, *In Search of the Lost Chord,* Deram DES 18017

The Mothers of Invention, *Freak Out!* Verve V6-5005-2X—*Absolutely Free,* Verve V/V6-5013X

Graham Nash, *Wild Tales,* Atlantic SD 7288

Newport Folk Festival (1960), Vanguard VSD 2087/88

Harry Nilsson, *Nilsson Sings Newman,* RCA LSP 4289

Phil Ochs, *All the News That's Fit to Sing,* Elektra EKS 7269—*Pleasures of the Harbor,* A&M SP 4133—*Tape from California,* A&M 4148—*Rehearsals for Retirement,* A&M SP 4181—*Chords of Fame,* A&M 4599

Tom Paxton, *Ramblin' Boy*, Elektra EKS 7277

Peter, Paul, and Mary, *Peter, Paul and Mary*, Warner WS 1449—*In the Wind*, Warner WS 1607

Wilson Pickett, *The Best of Wilson Pickett*, Atlantic SD 8151

Elvis Presley, *The Sun Sessions*, RCA AFM 1-1675—*Elvis' Worldwide 50 Gold Award Hits*, vol. 1, RCA LPM 6401

Procol Harum, *Procol Harum*, Deram DES 18008

Otis Redding, *History of Otis Redding*, Atlantic SD 33-261

The Rolling Stones, *Their Satanic Majesties Request*, London NPS-2—*Beggar's Banquet*, London PS 539—*Get Yer Ya Ya's Out*, London NPS-5—*Sticky Fingers*, Rolling Stones COC 59100—*Hot Rocks, 1964–1971*, London 2PS 606/7—*Exile on Main Street*, Rolling Stones COC 2-2900—*Some Girls*, Rolling Stones COC 39108

Pete Seeger, *We Shall Overcome*, Columbia CS 8901—*Dangerous Songs!?*, Columbia CS 9303

Paul Simon, *There Goes Rhymin' Simon*, Columbia KC 32280

Simon and Garfunkel, *Sounds of Silence*, Columbia CS 9269—*Parsley, Sage, Rosemary and Thyme*, Columbia CS 9363—*Bookends*, Columbia KCS 9529—*Bridge over Troubled Water*, Columbia KCS 9914

Sly and the Family Stone, *Stand!* Epic BN 26456

The Weavers, *Travelling On*, Vanguard VSD 2022

The Who, *Tommy*, Decca DXSW 7205—*Who's Next*, Decca DL 79182—*Quadrophenia*, MCA MCA2-10004

Woodstock, Atlantic SD 3-500

Neil Young, *After the Goldrush*, Reprise 6383

Index

A

Absorption, 153–177, 212–213
Absurdity, 72–75, 184, 202–212, 213
Acid, 96, 113–116, 118, 126, 155, 170, 219
Acid rock, 113, 125, 128–130
Adventures of Ozzie and Harriet, 2
Agnew, Spiro, 51
Alcohol, 117, 170
"All My Trials," 56
Allen, Steve, 2, 19, 26–27
Allen, Woody, 26
"Alley-Oop," 47
"Along Came Jones," 47
Alternative life styles, 111–151
American Bandstand, 43, 80, 148, 159–160, 170
American Graffiti, 7
"American Pie," 223
Anarchism, 54, 66, 212
Angry young men, 37
Anka, Paul, 39
Ann-Margret, 8, 198
Anti-heroes, 47, 83
Anti-nuclear protest, 28–31, 55, 56
Anti-theater, 200
Anti-war protests, 28, 30, 54, 59, 61–77, 79, 134, 193, 201, 202, 213
Armies of the Night (Mailer), 79, 144
Aronowitz, Alfred, 39
Art protest songs, 192–195
Art rock, 183–196
Artiness, 179–212, 213

Artist as social critic, 78–89
Association, 119
Astrology, 96
Atlantic Records, 133
Atomic bombs, 28–30
Audience participation, 200–203
Avalon, Frankie, 39, 159

B

Baez, Joan, 57, 59, 79, 101, 139, 150, 170, 190, 227
Baptism, 190
"Birmingham Sunday," 59
Come from the Shadows, 227
David's Album, 139
Joan Baez, 2, 59
Balin, Marty, 102, 219
"Ballad of Caryl Chessman, The," 20
Ballard, Hank, 40
Ban the Bomb, 28–31, 55, 56
Bay of Pigs, 69, 195
Beach Boys, 125, 147, 191
Beat Scene, 35
Beatles, 13, 18, 62, 64, 76, 79–80, 82, 89, 93–94, 96, 100, 107, 110, 118, 123–124, 148, 156–157, 161, 164–165, 172, 177, 186–189, 195–196, 206, 215, 225, 227
Abbey Road, 82, 99, 191, 215
"All You Need Is Love," 186
"Being for the Benefit of Mr. Kite," 187
"A Day in the Life," 81
"Dr. Robert," 62
"Eleanor Rigby," 186–187

"Boll Weevil Song," 55
Bomb, 4, 9, 28-31, 55, 56, 63
Bomb Culture (Nuttall), 31
Boone, Pat, 8, 39
Braceland, Francis, 38
Brando, Marlon, 17, 19
Bridge Too Far, A, 1
Broadside, 58
Brooks, Mel, 26
"Brother, Won't You Roll Down
    the Line," 32
Brothers Four, 55
Bruce, Lenny, 26, 28
Brunner, John, 29
Bubble-gum music, 163
Buddhism, 21
Buffalo Springfield, 73, 75, 138,
    161, 170
Bulletin of the Atomic Scientists,
    28
Bunche, Ralph, 109
Bureaucracy, 13, 51
Burroughs, William, 21, 23, 116
    Naked Lunch, 21
Buy-off, 155-156, 165-168
"Bye Bye, Love," 40
Byrds, 62, 114, 142, 181, 183
    "Turn, turn, turn," 114, 183

C

Caesar, Sid, 26
"California Dreamin," 87
Capital punishment, 19, 58, 221
Capra, Frank, 52
Carawan, Guy, 32
Carlos, John, 54
Carmichael, Stokely, 131, 133,
    154
Carter, Asa, 38
Cash, Johnny, 40
Cassady, Neal, 21

Catch-22 (Heller), 74
Cell 2455, Death Row (Chess-
    man), 19
Censorship, 51, 71, 171
Central Intelligence Agency
    (CIA), 66-68, 175
"Change Is Gonna Come, A," 62
"Chantilly Lace," 44
Charles, Ray, 40
Checker, Chubby, 40
Cher, 122
"Cherish," 109
Chess Records, 133
Chessman, Caryl, 18-19, 47, 74,
    106, 208
Chorus Line, 28
Christgau, Robert, 73, 183
Christian Science Monitor, 28
"Civil Disobedience" (Thoreau),
    52
Civil rights, 25-27, 54-57, 59, 61,
    64-69, 185
Civil Rights Act (1968), 210
Clapton, Eric, 171, 198
Clark, Dick, 43, 69, 121, 146,
    159-161, 164, 170
Clark, Thomas, 110
Clay, Cassius, 54
Cleaver, Eldridge, 155
Cleveland, Bradley, 58-59
Clockwork Orange, A, 16
Clooney, Rosemary, 8
Coasters, 40, 46-47, 170
    "Charlie Brown," 46
    "Searchin'," 40
    "Yakety-Yak," 48
Coca, Imogene, 26
Cocaine, 114, 116
Cochran, Eddie, 39
Cohen, Leonard, 85-86, 107, 184,
    194-196, 215
    "Joan of Arc," 101

DATE DUE

GAYLORD	PRINTED IN U.S.A